MINORITIES AND MEDIA

This book is dedicated to our fathers:
Clint C. Wilson, Sr., award-winning editorial cartoonist,
Los Angeles Sentinel, and the late
Félix J. Gutiérrez, journalism educator and founding editor,
the *Mexican Voice*.

Their example helped us understand the importance of media for people of all races and the value of encouraging all students to develop their communication talents.

MINORITIES AND MEDIA

Diversity and the End of Mass Communication

Clint C. Wilson II
Félix Gutiérrez

SAGE PUBLICATIONS
The Publishers of Professional Social Science
Beverly Hills London New Delhi

For information address:

SAGE Publications, Inc.
275 South Beverly Drive
Beverly Hills, California 90212

SAGE Publications India Pvt. Ltd.
M-32 Market
Greater Kailash I
New Delhi 110 048 India

SAGE Publications Ltd
28 Banner Street
London EC1Y 8QE
England

Printed in the United States of America

Library of Congress Cataloging in Publication Data

Wilson, Clint C.
Minorities and media.

Includes bibliographies and index.
1. Mass media and minorities—United States.
I. Gutiérrez, Félix. II. Title.
P94.5.M552U69 1985 305.8′00973 85-2212
ISBN 0-8039-2454-2
ISBN 0-8039-2455-0 (pbk.)

SECOND PRINTING

CONTENTS

ACKNOWLEDGMENTS

We wish to acknowledge the assistance of those who contributed to the realization of this effort, including both the scholars and journalists whose works are cited in the text and those who have worked directly in the development of the book. Carey Jue and David Tomsky were dedicated graduate research assistants. Luther Luedtke provided needed support as Interim Director of the University of Southern California School of Journalism.

Appreciation is extended to Erwin Kim, a former colleague, and to students in our Minorities and the Media courses at the university, whose enthusiasm for the subject was a source of intellectual stimulation and encouragement. Lena Chao and Stanley Rosen of the East Asian Studies Center of the University of Southern California provided timely and much-appreciated assistance in translating portions of the first Asian American newspaper, as did graduate journalism student Stanley Chung.

Important in the development of the historical information in the book were Michael Emery and Tom Reilly of the journalism faculty at California State University, Northridge. Jorge Reina Schement of the University of California, Los Angeles, and Hugo Garcia of the Northeast Newspapers in Los Angeles provided much of the stimulation for the chapter on audience segmentation. Armando Valdez of Stanford University and Don Carson and Edith Auslander of the University of Arizona provided speaking opportunities and comments that led to some of the concepts developed in that chapter. Carolyn McIntosh, research librarian at the University of Southern California, also provided invaluable assistance in locating material on the topics covered in the book. Staff members of the Margaret Herrick Library, Academy of Motion Picture Arts and Sciences, and Alice Marshall of Wave Publications were gracious contributors. Our friends at Sage

Publications offered helpful advice on the manuscript and exhibited admirable patience. The text for the book was prepared on Apple Macintosh personal computers, which made the writing and inevitable editing not only easier, but a more enjoyable experience.

Finally, and most important, we could not overlook the importance of the moral support and sacrifices of our families during the preparation of the manuscript; we hereby express sincere gratitude to Clarisa and Clint C. Wilson III and to María Elena, Elena Rebeca, Anita Andrea, and Alicia Rosa Gutiérrez.

PREFACE

In the mid-1960s the authors were college undergraduates with strong interests in professional journalism careers. Both faced discouraging incidents in their quest to attain those careers, not for lack of talent and ambition, but because they were made to feel the profession was not open to members of racial minority groups. Wilson was counseled by his academic journalism adviser against nurturing high expectations for a daily newspaper job. Although acknowledging his student's talent, the professor warned, "There just are no jobs out there for Negro reporters." Gutiérrez, after making the campus newspaper staff as a freshman, was told by his college journalism adviser that his services would not be missed should he decide not to enroll in the newspaper staff course for a second semester. Gutiérrez did return after sitting out a semester, however, and eventually became the paper's editor-in-chief. Upon graduation, neither author was successful in obtaining a reporting job with Los Angeles area daily newspapers. Before the Kerner Commission report in 1968, fewer than six racial minority reporters were employed in White-owned news media in Los Angeles, one of the three largest and most racially diverse media markets in the United States. Their personal encounters with news media organizations that were virtually closed to non-Whites contributed to the authors' decisions to pursue graduate study in the field. This book, therefore, is a result of those encounters and has been written in the hope that it will help others appreciate both the contributions of racial minorities to communication media and the obstacles they have faced.

It is the purpose of this book to examine the relationships between mass communication media and the four largest racial minority groups in the United States. It traces the historical development of those relationships and reveals the commonalities in media treatment of minorities. Additionally, the authors offer analyses of the past and present state of minorities and the media in the context of current trends that may point to the future.

The work is limited in several respects. It concerns itself only with the four largest racial minority groups in the United States: Native Americans, Blacks, Latinos, and Asian peoples. Other racial groups or other social groups sometimes categorized as minorities (the handicapped, homosexuals, women in the work force, and so on) are not subjects of this work, although some parallels may be seen in their relationships to mass media. Similarly, this book does not attempt to address every mass communications medium. Therefore, music recording, book publishing, and magazine fiction are not within the scope of this work. The authors have found in their research that material on the subject of ethnic groups is uneven in many respects. For example, there is much less literature on Asian media in the United States than on Black media and less on Indian employment in television than on Indian images in motion pictures. Thus it was not possible to tell the complete story of each group in every chapter. Such gaps, however, do suggest areas for future study by students and scholars who are seriously interested in documenting the role of media as they have related to racial minority groups.

In this book the terms "Asian" and "Asian American" are used to describe people who trace their origins to the Asian continent, as well as those from the Pacific Islands. The term "Black" is used to describe Afro-Americans and others who trace their origins to the sub-Saharan part of the African continent. "Latinos" is used as an inclusive term for persons of Latin American or Spanish background, including the Caribbean region. The terms "Native American" and "Indian" are used to describe the native peoples of the continent that Europeans and other immigrants have called America. The terms "White" and "Anglo" are used as applied by the U.S. Bureau of the Census and describe persons of European background who are not Latinos. All terms are capitalized in the text when referring to people of different races and cultures.

—Clint C. Wilson II
Félix F. Gutiérrez

I

Introduction

"The growth of minority people in the United States has forced the media to reexamine the ways they have traditionally dealt with minority groups. As these groups grow in number . . . at a rate that outstrips the Anglo population, the media will have to continue to look for new ways to deal with them."

1

RACIAL DIVERSITY IN A LAND OF IMMIGRANTS

WHEN USED IN ITS statistical sense, the term "minorities" refers to groups that are small in number, less than the majority. It has often been applied to people of color in the United States because as individual groups, Blacks, Latinos, Asians, and Native Americans do not constitute a large percentage of the national population. It has become a convenient umbrella under which to put any group that is not White.

But it is also a misleading label. It misleads the person using the term to think of those who carry the label as small not only in number, but in importance. It also can make the interests and issues raised by "minorities" appear to be less meaningful than those of the majority. And, finally, it is no longer a statistically accurate term in many cases. In many cities across the United States the people labeled as racial "minorities" are actually the majority of the population when the members of the individual groups are added together.

The projected growth rates of these groups indicate that they will continue to grow at a faster rate than the White population through the early part of the next century. Thus, while they may be described in terms that make them appear to be a relatively small part of the current population, demographers who have analyzed factors such as immigration, birthrate, and average family size conclude that the people called "minorities" will grow at a strong rate through the near future. These population changes are part of a changing racial mix that has been part of the land that is now the United States since the arrival of the first European settlers in the early 1600s.

In a 1982 report, population analysts Leon F. Bouvier and Cary B. Davis wrote:

> The region changed from predominantly Native American to predominantly White Anglo-Saxon Protestant (WASP) in large part due to high mortality on the part of the former and high immigration and fertility on the part of the latter group. In 1800 close to 20 percent of what, by then, was the United States of America, was Black—in large part, the result of high levels of immigration, albeit forced. By 1900, more significant changes had occurred. Blacks were only 10 percent of the population, but among Whites the proportion coming from southern and eastern Europe had grown substantially . . . . What had once been a predominantly WASP society with a Black minority was becoming much more heterogeneous. The proportions Black and WASP were falling, as immigration reached new highs. At first this gave rise to predictions of a "melting pot" society. Later, however, that theory was questioned as advocates of cultural pluralism became more vocal.[1]

The analogy of the "melting pot" was a popular way of describing the assimilation of European immigrants into the United States in the late 1800s and early 1900s. Proponents of the model held that immigrants who came to the United States would, within a relatively short period of time, lose their national identity, culture, and language and adopt the loyalties, customs, and language of their new home. It was held that within a generation the children of the immigrants would have "melted" into the population of the United States and would no longer be identifiable by the national origin of their parents. The idea was so dominant that some factories had a ceremony in which immigrant workers would enter a stage from one side in their national costumes, pass and change clothes behind a large symbolic melting pot, and emerge from behind the stage prop pot dressed in the clothes of the American working class. Today the legacy of the melting pot is found among Americans who know little of their family histories, other than that their grandparents or great-grandparents came from Germany, Ireland, Italy, Poland, or some other European country.

But while the grandchildren of those who blended in the melting pot may not be able to speak the language or share the customs of their ancestors there was an increased curiosity about family roots, national heritage, and past customs during the late 1970s and early 1980s. At the same time, there are groups who, because of differences in race, legal status, or geographic proximity to the home country, have never blended, or in some cases been allowed to blend, into the melting pot of the United States. Rather than a huge melting pot, these groups have experienced the United States as a huge salad, in which each group retains its individual characteristics and identities while interacting with other groups to form the whole nation. The groups with the greatest identity outside of the melting pot are the groups that are the focus of this book: Native Americans, Blacks, Asians, and Latinos.

DEMOGRAPHIC STATISTICS

As a nation whose population growth has always been fueled by immigrants, the United States has always had racial, national, and ethnic minorities. But, as noted earlier, the European immigrants who have constituted most of the nation's immigrants for the past 120 years have largely been encouraged to follow the melting pot model of assimilation. Those groups who fell outside of the melting pot have been counted, with varying degrees of accuracy, as separate groups. For instance, in 1790 the first census counted 757,000 Blacks, 92 percent of them living as slaves. They made up 19.3 percent of the nation's population.[2]

The 1980 census reported that slightly more than 1 in 5 persons of the 226 million residents of the United States was either Black, Hispanic (Latino), Asian/Pacific Islander, or Native American. These included 26.5 million Blacks (11.7 percent of the population), 14.6 million Hispanics or Latinos (6.5 percent), 3.5 million Asians and Pacific Islanders (1.5 percent), and 1.4 million Native

Americans, counted as Indians, Eskimos, and Aleuts (.6 percent).[3]

Perhaps more telling than the actual figures were the growth rates for the racial minority groups that the census figures revealed for the decade between 1970 and 1980. The census figures showed that the minority group growth rates had outpaced the national averages and, as a result, minorities substantially increased their share of the national population in the ten-year period. The biggest growth was found in the Latino and Asian/Pacific Islander groups, although Blacks and Native Americans also posted percentage gains. Between 1970 and 1980 Latinos grew from 4.5 to 6.4 percent of the United States population, Asians and Pacific Islanders from .8 to 1.5 percent, Blacks from 11.1 to 11.7 percent, and Native Americans from .4 to .6 percent.[4] There were many causes cited for the accelerated growth of minorities when compared with overall population trends.

One reason is that most minority groups have a younger median age than the overall population and thus are within the child-bearing, family-rearing ages. For instance, while the median age for Whites in 1980 was 31.3 years, for Blacks and Latinos it was 23.2 years. More than 12 percent of the White population was over 65 years old, while only 7.9 percent of the Blacks and 4.9 percent of the Latinos were over 65.[5] This means not only that members of these groups are within the ages for bearing and raising children, but also that they have children who will most likely bear and raise families in the near future.

Another reason was increased immigration from Asia and Latin America to the United States. While in earlier decades Europe had supplied large numbers of immigrants to the United States, during the 1970s legal and illegal immigration to the United States from Asia and Latin America increased sharply. Some of this was spurred by warfare and political turmoil in certain countries in these regions. Other immigrants were driven by the desire for an improvement in economic status. For whatever reason, the United States continued to be the land of opportunity for these new residents, just as it had been for the earlier European immigrants. The Population Research Bureau reported in 1982 that between 1977 and 1979 immigrants from Latin America and Asia accounted for 42 percent and 39 percent, respectively, of the immigrants admitted to the United States, accounting for 81 percent of the immigrants to the country. Europe accounted for only 13 percent. In contrast, between 1931 and 1960, Europeans constituted 58 percent of the immigrants, Latin Americans 15 percent, and Asians 5 percent.[6]

The difference in the birthrate between Whites and minorities was another factor that spurred the population growth of the 1970s. For instance, Blacks have substantially higher fertility rates than Whites and, despite the projections of the Census Bureau, appear to be staying that way. In 1976 the Census Bureau projected that Black and White fertility rates would eventually reach the same level, that by 1978 Black fertility would be 19.1 percent higher than that of Whites and by 1985 only 6 percent higher. Instead, the 1980 census revealed that Black fertility was 30.3 percent higher than that of Whites, about the same difference as in 1970.[7] In the early 1980s White women averaged 1.76 children, while for Latinos the average was 2.6 children and for Blacks 2.3 children. This meant that Latinas were bearing 50 percent more children and Black women 32 percent more children than White women.[8]

Immigrants also probably do not have the same fertility rate as Whites, although the Census Bureau has assumed that immigrants have children at the same rate as the U.S. population averages for people of the same age, sex, and race. "An assumption is necessary because vital statistics do not record immigrant status," wrote demographers Gregory Spencer and Signe Wetrogran in 1981, "but the assumption is not always accurate."[9]

Other possible causes of the minority population boom cited by analysts of the 1980 census is a possible increase in the number of persons designating themselves as members of minority groups, a change in the racial categories used on census forms, and a stepped-up effort by the Census Bureau to count members of different minority groups accurately. Whatever the reason, the bottom line is clear. Minorities have grown at a substantially higher rate than the rest of the nation's population and, as a result, constitute an even larger percentage of the United States than they have before. Even more important for the future are the projections that members of minority groups will continue to grow at an accelerated pace well into the next century.

PROJECTED GROWTH RATES

Based on the trends noted in the 1980 census, it seems clear that people of color will continue to grow, both in actual numbers and as a percentage of the United States population for the near future. The rate of growth and its relationship to the White population's trends are a matter of debate among demographers. However, although they may argue over the slope of the ascending minority growth rate curve, they are in agreement about its upward direction.

"The non-White population will increase one-third by the turn of the century and double by 2040. As a consequence, the percent of the population that is not White will rise from 14.4 percent at the present time to almost 17 percent in 2000, and 22 percent in 2040," predicted two Census Bureau demographers, Gregory Spencer and John F. Long, in a 1983 article for *American Demographics* magazine. They took into account factors such as birthrate, immigration, and age.[10]

Some projections have gone so far as to predict a day when the so-called minorities will be the majority of the United States population. The Population Reference Bureau has predicted that by the year 2080 Whites will no longer be the majority of the people in the United States. The bureau's projections, based on its analysis that Latinos, Blacks, and Asians were 20 percent of the nation's population in 1982, estimated that Whites would decline to 49.8 percent of the population in the year 2080. Primary causes for the population shift were the continuation of current inflow of people from Asia and Latin America as immigrants to the United States and continuation of the current differences in fertility among Whites, Blacks, and Latinos.[11] The authors of the study, Leon F. Bouvier and Cary B. Davis, commented on the implications of such racial changes in a 1982 report:

> There are those who would prefer a "status quo" society. That is to say a continuation of the present racial and ethnic composition under an Anglo-conformity umbrella. There are those who see the future demographic changes as marking the onset of a new phase in the ever changing American society—a "multi-cultural" society. In

the late 19th century and early 20th century the United States successfully changed identity from WASP to multi-ethnic culture within the White community. In the late 20th and early 21st century, it may once again change towards being the first truly multiracial society on the planet earth, a multi-cultural society which while still predominantly English speaking would tolerate and even accept other languages and other cultures.[12]

The projected changes have already caused some rethinking among those who became accustomed to the "melting pot" model of assimilation in the United States. In a 1981 interview Daniel Levine, acting director of the U.S. Bureau of the Census, commented that he didn't see the United States as a melting pot anymore. Instead, he said, he saw the nation developing as a "confederation of minorities" from different groups, each demanding to be counted by the census and, in his words, demanding immediate political representation:

> What bothers me at this point is recent legislation fostering the confederation I'm talking about. Bilingual education is an example. The very fact that we have passed legislation recognizing that these people are disenfranchised, recognizing that these people may have been discriminated against, encourages just what we don't want to happen. When you start passing legislation that says if you're Hispanic you get this type of program participation or you get this benefit, you've escalated the situation where people now are going around and saying, "make sure you save your cultural heritage and affinity because it benefits our particular group."[13]

In the same interview, Bruce Chapman, director designate of the Census Bureau, sounded a more optimistic note regarding the impact of growing numbers of minority groups in the United States. He argued that what have long been identified as "traditional American values" were also part of the value structure of the nation's newest immigrants, particularly Asians and Latin Americans. He cited the strong family relationships of members of these groups and also predicted that they would become assets to the nation. "They may want to retain some cultural identification with the old country, but they also want to be unhyphenated Americans," he said.[14]

RACIAL MINORITIES: AN INTERNATIONAL PHENOMENON

The United States is not the only country with substantial and growing minority populations. In fact, most nations of the world have religious, ethnic, or racial minority groups within their boundaries. The treatment of members of these groups varies from nation to nation, depending on the political and economic systems of the country, as well as the historical relationship between the dominant and subordinate groups.

For instance, in most colonial situations in which a nation conquers or colonizes the people of another land there are rigid separations based on class and race. The British, who colonized much of North America as well as parts of Africa, Oceania, and Asia, maintained strict lines of distinction between the predominantly Anglo colonizers and the people they conquered. As Raymond Kennedy wrote in 1945:

> The British colonial code draws the most rigid color line of all. . . . The British have been in contact for a longer time with more dark peoples than any other western nation, yet they hold aloof from their subjects to an unequalled degree. They refuse to associate freely or make friends with other races, and their exclusiveness has engendered a reciprocal feeling toward them on the part of their colonial peoples.[15]

In Latin America, which was colonized by Spain and Portugal, the situation was less clearly defined. In all countries the European nation expropriated the lands of the indigenous peoples, making them slaves or peons working the land in some countries and importing African slaves in others. But, although there were class distinctions between Europeans and native Indians, there was also more intermarriage. As a result, a mixed racial population of mestizos emerged in Indian countries and mulattoes in countries such as Brazil, where Africans were brought to work. The process went so far that one country, Mexico, is considered by many to be a mestizo nation with scattered pockets of native people.

Colonialism in Southeast Asia was shared by several nations, including Britain, France, the Netherlands, and Spain, each with different policies toward the indigenous residents of the area. Like the Portuguese in Brazil, some colonizing nations also brought in laborers from other areas, Indians to Burma and Malaya and Chinese to most of Southeast Asia. As a result, these colonized areas became stratified on three levels: Europeans, immigrant workers, and the natives.[16]

In all of these colonial situations the relationship between minorities and majorities were reversed from what racial minorities have experienced in the United States. In the colonial situation the numerical minority groups were the European colonizers, who conquered and then governed the native people who outnumbered them. In this case, the term "minority" could be applied to the Europeans, who, though smaller in number, exerted military, political, economic, and social control over the native populations. Thus, while the Europeans may have been a *numerical* minority, they were not a *power* minority. However, as in the United States, the different social strata were distinguished by racial criteria as well.

The legacy of colonialism and distinctions based on race are still found in other countries of the world. As Charles F. Marden and Gladys Meyer point out in their book *Minorities in American Society*, nations as diverse in political and economic structure as South Africa, Israel, Soviet Russia, and the People's Republic of China have substantial divisions based on ethnic and racial divisions between dominant and subordinate groups.[17] The heated conflicts between Blacks and Whites in South Africa and between Jews and Arabs in Israel and other parts of the Middle East have been widely reported, as has the plight of Soviet Jews. Less well known in the United States is what Marden and Meyer call "the virtual destruction of small tribal people in Asiatic Russia"[18] and the integration through annexation of people in Baltic and Serbian territories now within the Soviet Union. Similarly, the People's Republic of China annexed people of a different culture and nationality when they annexed Tibet in the late 1940s.

Except for the Native Americans, who were subjected to colonization by the Spanish and extermination by the English, minority groups in the United States have followed patterns that are different from other nations. This is because the predominantly White Europeans who were to come to dominate the nation were themselves immigrants who became the numerical majority. Rather than exert their control through a rigid class system, they exterminated or confined the Native Americans, waged war to take lands held by the Native Americans and Mexicans, imported Black, Asian, and Latino labor as it was needed, and encouraged more European immigrants to come, settle, and develop a new society of White European immigrants in the United States. Between 1820 and 1970, 45 million immigrants entered the United States, 75 percent of them from European nations.[19] It is these immigrants, their children and grandchildren, who became the new majority in the United States, leaving the people of color to be designated as racial minorities.

DOES THE TERM "MINORITIES" DESCRIBE THE PRESENT AND FUTURE?

In the United States when the terms "majority" and "minority" are used in a racial context they usually refer to White Europeans as the majority and people of color (Native Americans, Asians, Blacks, and Latinos) as the minority. These have long represented both power and numerical relationships in which the White majority both outnumbered and dominated the more racially diverse minority groups. As a result, the word "minorities" became an umbrella term encompassing any group in the United States that was not White.

But the use of the term, though widespread by people of all races, masked the more complex distinctions between dominant and subordinate groups and the diversity between the groups bunched under the umbrella. It also distorted the reality of the racial situation in the United States and in the world. For instance, the use of the term has made it appear that racially diverse people such as Asians, Blacks, and Latinos are a minority in the world's population, when, in fact, as a group they far outnumber the Whites. Thus people who may have felt that they were permanent minorities in the United States and elsewhere were, in fact, a much more substantial part of the population elsewhere.

In addition, the term "minority" no longer accurately describes the situation in many urban areas of the nation. As a 1984 article in *American Demographics*[20] magazine pointed out, Blacks, Latinos, Asians, and other "minorities," when added together, already make up the majority of the population in many of the nation's largest cities. By identifying the number of Spanish-origin people originally listed as White, Black, or "other," John D. Kasarda, chairman of the Department of Sociology at the University of North Carolina, was able to calculate a more accurate enumeration of the percentages of minorities in cities across the United States. The results, according to Kasarda, show a much larger percentage of minorities in many cities than when they are reported on the basis of race only.

Kasarda's figures show that in 1983, 52 percent of New York City's population was Black, Latino, or Asian. Racial "minority" groups were also more than half of the people in such cities as Los Angeles, Chicago, Detroit, San Antonio, Miami, Washington, D.C., El Paso, Atlanta, Newark, Honolulu, and Gary, Indiana. In the South, Baltimore, New Orleans, Savannah, Corpus Christi, Richmond, Virginia, and Hialeah, Florida, were cities where "minorities" were the majority. In the North, Jersey City and Paterson, New Jersey, and Hartford, Connecticut, were listed as cities where the White "majority" was actually the minority. In the West, Oakland, Santa Ana, and Oxnard, California all had more Latinos, Blacks, and Asians than Anglos in 1983. Thus, in these cities, the term "minority" used in the numerical sense, is best applied to Anglos (Whites who are not of Latin American heritage), rather than people of color. Other cities, such as Philadelphia and Houston, were nearly half "minority," and Kasarda predicted that before 1990 the minority proportions would top 50 and 60 percent in even more cities in the United States.

But even if the term "minority" were an accurate description of the numerical relationship between Whites and non-Whites across the board, the use of the term would still cause unnecessary problems. The umbrella term "minority" may be useful in adding focus and emphasis to the issues that separate people of color from White Americans, such as differences in income, education, and employment. But it also groups people together inappropriately. While Blacks, Asians, Latinos, and Native Americans may fit conveniently under the label of "minority," there are as many differences between these groups as there are between each group and the White majority. In fact, the only characteristic they universally share is that they are not Anglo Europeans, but then neither are a lot of other groups that are not designated as minorities.

Los Angeles, which has been portrayed as a multiracial city that may be the prototype for changes to come in other parts of the country, offers an excellent example of minority growth and diversity in a region once dominated by White European immigrants. Between 1970 and 1979, according to figures compiled by the *Los Angeles Times* Marketing Research Department, Blacks, Latinos, Asians, and other racial minorities accounted for nearly all of the net natural increase (births minus deaths) in population in Los Angeles county. Latinos alone accounted for more than 70 percent of the population growth and Anglos less than 1 percent.[21] According to a 1984 Rand Corporation report, the number of foreign-born residents of Los Angeles County doubled from 1970 to 1980, and Anglos now make up less than half of the city of Los Angeles's residents. In the same decade the Latino population grew by nearly 75 percent and the Asian population more than doubled.

Although the Blacks, Latinos, Native Americans, and Asians in Los Angeles are still called minorities, they collectively make up more than half of the city's population. As minority groups they share some common experiences, particularly in dealing with predominantly Anglo institutions. But there are also differences between the minority groups. For instance, while minorities are usually described as having a lower median age than whites, there is much variation between the minority groups in Los Angeles and neighboring Orange County, according to data compiled by the *Los Angeles Times* Marketing Research Department. The median age of heads of households is 47 years for Whites, but is lower for the individual minority groups: Blacks, 41; Asians, 39; and Latinos, 37.

However, in other areas, individual minority groups have characteristics that are more like Anglos than they are like the other minority groups. For instance, the *Los Angeles Times* report showed that Asian families in Los Angeles and Orange counties had a median income of $21,509 in 1979-1980, just short of the White median household income of $21,929. Blacks and Latinos had median household incomes of $13,719 and $15,172, respectively. Thus in this case the Asian minority group had incomes closer to the majority Whites than to the other two minority groups of Blacks and Latinos.[22]

But even these data can be deceptive. For instance, while the *Los Angeles Times* marketing data show that incomes of Asian and White households are comparable, a closer look at the data reveals a marked difference. The median household income figures are very close together, at $21,929 for Whites and $21,509 for Asians. But another table shows that in 65 percent of the Asian families had the female head of the household employed, while only 48 percent of the White families had the woman head of the household working. Thus, while the household income amount is nearly the same, that income is produced by two people in most Asian households, and by only one in most White households.[23]

There are also differences between members of the same racial group. Reynolds Farley and Suzanne M. Bianchi in a 1983 article for *American Demographics* discussed what they called "the growing gap between Blacks."[24] Pointing to differences in education and income within the Black population, the two researchers cited data they said showed "blacks risk becoming polarized economically and socially." They contrasted the gains of "middle-class blacks" in education, employment, and housing against the problems of "a large black underclass" beset by poor schools, few jobs, and small welfare support payments. Noting the wide income gap between the richest and poorest Black families, the researchers found that while Black households headed by women "make up an increasing share of the poorest quarter of families" the Black households with both husbands and wives in the homes "are approaching parity with whites." Thus, while the term "Black" may be a useful label for persons of Afro-American descent in the United States, the data derived for that group tend to mask the differences among Blacks, just as use of the term "minority groups" lumps together different racial groups that have many differences.

Rather than portraying race relations in the United States in terms of a majority and minorities or dominant and subordinate groups, it is probably more accurate to avoid broad umbrella terms and speak in terms of racial diversity. Rather than classifying racial groups as majorities or minorities (and thereby masking the differences within these categories), the term "racial diversity" suggests a nation with a variety of races, each with similarities and dissimilarities within itself and with other groups. Rather than masking the differences within different racial groups designated as majority or minorities, the term "racial diversity" describes a nation of different and diverse races. It is a more accurate description of racial conditions in the United States as the nation approaches the twenty-first century.

It is this growing racial diversity that will characterize the nation's population through the near future. The census and projected growth figures clearly show where the United States is headed. How the media and other institutions react to these changes will, to a large extent, determine whether or not the United States will continue to be thought of as the land of opportunity. For, while the figures are clear, it is not so certain that the people of different races will not suffer the same discrimination that has historically faced Blacks, Latinos, Native Americans, and Asians in the United States as they seek education, employment, and housing. For these groups, discrimination continues to be a problem that stands in the way of opportunity.

At the same time, the growing racial diversity can be described as either a problem or an opportunity by the rest of American society. The increasing heterogeneity of the American people forces changes on education, government agencies, and businesses that have become used to conducting their affairs in a certain way. Now, as people come speaking different languages, following different religions, and bringing different cultural traditions, these institutions must respond. Some may see the changes as a problem, others as an opportunity to serve new students and consumers. But, whatever the reaction, the trend of the numbers is clear. As John D. Kasarda wrote in *American Demographics* in 1984:

> The message is clear. Our major cities are becoming increasingly diverse as their resident populations transform from white, European heritage to black, Hispanic and other minority groups. . . . These trends are creating not only powerful political

bases for minorities (blacks already govern many of the largest cities, including Los Angeles, Chicago, Philadelphia, Detroit, Washington, D.C., Atlanta, and New Orleans) but also unique opportunities for businesses cognizant of rapidly changing urban markets.[25]

ANALYSIS

As census reports and other data clearly indicate, the current and projected growth of non-White groups in the United States ensures that the nation will be less racially homogeneous in the future than it has been in the past. This growth of racial diversity in a land that has been largely populated by immigrants will continue to create new opportunities in the nation that prides itself as "the land of opportunity." At the same time, as a more racially diverse population challenges the commonly held melting pot theory that once characterized thinking in this country, there will be new stresses and strains.

The communication media of the United States bear a special responsibility in these circumstances, because they share a portion of the responsibility for educating older residents about the newcomers. The media also penetrate the homes of all members of the population through both print and broadcast outlets and assist minority group members by defining the society to newcomers and others outside the mainstream. In the past, media have chosen either to ignore racially diverse populations or to treat them in an unequal manner. However, the growing number of Blacks, Asians, Latinos, and Native Americans throughout the country, particularly in urban areas, forces the abandonment of this reaction and the adoption of new strategies. As the media move beyond tokenism in hiring and content, they will grapple with ways to reach audiences, cover news, and provide entertainment programming to a racially diverse society.

It is still too early to project all of the changes media will undergo as they seek to capitalize on the rainbow of races that will characterize the United States in the future. However, it is clear that the media that choose to avoid the clearly marked trends will have an increasingly difficult time in capturing a fair share of the audience in areas where non-White groups constitute a substantial and growing portion of the population. The media that do successfully penetrate those audiences will be the media with the greatest chances for success and profitability in the future.

NOTES

1. Leon F. Bouvier and Cary B. Davis, *The Future Racial Composition of the United States* (Demographic Information Services Center of the Population Reference Bureau), August 1982, pp. 1, 3.

2. "U.S. population: Where we are, where we're going," *Population Bulletin*, Vol. 37, No. 2, June 1982, p. 6.

3. Bureau of the Census, "Age, sex, race and Spanish origin population: 1980," *1980 Census of Population, Supplementary Reports*, PC-S1-1, May 1981.

4. "Big stories of the decade," *Public Opinion*, August/September 1981, pp. 18-19.

5. Philip M. Hauser, "The Census of 1980," *Scientific American*, Vol. 245, No. 5, November 1981, p. 61.

6. Bouvier and Davis, *Future Racial Composition*, p. 2.

7. Gregory Spencer and Signe Wetrogan, "Projecting the census," *American Demographics*, April 1981, p. 3.

8. "Non-Anglo majority projected for U.S. by 2080," *Public Management*, September 1983, p. 17.

9. Spencer and Wetrogan, "Projecting the census," p. 3.

10. Gregory Spencer and John F. Long, "The new Census Bureau projections," *American Demographics*, April 1983, pp. 30-31.

11. "Non-Anglo Majority Projected for U.S. by 2080," pp. 17-18.

12. Bouvier and Davis, *Future Racial Composition*, p. 57.

13. "What does the 1980 Census show? Looking ahead and looking back," *Public Opinion*, pp. 15-16.

14. Ibid., p. 17

15. Raymond Kennedy, "The colonial crisis and the future," in *The Science of Man in the World Crisis*, ed. Ralph Linton (Columbia University Press, 1945), p. 320, as cited in Charles F. Marden and Gladys Meyer, *Minorities in American Society* (D. Van Nostrand, 1978), p. 5. For an analysis of the role of the media in Great Britain and their relationship to racial minorities, see Paul Hartmann and Charles Hubbard, *Racism and the Mass Media* (Rowman & Littlefield, 1974).

16. Marden and Meyer, *Minorities in American Society*, pp. 6-7.

17. Ibid., pp. 10-15.

18. Ibid., p. 14.

19. Ibid., p. 63-64.

20. John D. Kasarda, "Hispanics and city change," *American Demographics*, November 1984, pp. 25-29.

21. Félix Gutiérrez, "Ethnic diversity in Los Angeles," *Urban Resources*, Vol. 1, No. 4, Spring 1984, pp. LA4-LA6.

22. "Factors for effective marketing to Latinos," *Los Angeles Times* Marketing Research, March 1982, p. 2.

23. Ibid., p. 14.

24. Reynolds Farley and Suzanne M. Bianchi, "The growing gap between Blacks," *American Demographics*, July 1983, pp. 15-18.

25. Kasarda, "Hispanics and city change," p. 29.

2

COMMUNICATION MEDIA IN A RACIALLY DIVERSE SOCIETY

HOW MUCH DO YOU KNOW about the people who first lived on what is now called the American continent? Think about it. How much do you know about the people who lived in the nomadic tribes and the villages across what is now the United States? Do you know what languages they spoke? What they liked to eat? What their customs were? Can you describe how they dressed? Or what their villages looked like? Or how they battled the European settlers who came into their land?

If you are like most people in the United States you probably know some, but not all, of the answers to the questions above. You know some things about Native Americans, but probably not as much as you think you should know. At one time or another you have probably seen a movie or a television documentary, or read a book, about Native Americans and their fight to survive on the land that was once theirs.

Now try to forget about what you have learned from personal experience, textbooks, or school. Try to remember what you know about Native Americans from what you have seen from the communication media—from radio, television, newspapers, and magazines. Chances are you will not remember very much factual information, since, aside from western movies and an occasional news story, Native Americans are still an invisible minority in the communications media of the United States. The images that have been portrayed often do not do justice to the people they are supposed to represent. Movies and television programs have traditionally treated Native Americans as savages who were vanquished by a superior people and civilization. Contemporary Native Americans have been treated by news reports as either a group overburdened by its own problems or the source of problems for the larger society.

In a media-dominated society such as the United States, all of us depend on the media of communication to portray and define those things we have not experienced for ourselves. Thus we "learn" about others through radio, television, movies, newspapers, and magazines. The portrayals and news coverage of Native Americans and other groups in these media can become reality in our minds, especially if we have no personal experiences to balance them against. This pervasive influence of the media in our society has been amply described and documented by other scholars who have analyzed communication media in modern society.

FUNCTIONS OF MASS COMMUNICATION IN SOCIETY

The functions of media in modern society have been described in different terms by different scholars, all of whom agree on the pervasive influence of media on American society. In a 1948 essay often cited by other researchers, pioneer communication scholar Harold Lasswell described the three major functions of communication as follows:

(1) *surveillance* of the environment, disclosing threats and opportunities affecting the value position of the community and of the component parts within it

(2) *correlation* of the different parts of society in responding to environment

(3) *transmission* of the social heritage from one generation to the next[1]

Examined in the context of a society containing several racial minority groups and a majority group that, to a large extent, controls the mass communication media of that society, Lasswell's surveillance function assigns to the media the responsibility of looking across the society in order to define and describe the different minority groups within it. The correlation function of the media helps members of the media's audience take stock of the different groups and determine how and where they fit in the society. Finally, the transmission function both defines what the social culture and heritage of the society are and transmits it to other members of the society.

Lasswell noted that although the United States prides itself on being a democratic society built on rational public opinion formed through broad dissemination of information, there is often a gap of information between the leaders and the public. He also noted that communication can be altered when the ruling elements of the society sense a threat:

> In society, the communication process reveals special characteristics when the ruling element is afraid of the internal as well as the external environment. In gauging the efficiency of communication in any given context, it is necessary to take into account the values at stake, and the identity of the group whose position is being examined. In democratic societies, rational choices depend on enlightenment, which in turn depends upon communication; and especially upon the equivalence of attention among leaders, experts, and rank and file.[2]

Lasswell's addendum, which is the last paragraph in his article, reinforces the importance of understanding that communication systems may behave differently when a threat is perceived by the leaders of the systems, especially when a particular group has been identified. In such cases, the media must portray a consistent message that develops a cohesive opinion among the various components of the society about that threat or group.

Applying Lasswell's functions, it is not surprising to discover that most people in the United States know very little about Native

Americans. The news media historically treated the native populations as part of the surveillance function, watching the horizon and reporting on them as they defended their lands and culture from the intrusion of the westward-moving Europeans who came to the American continent in the eighteenth and nineteenth centuries. In terms of correlation they were defined as a primitive and pagan people who blocked the manifest destiny of the Whites destined to populate the North American continent. The native population was worthy only of annihilation, subjugation, or consignment to reservations. Finally, the social inheritance of the continent—the true American culture—was defined as the culture developed by the European settlers, not by the Native American inhabitants.

While most of us may have limited knowledge about the culture and civilizations of the Native Americans, it is not because we are readers of the newspapers and magazines published during the European westward expansion in the last century. For the most part, the image of the people the Europeans called Indians has been shaped by the movies, television programs, and Western novels we have seen or read. These media are not designed primarily to be informative, but to serve as a diversion for their audiences. That is why in 1959 Charles Wright added a fourth dimension to Lasswell's three functions. Wright's fourth function, *entertainment*, emphasized that communication can also entertain the members of the society.[3] In the case of Native Americans, portrayals presented as entertainment have become reality in the minds of those who have seen Native Americans in movies and on television but nowhere else.

In addition to these functions, other scholars have noted that the mass media also perform important economic functions in the society. Wilbur Schramm and William Porter wrote in 1982 that, while no economist had outlined the economic functions of the media with the specificity of Lasswell, it is possible to enumerate them:

> For one thing, communication must meet the need for an economic map of the environment so that each individual and organization can form its own image of buying and selling opportunities at a given moment. For another, there must be correlation of economic policy, whether by the individual, the organization, or the

> nation. . . . Finally, instruction in the skills and expectations of economic behavior must be available.[4]

Other scholars have had a more bottom-line approach to describing the economic role of media in American society. In a mass communication textbook, Peter Sandman, David Rubin, and David Sachsman once described the economic function of the media as "to make money."[5] In a later edition, they changed the function to "to serve the economic system," but listed it as the first function and emphasized its central role in the functioning of media in this society:

> The fundamental economic purpose of the mass media in the United States is to sell people to advertisers. Economically, the articles in your newspaper and the programs on your radio and TV sets are merely come-ons to catch and hold your attention. Advertisers buy that attention from the media, and use it to sell you their products and services. In the process, both the media and the advertisers earn substantial profits.[6]

They could easily have added that the media, including those that do not depend on advertiser support—such as movies, records, and some cable television channels—also serve the economic system by functioning within the private sector as corporations that sell stock and generate profits or losses for their owners and stockholders. Thus the media must serve the needs of the economic system because, as part of the corporate community, they are private-enterprise institutions, rather than tax-supported institutions, such as schools or libraries. Because they are part of the private-enterprise system they must behave as other corporations and businesses do, seeking revenues and profits by maximizing consumption of their product while lowering the costs of production and distribution.

Combining the work of these and other scholars who have examined the functions of media in society we find that five central functions emerge for media in the United States:[7]

(1) *Surveillance*: the sentinel or lookout role of the media watching the society and horizon for threats to the established order and information on people or places of public interest

(2) *Correlation*: interpretation and linking function of the media, which helps the audience understand, interpret, and comprehend the different things that are happening in and out of society and how they affect each other, as well as stay in touch with others in the society

(3) *Transmission*: the socialization function of the media, which defines the society, its norms, and its values to the audience and, through their portrayals and coverage, assists members of the society in adopting, using, and acting on those values

(4) *Entertainment*: the function of the media for diversion and enjoyment, which provides stories, features, music, and films designed to make the audiences laugh, cry, relax, or reflect, rather than gain information

(5) *Economic service*: the role of the media within the economic system of the society, which in the United States means that most media function as corporations serving the needs of their shareholders and other corporations by attracting audiences that will either pay for the media product or serve as the target for advertising messages

MASS AUDIENCE, MASS MEDIA, AND MINORITIES

The media might be fulfilling all of these functions in American society today without treating members of racial minority groups any differently from those in the majority if it had not been for an economic transformation that dictated the direction and form of communication media in the industrial society taking shape in the United States in the early nineteenth century. As originally envisioned by the framers of the U.S. Constitution, media in the United States were supposed to operate in a free marketplace of ideas in which every political group, interest group, or anyone else with the wherewithal and motivation would be able to print and disseminate newspapers. It was felt that the new republic's voters, at that time a population limited to White males, would choose from the wide variety of periodicals available to them and, after weighing the different shades of opinion, would make an informed choice at the polling place. Media were seen as both the watchdogs of the government and the critical communication link on which the new democratic society would depend for information. For this reason, the First Amendment to the Constitution prohibits legislation limiting the freedom of the press, the only portion of the private sector afforded constitutional protection.

But in freeing the press from governmental restraints, the framers of the Constitution also denied the press the licensing and underwriting that had been afforded to official government or sanctioned periodicals in Europe and other parts of the Americas. Therefore, the press, while freed from the laws of Congress, was forced to function as a business within the economic system and follow the unwritten laws of capitalism that govern businesses in the United States. While a subsidized partisan press played an important role in the development of early newspapers in the United States, the media that would come to dominate the United States through the 1980s emerged in the 1830s in the form of a popular newspaper.

The newspaper was the *New York Sun*, which appeared in 1833 and sold for only a penny. This first "penny press" was uniquely adapted to the free enterprise system. Although it sold for only a penny, it did not depend on subsidies from a political party, from a government in the form of public notices, or from the subscriptions of readers. Instead, the newspaper's revenues and profits came primarily from advertisers who paid for space in the newspaper in order to reach the large readership attracted by its low price.

Benjamin Day, founder of the newspaper, envisioned the penny press as a newspaper for the mass audience of city-dwelling workers who would be attracted by the newspaper's lively content, its low price, and the promise of the *New York Sun*—"It Shines for ALL." The newspaper's formula, which was widely imitated, attracted the loyalty of readers. But they were not the only ones to take an interest in the penny press. According to journalism historians Edwin Emery and Michael Emery,

> Another person began to take a special interest in the newspaper for the masses. This was the advertiser, who was impressed by the amazing circulation of the new medium. Putting an ad in every publication bought by small splinter groups was expensive and ineffective sales promotion. The large circulation of the penny papers

> now made it feasible to publicize articles for sale that formerly would not have warranted advertising expense.[8]

Given the formula developed by the penny press, communication media in the United States developed as mass-audience media, with content designed to attract a wide audience and deliver that audience to advertisers. The space for the advertisement in the newspaper or on the television screen has no intrinsic economic value of its own. Its worth is derived from the size of the audience that has been attracted to that space by the news or entertainment content of the newspaper and broadcast station. As media strove to accumulate large audiences, they developed content that would attract the widest audience possible and offend the fewest people. Rather than including a variety of small outlets, each addressing the needs of segments of the society, media in the United States became synonymous with the mass audience. In fact, the terms "mass media" and "mass communication" are used interchangeably to describe the media system of the nation. As a result, media geared for political, national, or racial minorities have been consigned to economic second-class standing, and members of those groups have been either ignored in the mass media attracting the majority society or portrayed in ways that made them palatable to the majority. Mass society in the United States did not necessarily mean a society of the masses, but a society in which the people were amassed into an audience for the messages of the mass media of communication.

The function of the content of the mass media in the nineteenth and twentieth centuries has been to reach the lowest common denominator in the society and address the media content (news, entertainment, or information) to that level. While different media might target different strata within the masses, the basic goal of attracting the largest number of persons at that level has remained the same. The media successful in attracting the mass audience were rewarded by being able to charge higher prices to advertisers or, in the case of records and movies, to purchasers of their products. And it was the advertisers, with their seemingly insatiable appetite for larger audiences for their advertisements, who fueled the media's chase of the mass audience. The critical role of advertising in shaping and directing the development of the mass-audience mentality by the media has not always been appreciated by scholars describing the development of communication media in the United States. In 1954, historian David Potter wrote:

> Histories of American periodicals and even of the mass media deal with advertising as if it were a side issue. Students of the radio and of the mass-circulation magazines frequently condemn advertising for its conspicuous role, as if it were a mere interloper in a separate, pre-existing, self-contained aesthetic world of actors, musicians, authors, and script-writers; they hardly recognize that advertising created modern American radio and television, transformed the modern newspaper, evoked the modern slick periodical, and remains the vital essence of each of them at the present time.[9]

Although the range of media has greatly increased in the three decades since Potter wrote, and now afford a wider range of content for different segments of American society, the fundamental relationship that he described between advertising and the media has not changed. In the period when the mass audience media dominated all other forms this relationship dictated that minority groups were treated in the mass media in terms that did not offend or, in fact, reinforced the attitudes of the dominant society toward those groups.

MASS MEDIA AND THE COLLECTIVE CONSCIOUSNESS

Advertisers demanded mass audiences to advertise their products; the communication media responded by adopting news and entertainment strategies that would attract the largest numbers of people. Since nearly all of the people in the United States were White, many of them immigrants, this meant that Blacks, Latinos, Native Americans, Asians, and other people of color were treated as fringe audiences, not important enough in numbers to dictate the content that would be directed to the mass audience.

The media reinforced a collective consciousness in the members of the audience that was necessary to attract large numbers of undifferentiated people. It was the task of the mass media to look for commonalities among members of the audience—

common themes, ideas, and interest areas that would attract and not offend the mass audience. With few exceptions, this meant that the content of the mass media reinforced, rather than challenged, the established norms and attitudes of the society. To do otherwise would be to risk offending significant numbers in the mass audience and, in the process, losing the large audience demanded by the advertisers.

The society of the United States, characterized by a melting pot mentality through which immigrants from different nations have tried to blend together, has often treated members of groups who had not blended or could not blend into the mainstream as outsiders. Racial minorities that could be identified by color or facial characteristics were often "beyond" the melting pot, unable to blend over the period of a generation because of physical characteristics. Blacks, Native Americans, Asians, and Latinos were groups whose physical appearance permanently identified them as different from the European Whites who had come from different countries and "melted" into the society of the United States.

They were not only beyond the melting pot, but outside the focus of the mass audience. Their numbers were relatively insignificant compared with the White majority and, as a result, they were not considered important components of the mass audience. For the most part, the mass media treated groups not in the mass audience or mainstream by either ignoring them or stereotyping them. Movies, radio programs, newspapers, and newsmagazines generally ignored the issues confronting people of color in the United States, as well as their culture and traditions. When they were treated, it was often in stereotyped roles, such as a Black mammy, an Indian maiden, a Latin lover, or sinister Asian warlord. These characterizations of minorities were largely based on the perceptions and preconceptions of those outside the groups, rather than the realities of the groups themselves. They were pictures of racial minorities as seen through Anglo eyes.

The images served a useful economic purpose in attracting the mass audience. One characteristic of the mass audience was that it represented people who really were different from each other—people who lived in different parts of the country, had different levels of income and education, and came from different cultural backgrounds. It included men and women, young and old, rich and poor. The media needed to communicate across these barriers and develop a common content denominator to which all in the potential audience could relate.

The technique developed by the mass media in dealing with racial minorities and others outside the mainstream involved symbols and stereotypes. The mass media, because they dealt with a wide audience, came to rely on symbols and stereotypes as shorthand ways of communicating through headlines, characters, and pictures. Dramatic portrayals such as those of rich bankers, heroic cowboys, or old spinsters were used so audiences would understand the character the first time he or she appeared on the screen or in the short story. At the same time, newspapers used symbols such as "right wing," "leftist," and "moderate" in headlines to characterize people or parties in different places on the political spectrum.

These symbols were a useful shorthand for the mass media, since they allowed the entertainment and news media to capsulize complex personalities and issues in shortened characterizations or terms. Thus when the audience at a western movie saw a man come on the screen with a white hat, they knew he was supposed to be the hero. Or when the term "leftist" was used in a headline, that meant that the group to which the term was applied was on the liberal extreme, bordering on communist. The terms themselves were useful because they became symbols that triggered stereotypes, which Walter Lippmann long ago described as "pictures in our heads." The symbol was the term that called up a whole set of characteristics ascribed to those associated with the term in the minds of the mass audience. Those characteristics became the stereotype in the mentality of the audience.

Racial minority groups were among the groups portrayed by symbols and stereotypes in the entertainment and news media. Stereotyped characterizations of Native Americans, Blacks, Asians, and Latinos dominated the portrayals of members of these groups in the entertainment media of movies, radio, fiction, and television through the 1960s. Similarly, news media rarely covered activities in these communities unless, in accordance with their surveillance function, they were perceived as posing a threat to the established order or, in accordance with the correlation function, they were covered during colorful cultural festivals. Thus the mass audience saw only a slice of the minority communities, one that did not jar their preconceptions of these groups. In fact, the media portrayals probably helped legitimize and reinforce such preconceptions.

In the absence of alternative portrayals and broadened news coverage, one-sided portrayals and news articles could easily become the reality in the minds of the audience. Whites might be seen in a wide range of roles in a movie, ranging from villains to heroes. In contrast, Blacks were seen only as comical mammys, wide-eyed coons, or lazy, shuffling no-goods. There were no alternative portrayals to counter the stereotype.

DO THE MEDIA HAVE AN EFFECT?

Although it was once thought that the mass media constituted a "magic bullet" that entered the minds of the audience and could convert them to any opinion or attitude, scholars who have examined the effects of media on society since the 1940s have found that the influence of media is both more limited and more complex than that. They have found that media have their greatest influence when they reinforce, rather than change, the opinions of those in their audience. Rather than a mere target for a bullet, the mass audience is more accurately described as a complex set of groups and individuals who make selective decisions about which media to use, what information to retain from the media, and how to interpret what they see and remember. Media have their greatest effect when they are used in a manner that reinforces and channels attitudes and opinions consistent with the psychological makeup of the person and the social structure of the groups with which he or she identifies.

Because of the wide range of social and psychological factors affecting how a person thinks and acts, it is difficult to pinpoint specific effects of media on how people think and act. However, the reinforcement and channeling effect of media, when coupled with the content analyses that have been made on coverage and portrayal of minorities in news and entertainment media, provide an insight into the negative effects of one-sided media images on both Anglos and the members of the minority groups portrayed. Effects do, of course, vary by the age and psychological makeup of the people receiving the messages, and the research in this area is not as well developed as are some other areas of communication research. Nevertheless, the studies that have been done show that negative, one-sided, or stereotyped media portrayals and news coverage do reinforce racist attitudes in those members of the audience who have such attitudes and can channel mass actions against the group that is stereotypically portrayed. The studies also show that bigoted persons watching television programs ridiculing bigotry interpret such programs as reinforcing their preexisting beliefs. The studies also show that children, both minority and majority, are especially affected by entertainment characters that portray minority groups. While it is unwise to make general statements about the effect of coverage and portrayals of minorities on the society, it is useful to look at three studies that illustrate cases in which the broad principles of media effects have been found useful in assessing the impact of media in this area.

News Coverage and Mob Violence: The Zoot Suit Riots of 1943

In the midst of World War II, Los Angeles was the scene of violent attacks by battle-trained American servicemen stationed in Southern California on Mexican, Black, and Filipino youths on the streets of downtown Los Angeles. The attacks targeted minority youth wearing "zoot suits"—long suitcoats, pants pegged at the cuff with deep pleats at the waist—and a full head of well-greased hair. The attacks followed and were accompanied by a news media campaign targeting the zoot-suited youths as antisocial elements whose dress was out of step with the nation's war effort. Accounts of the zoot suit riots, which occurred in June 1943, often include references to the one-sided coverage of the predominantly Mexican youths in the Los Angeles press.

In 1956, two sociologists, Ralph H. Turner and Samuel Surace, analyzed coverage of Mexicans in the Los Angeles press in an effort to determine how it may have affected the violent attacks on the teenaged youths.[10] Turner and Surace, hypothesizing that the period preceding the riots was characterized by steady negative coverage of Mexicans in Los Angeles, first studied the coverage of Mexicans in the *Los Angeles Times* from 1933 to 1943. Articles were categorized into one of five categories. First was *favorable*—stories that emphasized the area's Old California tradition: the romantic, brave, dashing image of Mexicans; religion in the Mexican community; or Mexican culture. Second was *unfavorable*—articles on delinquency and crime or Mexicans as a public burden. Third was *neutral*—miscellaneous articles including people with Spanish surnames, but not identified as Mexicans in the article.

Fourth was *negative-favorable*—articles that stated and then refuted accusations against Mexicans with such statements as "Not all zoot-suiters are delinquents." Fifth was *zooter theme*—articles identifying the zoot-suit dress with crime, sex, violence, or gang activities.

The two sociologists hypothesized that the uniform crowd behavior, such as the organized attacks on Mexican youths by servicemen stationed in the area, was preceded by media coverage in which the term "Mexican" would be used as an unambiguous negative symbol. They also hypothesized that because of the negative behavior ascribed to those labeled with the symbol, mob violence against the Mexican youths that would not be tolerated in other circumstances would be sanctioned by the larger society. Turner and Surace felt that both favorable and unfavorable sentiments could be triggered by ambiguous symbols, noting that "even the most prejudiced person is likely to respond to the symbol 'Negro' with images of both the feared invader of white prerogatives and the lovable, loyal Negro lackey and 'mammy.'"[11] But unambiguous symbols representing people outside the boundaries of normal, accepted behavior would trigger "the dictum that 'you must fight fire with fire' and the conviction that a person devoid of human decency is not entitled to be treated with decency and respect."[12] When the symbol loses its positive or neutral elements, the people associated with the symbol could become targets for mob violence that would not normally be allowed in the society, the sociologists wrote. Therefore, in looking at the news coverage, the sociologists expected to find a decline in the number of times the term "Mexican" was used in favorable news coverage in the period preceding the mob violence, resulting in the development of an unambiguously negative image for the people labeled with the term.

Their hypothesis was not fully supported by the data gathered before the rioting. In fact, themes classified as favorable by the researchers (primarily those that tended to romanticize the Mexican culture) covered between 80 percent and 90 percent of the stories in which the term "Mexican" was used in the 10-year period before the riots. In taking a closer look at the data, however, they did find support for their hypothesis on the importance of unambiguous negative symbols. While the percentage of favorable mentions of "Mexican" in the three-year period preceding the 1943 riots did not decrease, the researchers noted a sharp decline in the number of articles using "Mexican" at all. The term was used in 27 articles sampled between January 1933 and June 1936 and 23 times in articles between July 1936 and December 1939. But it was used in less than half that number, only 10 articles, between January 1940 and June 1943. Thus, given what the researchers considered to be the "favorable" image of the term "Mexican" in the 1930s, the researchers found what they described as "a shift away from *all* the traditional references to Mexicans during the period prior to the riots."[13]

Their data analysis showed there had been no lessening of coverage of stories concerning Mexicans during the ten-year period. In fact the number of articles rose steadily in the three periods between 1933 and 1943. But there was a decline in the number of articles using the term "Mexican" and an increase in the percentage of articles classified as neutral, negative-favorable, and zoot-suiter. In the first period, favorable articles constituted 80 percent of the articles coded, but in the last period only 25 percent of the articles were favorable. The percentage of articles coded as neutral increased sharply to 32 percent, and the authors noted that the category "actually consists chiefly of unfavorable presentations of the object 'Mexican' without overt use of the symbol 'Mexican.'"[14] The percentage of articles in the negative-favorable category also increased, although the increase was smaller than the others, and, as the authors noted, is based on the overall negative image of Mexicans.

The most startling shift, and the one most supportive of the secondary hypothesis of the researchers, was the sharp increase in the use of the "zoot suit" term and theme as a strictly negative symbol. The zoot-suit theme, which was not used before 1940, accounted for a third of all the articles from 1940 to June 1943. The authors concluded that the introduction of the term and its heavy use in unfavorable circumstances resulted in the development of a strictly negative symbol that triggered no unambiguous or positive stereotypes. The association of that symbol with Mexican youth portrayed as displaying antisocial behavior helped spur the indiscriminate attacks of servicemen on Mexican youths, including those not wearing zoot suits. According to Turner and Surace:

> Unlike the symbol "Mexican," the "zoot-suiter" symbol evokes no ambivalent sentiments but appears in exclusively unfavorable contexts. While, in fact, Mexicans were attacked *indiscriminately* in spite of apparel (of two hundred youths rounded up by the police on

> one occasion, very few were wearing zoot suits), the symbol "zoot-suiter" could become a basis for unambivalent community sentiment supporting hostile crowd behavior more easily than could "Mexican."[15]

The researchers found that in the period just before the violent attacks on Mexican teenagers, the newspaper's coverage of the Mexican community in the issues sampled was characterized by the predominance of the zoot-suiter theme in unfavorable coverage, less use of the term "Mexican" in favorable coverage, and an increased coverage of Mexicans in articles not using the term "Mexican" but portraying the community unfavorably. Of the 15 articles analyzed in the six months just prior to the June 1943 attacks, 10 concerned zoot-suiters, 3 were negative-favorable, 2 were neutral, and none was in either the traditional favorable or unfavorable categories. In the month just before and including the attacks by servicemen on Mexican youths, 74 percent of the 61 articles on the Mexican community concerned zoot-suiters, 23 percent were negative-favorable, and 3 percent were neutral.

While not ascribing all the blame to the news media for the violent attacks on Mexican youths, the researchers felt that the news coverage may have contributed to the violence and the general public support of the servicemen in two ways. One way was by showing a Mexican name or picture, or using a reference to "East Side hoodlums," without using the term "Mexican" or any other symbol. The second and, according to the authors, more effective, method was the introduction and use of a new symbol in a strictly unfavorable context. As Turner and Surace wrote:

> It [the new symbol] provided the public sanction and restriction of attention essential to the development of overt crowd hostility. The symbol "zoot-suiter" evoked none of the imagery of the romantic past. It evoked only the picture of a breed of persons outside the normative order, devoid of morals themselves, and consequently not entitled to fair play and due process. . . . The "zooter" symbol had a crisis character which mere unfavorable versions of the familiar "Mexican" symbol never approximated. And the "zooter" symbol was an omnibus, drawing together the most reprehensible elements in the old unfavorable themes, namely, sex crimes, delinquency, gang attacks, draft-dodgers, and the like and was, in consequence, widely applicable.[16]

The Turner and Surace article is valuable because racial symbols triggering commonly accepted images in the minds of the audience have often been used in the news coverage of minorities. Since racial minorities historically have not been well reported in the news media, these symbols are often used at a time when the surveillance and correlation functions of the media are called upon to describe a change in the environment created by minorities, or to define how and where minorities fit into the society. A study of national magazine coverage of Mexicans in the United States from 1890 to 1970 revealed a near-absence of coverage except when elements of the Mexican population were seen as a threat to society and subject to discriminatory acts by the public or law enforcement officials. In these periods symbols such as "zoot-suiters," "wetbacks," and "Chicanos" (in the militant sense) dominated the headlines of national magazines. More recently, the term "illegal alien" has been used to symbolize a person who enters the country illegally and is said to constitute a burden on public resources.[17] A survey of 114 randomly selected articles from California newspapers on undocumented immigration from January 1977 through March 1978 found that nearly half of the articles used the symbols "alien" or "illegal alien" in the headlines. The largest categories of headlines dealt with immigrants as a law enforcement problem or as a drain on public resources, or focused on their illegal entry into the United States or federal efforts to cope with the issue.[18]

Bigotry and Bigots Reinforced: The Case of Archie Bunker

When the situation comedy program *All in the Family* hit the airwaves in January 1971 it immediately triggered a debate over the breaking of traditional barriers against racial and ethnic humor in network television. The story line of the program pitted a rascally but hard-working bigot, Archie Bunker, against his liberal minded son-in-law, Mike. Mike, a graduate student, lived in the Bunker household and engaged in lively and humorous debates with Archie, who had dropped out of high school and had a blue-collar job. Some lauded the program for tackling racial prejudice and exposing the foolishness of bigotry through the use of comedy. Others argued that the program, by portraying Archie as a lovable bigot, had the effect of sanctioning and even encouraging bigotry.

Norman Lear, the producer of the program, answered critics of the program by arguing that the comedy's story lines countered bigotry because Mike effectively rebutted Archie; Lear said that Mike was the one "who is making sense." Archie, Lear wrote in 1971, was seen by the audience as an advocate of "convoluted logic."[19] The program's dependence on racial themes would bring bigotry out in the open and would allow parents to answer children's questions about it, Lear contended. The CBS television network, which aired the program, commissioned a study that showed the program could contribute to a lessening of racial bigotry by humorously exposing its shortcomings. Others defended the program for using a comedy format to belittle those with prejudiced opinions. The Los Angeles chapter of the National Association for the Advancement of Colored People (NAACP) even gave its 1972 Image Award to *All in the Family* for contributing to better race relations.

The television program continued for more than a decade and the basis of its humor moved into other areas as the program and characters evolved. Although several research projects dealt with the impact of the program on its viewers, one of the most important was also one of the first. In 1974, psychologist Neil Vidmar and sociologist/psychologist Milton Rokeach published an article analyzing viewers of the program in the United States and Canada and the apparent impact of the program on them. Noting the debate then taking place over the effect of Archie Bunker on bigotry and prejudice, the researchers tested the audience reaction to the program in terms of the previous studies, showing the way audiences use selective perception and selective exposure to regulate and filter the media.

Under the selective perception hypothesis, Vidmar and Rokeach theorized that viewers with different degrees of prejudice or racism would have different reasons for watching the program, would identify with different characters, and would find different meanings in the outcomes of the programs. Under the selective exposure hypothesis, the researchers proposed that low-prejudiced and high-prejudiced people would not watch *All in the Family* to the same extent. To test the hypotheses they surveyed 237 high school students in a small town in the midwestern United

States and 168 adults in London, Ontario. The people surveyed were asked to respond to a questionnaire with eleven items designed to probe their reactions to the television program and six questions to measure their ethnocentrism or prejudice.

The initial analysis of the results showed that more than 60 percent of the respondents liked or admired Archie more than Mike, that 40 percent of the U.S. respondents felt that Archie won at the end of the show, that 46 percent named Mike as the one most made fun of, and that 35 percent saw nothing wrong with Archie's use of racial and ethnic slurs. Results from the Canadian sample followed the same pattern. Vidmar and Rokeach then compared the exposure and interpretations of the program between respondents who were rated as high prejudiced and low prejudiced on the six items designed to measure ethnocentrism and prejudice. While both groups found the program equally enjoyable, there was a big difference in their reactions to the program. The analysis of data testing the selective perception hypothesis found a number of significant differences showing that people at different levels of prejudice drew different conclusions from watching the same television characters.

"High prejudiced persons in both the U.S. and Canadian samples were significantly more likely than low prejudiced people to admire Archie over Mike and to perceive Archie as winning in the end," the researchers wrote.[20] The high-prejudiced U.S. adolescents were also more likely to report that Archie made better sense than Mike and to report that their attitudes would be similar to Archie Bunker's in 20 years. High-prejudiced Canadian adults also condoned Archie's racial slurs more often and saw the show as poking fun at Archie less often than did low-prejudiced viewers. The researchers summarized that the data "tend to support the selective perception hypothesis—namely, that prejudiced persons identify more with Archie, perceive Archie as making better sense than Mike, perceive Archie as winning."[21] Furthermore, high-prejudiced viewers indicated a number of things they disliked about Mike and low-prejudiced viewers indicated things they disliked about Archie.

Vidmar and Rokeach also found support for the selective exposure hypothesis, but in a different direction than the one proposed by a report commissioned by the CBS television network. Network researchers, assuming that the program would be interpreted as satirizing bigotry, speculated that low-prejudiced persons would be the most avid viewers. But Vidmar and Rokeach found that U.S. teenagers who were the most frequent viewers of *All in the Family* were those in the high-prejudice group. No significant differences were found in the Canadian sample. The data also showed that the most frequent viewers admired Archie more than Mike and condoned Archie's ethnic slurs more than infrequent viewers. The researchers concluded that the testing of the selective exposure hypothesis showed that "*All in the Family* seems to be appealing more to the racially and ethnically prejudiced members of society than to the less prejudiced members."[22] They added:

> Despite the fact that the present study is not an experimental study, the findings surely argue against the contention that *All in the Family* has positive effects, as has been claimed by its supporters and admirers. We found that many persons did not see the program as a satire on bigotry and that these persons were even more likely to be viewers who scored high on measures of prejudices. Even more important is the finding that high prejudiced persons were likely to watch *All in the Family* more often than low prejudiced persons, to identify more often with Archie Bunker and to see him winning in the end. All such findings seem to suggest that the program is more likely reinforcing prejudice and racism than combating it.[23]

Contrary to the claims of the program's producer and network researchers, the findings of Vidmar and Rokeach, as well as those of subsequent scholars examining the impact of *All in the Family*, were consistent with previous studies on the way the social and psychological makeup of members of the audience influences the manner of choosing which media to use and how to interpret what they see, hear, or read. In the classic "Mr. Biggott" studies in the late 1940s, prejudiced individuals were shown cartoons in which the bigoted attitudes of Mr. Biggott were portrayed in an unfavorable light. Instead of seeing the shortcomings of such attitudes, the respondents reinterpreted the meaning of the cartoons to avoid ridiculing Mr. Biggott or to reinforce their own attitudes.[24] These and other studies have shown that the impact of media is to reinforce attitudes already held by members of their audience, rather than to persuade people to change them. When the content of the media plays on racial prejudice and bigotry, even if these themes are ridiculed, prejudiced persons interpret the message to reinforce their bigoted attitudes rather than to reject or change them.

Learning from Television: Effects of Black Portrayals on Children

The late 1960s and the 1970s witnessed an increase in the percentage of minority characters, particularly Blacks, in prime-time network television programming. In 1969-1970, half of the television dramatic programs had a Black character, and from that season through the early 1980s annual surveys of Blacks in network programming showed that 6 percent to 9 percent of all television characters were Black. However, the increase in the number of characters did not necessarily mean that Blacks were treated equally with characters of other races. Research cited by communication researchers Charles K. Atkin, Bradley S. Greenberg, and Steven McDermott revealed that Black characters were more often in minor roles and less prestigious jobs than White characters, but were just as industrious, competent and physically attractive. Blacks were also portrayed as more kind, moral, and altruistic, more often crime victims, and more often involved in violence and killing than Whites. Blacks also tended to be dominated by Whites in crime dramas, although they dominated Whites in situation comedies. By the late 1970s, most of the Black characters were found in situation comedies, where they most often played stereotyped characters who were lower in social status and more beset by problems than Blacks in integrated programs.[25]

To test the impact of such portrayals on White youths, in 1983 Atkin, Greenberg, and McDermott surveyed 316 White students in the fourth, sixth, and eighth grades in schools in Michigan and Northern California. The students were asked how often they watched six network television programs featuring Black casts, if they tried to learn from television, whether television Blacks were like real Blacks, and how much they identified with Black characters. They were also asked to compare portrayals of Blacks and Whites, to compare traits of real Blacks and Whites, and to estimate the proportion of Blacks in the population. In addition, they were asked what they learned from television about Blacks, and how much contact they had with Blacks.

In analyzing the responses, the researchers found that 30 percent of the youths watched the six programs weekly or almost weekly. Although only 14 percent said they watched television to learn about how other people behave, talk, dress, and look, it was clear that the televised portrayals of Blacks had affected the students' "knowledge" of Blacks. Less than a third of the students said they used television to learn about how Blacks dress, behave, and talk, but 66 percent said television Blacks "talk" like Blacks in real life. Black teenagers on television were seen as realistic by 56 percent, Black men by 45 percent, and Black women by 44 percent of the youths surveyed. The researchers also found that the impact of the portrayals on television was mitigated by how the youths interpreted those portrayals. While finding no direct stimulus-response relationship between the way television portrayed Blacks and how real Blacks were perceived by the children, the researchers found that the selective perception of the young viewers could interpret the television programming to reinforce existing racial attitudes:

> The data showing that belief effects depend on the perceptions of the viewer indicate that television's role may be to reinforce prior dispositions rather than cause dramatic changes. This suggests the important role that parents and schools might play in shaping the process of learning from television, since these sources directly influence attitudes that the viewer brings to the set.[26]

The researchers wrote that their findings supported the traditional viewpoint that "what the child brings to TV" is just as important as "what TV does to the child."

While the portrayals of Blacks may not have a predictable straight-line effect, it has also been shown that Black and White children may learn different things from those portrayals. In an earlier study, Greenberg found that Black children were more likely than Whites to watch television programs with Black characters, were more often able to name a show featuring a Black character, and had more positive attitudes toward Blacks on television than did White children.[27] Researcher Alexis Tan concluded in a 1979 study that steady exposure to television entertainment programs that either ignore Blacks or relegate them to low-status roles could lead to low self-esteem among Black viewers.[28] Because of the statistical procedure used to analyze the data, the study did not show a cause-and-effect relationship between television portrayals and low self-esteem among Black adults. Other researchers have also shown that media portrayals may have a greater influence on the development of minority children than on White children.[29]

EFFECTS OF MEDIA ON SOCIETY

The findings in these and other studies are consistent. They show that the media's coverage and portrayal of minorities have an effect on members of both minority and majority groups. But it is a complex effect, one influenced by each person's psychological makeup, social status, and age and by how he or she uses the media. It is unlikely that scholars will ever be able to make definitive statements regarding the effect of media on minority groups or any other segment of society. This is because communication is not a physical science, but a behavioral process. The role and effect of media are not as predictable as the results when two chemicals are mixed at a certain temperature in a laboratory. Communication involves human beings and society, not physical elements undergoing experimentation in a laboratory.

Even when communication researchers replicate experimental conditions as much as possible, they encounter difficulties in generating findings that can be applied to all people in all situations. Furthermore, laboratory findings do not always reflect reality. While the laboratory may be the best setting for the observation of biological experiments under controlled conditions, it may be the worst setting for the observation of social happenings. People do not encounter the media in a sterile laboratory, but in homes, waiting rooms, bars, and many other social settings. What they see, hear, and read in those settings is influenced by the people around them and by their own psychological makeup.

However, even though it is difficult to assess the effects of mass communication on members of society, the research findings are clear that certain types of people—including the young, those with predispositions to view members of racially different groups in a certain way, and members of minority groups that are not well integrated into the coverage and programming of the media—are affected to a greater extent than others. As a result, studies show that the young, prejudiced people, and members of minority groups are more influenced by minority portrayals in the media than are others.

RACIAL DIVERSITY: A PROBLEM OR AN OPPORTUNITY?

The growth in minority populations in the United States has forced the media to reexamine the ways it has traditionally dealt with minority groups. As these groups grow in number and as a percentage of the population at a rate that outstrips the Anglo population, the media will have to continue to look for new ways to deal with them. And, as Census Bureau Director-Designate Chapman has pointed out (see Chapter 1), their continued identification with their own cultural backgrounds and racial groups will make it more difficult for the media to play their traditional role of homogenizing the members of disparate groups into a mass culture or society. Rather than try to address them as part of the melting pot, media may have to address them along their cultural and racial identities and, in the process, reinforce the differences rather than change them.

Too often the growth of a racially diverse population has been portrayed as a *problem* for the media and other institutions, forcing them to change their methods of doing business and making them cater to groups that tenaciously hang on to their cultural roots in a nation in which other immigrants have willingly shed theirs. There are differences in language, culture, religion, and lifestyle that are seen as a threat to traditional North American values. Some media organizations, while professing concern over the changing populations, have consciously adopted strategies that appear to be an attempt to avoid minority groups as they moved into the nation's cities.

At the same time that the inner cities were becoming increasingly racially diverse, many big-city newspapers were looking for ways to avoid the potential readers in their neighborhoods, but chasing those who were living in suburban cities and counties. Using circulation strategies that made it difficult, if not impossible, for residents of ghettos and barrios to subscribe to newspapers, some metropolitan newspapers refused to put newsstands in inner-city areas at the same time they were starting or expanding new editions in outlying areas. The strategies were defended as being based on economics, because the low-income characteristics of Blacks and Latinos made them undesirable newspaper readers. Mainstream advertisers, some publishers argued, wanted affluent readers who could afford the products that they advertised. Denying any racist intentions, the newspaper managers said they were merely following the more affluent readers who moved to the suburbs.

The strategies of newspapers in avoiding the inner city were described by Ben Bagdikian of the University of California at Berkeley in a 1978 article in *Human Behavior*. Bagdikian cited newspapers in different parts of the nation that consciously adopted circulation and news reporting strategies that avoided the growing numbers of minorities and low-income residents in central-city areas, while reaching out to readers in the predominantly Anglo and more affluent suburbs around those cities.

"We cut out unprofitable circulation, and we arbitrarily cut back some of our low-income circulation," Bagdikian quoted Otis Chandler, then publisher of the *Los Angeles Times*, as saying. He also quoted a 1976 memo by an editor of the *Detroit News* ordering staffers to aim the newspaper at people who made more than $18,000 a year and were between the ages of 28 and 40. Such stories, the editor wrote, "should be obvious: they won't have a damn thing to do with Detroit and its internal problems."[30] According to Bagdikian:

> The blackout of news to the central city is usually justified by publishers on grounds that it is harder to sell papers there, that it is harder to hire and keep delivery people on the job and there is a higher rate of nonpayment of bills. That is true, and it has always been true. The difference now is that advertisers don't want that population so now the publishers don't either.[31]

Because advertisers wanted affluent readers, newspapers and broadcast media targeted their content to audiences in the more affluent, and predominantly Anglo, suburban areas. Circulation percentages and actual numbers declined in the cities whose names the newspapers proudly wore on their front pages and broadcast stations claimed as their city of license. According to figures cited by Bagdikian in 1978, the *Los Angeles Times* was received by only 26 percent of the homes in Los Angeles and the *San*

Francisco Chronicle by only 36 percent of San Francisco's homes. Across the country, in New York, the *Daily News* got into only 37 percent of New York homes, the *New York Post* into 15 percent, and the *New York Times* into 11 percent.

Broadcasters, while they could not control who watched or listened to their stations and bore no additional costs for having low-income people tuned into their broadcasts, still have tried to target news and entertainment programming to more affluent viewers and listeners. Bagdikian noted that the American Broadcasting Company issued a demographic analysis of its audience titled "Some People Are More Valuable than Others." He wrote:

> In reporting and emphasis . . . both broadcast and printed news in metropolitan areas have turned their backs on their own cities. This despite a basic communications law that is supposed to exchange a monopoly on the dial for a station commitment to air local issues, and despite the fact that both broadcast stations and papers take their names from the cities they have reportorially abandoned.[32]

Given that many of the low-income residents of the central cities were members of racial minority groups, the economic strategies of the publishers and broadcasters had racial overtones as well. While media managers claimed their emphasis on affluent, suburban audiences was motivated only by their desire to reach the people advertisers sought, the fact remained that many low-income people in the inner cities who were unserved by the media were racial minorities.

In 1978 Otis Chandler, in response to a question by a television interviewer, admitted that the *Los Angeles Times* had "a way to go" in adequately covering Los Angeles's minority communities. But he added that it "would not make sense financially for us" to direct the newspaper to low-income readers because "that audience does not have the purchasing power and is not responsive to the kind of advertising we carry."

"So we could make the editorial commitment, the management commitment, to cover these communities," Chandler said. "But then how do we get them to read the *Times*? It's not their kind of newspaper: it's too big, it's too stuffy. If you will, it's too complicated."[33]

In a 1979 *Columbia Journalism Review* article Chandler and other *Times* executives were quoted as denying that the newspaper approached coverage and circulation from a racial standpoint, although one did admit the strategy meant the newspaper was directed at a predominantly Anglo audience. John Mount of the *Times* Marketing Research Department said, "We don't approach marketing from a racial standpoint. It just happens that the more affluent and educated people tend to be white and live in suburban communities."[34] The newspaper's advertisers were also pinpointed as spurring the strategy.

"Our major retail advertisers have said to us that 'We want a certain class of audience, a certain demographic profile of reader, whether that person be black, white, or brown or Chinese or whatever. We don't really care what sex or race they are. But we do care about their income,'" Chandler said. He also expressed optimism that more minorities would begin to read the *Times* "as their income goes up and their educational level comes up and they become interested in a paper like the *Times*. Then they become prospects for our advertisers."[35]

The situation at the *Los Angeles Times* and other newspapers has changed since the late 1970s, spurred by an upswing in the hiring of minority journalists. In 1978 the American Society of Newspaper Editors adopted a resolution calling for racial parity in the newsroom by the year 2000 and, although the representation of minorities in the newsroom is still far short of that, efforts have been made toward integrating minorities into the newsrooms and on the news pages. The employment story is amply told elsewhere in this book. The lesson that the media learned is that the development of a racially diverse population is something that cannot be avoided by the media. Instead of trying to bypass minority readers and coverage, the news organizations that have made the greatest gains are those that have seen the growing racial diversity as an opportunity, rather than as a problem.

The problem orientation of many media executives and corporations came about in the mid-1970s, just after the first wave of minority media hiring took place as a result of the civil rights movement and federal government pressures in the late 1960s and early 1970s. That first wave of hiring and coverage triggered gains based on tokenism, in which every respectable news organization tried to have at least one Black reporter and, possibly, a Latino, Native American, or Asian American. It was also motivated by a good dose of White guilt for past discrimination against minorities in hiring and coverage.

But by the mid-1970s much of that argument had run its course, as media organizations paid at least minimal lip service to the need for integration. By the latter part of the decade the argument for integration had switched to population demographics, focusing on the growing racial diversity in the nation. And, as in the previous decade, many well-meaning news organizations saw the growing minority populations as a problem to be solved. The changing racial mix of the nation was seen as something that had to be overcome, a problem that demanded a solution. Thus the response was often an increase in the tokenism, from one Black to two, or a broadening of attention to minorities to include Latinos, Asian Americans, and Native Americans. More attention was also given to coverage of minority issues and special events. These quick-fix solutions to what was seen as a problem sometimes compounded the issue.

For instance, the coverage of minority issues often focused inordinate attention on the more bizarre or unusual elements of minority communities, such as youth gangs, illegal immigration, or interracial violence. While these are all legitimate topics, the emphasis on such coverage and the near absence of other news stories or dramatic themes involving minorities resulted in a new stereotype of racial minorities as "problem people," groups either beset by problems or causing them for the larger society. Thus the problem orientation of the media managers was often reinforced by the coverage and dramatic portrayals that minorities were allowed.

ANALYSIS

There are other difficulties inherent in approaching minorities as a problem. A problem needs to be solved; once it is solved it can be set aside. In the late 1970s and early 1980s, the hiring of minority reporters or staffers became the quick solution to what was seen as a minority problem. Once a minority reporter or actor was hired, the minority problem was seen as solved. If the reporter didn't work out or was hired away, the problem reappeared.

Problems also often beg for single solutions, a perception that is perhaps a throwback to our training in mathematics, in which each math problem has only one solution. Thus if hiring was seen as a solution to a problem, more hiring of minorities would add more solutions if the problems resurfaced. Editors often looked simplistically at changes in coverage to try to find out what the Black, Latino, or Native American community "wanted" from the media. Some experimented with Spanish or Asian-language "simulcasts" of news programs. Some inserted special sections geared for the minority communities on a regular basis. Others did extensive special reports on the different minority communities in their circulation or broadcast areas. Not all of these were successful in gaining increased readership, viewership, or acceptance by the minority communities. And, as a result, some media managers were discouraged from trying other approaches.

Finally, a problem is, by definition, an obstacle, an obstruction, a puzzle that stands in the way of someone's progress. It is something that must be overcome, surpassed, or eradicated so that forward movement can continue. Thus, when the growing minority populations were seen as a problem by media managers, the approaches, however well intentioned or creative, were geared to overcoming or changing something that was seen as an obstacle. Instead of looking for ways to capitalize on the new opportunities presented by the changing population, media managers tried to overcome them because they were seen as a threat to "business as usual."

More recently, media corporations, spurred by pressure groups, their own minority employees, or even a growing social consciousness, have come to see the growing minority population as an opportunity, not a problem. Rather than simply trying to overcome a hurdle and put the obstacle behind them, they recognize that the United States is growing as a racially diverse nation and that the changing racial demographics are an opportunity for them to gain new audiences and readers. It is this attitude, coupled with the growing racial diversity of the nation, that presages the greatest progress of minorities and the media of communication.

NOTES

1. Harold Lasswell, "The structure and function of communication in society," reprinted in Wilbur Schramm and Donald F. Roberts, *The Process and Ef-*

fects of Mass Communication, rev. ed. (University of Illinois Press, 1971), pp. 84-99.

2. Ibid., p. 99.

3. Charles Wright, *Mass Communication: A Sociological Perspective* (Random House, 1959), cited in Wilbur Schramm and William E. Porter, *Men, Women, Messages and Media* (Harper & Row, 1982), p. 27.

4. Schramm and Porter, *Men, Women, Messages, and Media*, p. 27.

5. Peter M. Sandman, David M. Rubin, and David B. Sachsman, *Media: An Introductory Analysis of American Mass Communication* (Prentice-Hall, 1972), p. 14.

6. Peter M. Sandman, David M. Rubin, and David B. Sachsman, *Media: An Introductory Analysis of American Mass Communication*, 3rd ed. (Prentice-Hall, 1982).

7. See Joseph R. Dominick, *The Dynamics of Mass Communication* (Addison-Wesley, 1983), pp. 33-49, for a further elaboration of these functions as applied in contemporary media systems.

8. Edwin Emery and Michael Emery, *The Press and America*, 5th ed. (Prentice-Hall, 1984), p. 141.

9. David Potter, *People of Plenty* (University of Chicago Press, 1954), pp. 167-168.

10. Ralph H. Turner and Samuel J. Surace, "Zoot-suiters and Mexicans: Symbols in crowd behavior," *American Journal of Sociology*, Vol 67, No. 1, July 1956, pp. 14-20.

11. Ibid., p. 15.

12. Ibid.

13. Ibid., p.18.

14. Ibid., pp. 18-19.

15. Ibid., p. 19.

16. Ibid., p. 20.

17. Félix Gutiérrez, "Making news—Media coverage of Chicanos," *Agenda*, Vol. 8, No. 6, November/December 1978, pp. 21-22.

18. Ibid., p. 23.

19. Norman Lear, "As I read how Laura saw Archie," *New York Times*, October 10, 1971.

20. Neil Vidmar and Milton Rokeach, "Archie Bunker's bigotry: A study in selective perception and exposure," *Journal of Communication*, Vol. 24, No. 1, Winter 1974, p. 42.

21. Ibid., p. 43.

22. Ibid., p. 45.

23. Ibid., p. 46.

24. Eunice Cooper and Marie Jahoda, "The evasion of propaganda: How prejudiced people respond to anti-prejudice propaganda," in Schramm and Roberts, *The Process and Effects of Mass Communication*, pp. 287-299.

25. Charles K. Atkin, Bradley S. Greenberg, and Steven McDermott, "Television and race role socialization," *Journalism Quarterly*, Vol. 60, No. 3, Autumn 1983, p. 408.

26. Ibid., p. 414.

27. Bradley S. Greenberg, "Children's reactions to TV Blacks," *Journalism Quarterly*, Vol. 49, No. 1, Spring 1972, pp. 8-9.

28. Alexis S. Tan, *Mass Communication Theories and Research* (Grid Publishing, 1981), p. 261.

29. For a review and analysis of the literature on the effects of television on minority children, see Gordon L. Berry and Claudia Mitchell-Kernan, eds., *Television and the Socialization of the Minority Child* (Academic Press, 1982).

30. Ben H. Bagdikian, "The best news money can buy," *Human Behavior*, October 1978, pp. 63-66.

31. Ibid., p. 64.

32. Ibid., p. 66.

33. Ibid.

34. Félix Gutiérrez and Clint C. Wilson II, "The demographic dilemma," *Columbia Journalism Review*, January/February 1979, p. 53.

35. Ibid.

SUGGESTED READING

Davis, Cary, Carl Haub and JoAnne Willette. "U.S. Hispanics: Changing the Face of America," *Population Bulletin, 38* (June 1983), pp. 3-43.

Duncan, Hugh Dalziel. *Symbols in Society*. London: Oxford University Press, 1968.

Feldstein, Stanley (Ed.). *The Poisoned Tongue*. New York: William Morrow, 1972.

Fisher, Paul L. and Ralph L. Lowenstein (Eds.). *Race and the News Media*. New York: Frederick A. Praeger, 1968.

Frazier, P. Jean and Cecille Gaziano. *"Robert Ezra Park's Theory of News, Public Opinion and Social Control," Journalism Monographs*, No. 64, November 1979.

Glazer, Nathan and Daniel Patrick Moynihan. *Beyond the Melting Pot*. Cambridge: MIT Press, 1963.

Gossett, Thomas F. *Race: The History of an Idea in America*. New York: Schocken, 1963.

Greenberg, Bradley, Michael Burgoon, Judee K. Burgoon, and Felipe Korzenny. *Mexican Americans and the Mass Media*. Norwood, NJ: Ablex, 1983.

Gutiérrez, Félix. "Ethnic Diversity in Los Angeles," *Urban Resources*, 1 (Spring 1984), pp. LA4-LA6.

Horsman, Reginald. *Race and Manifest Destiny*. Cambridge: Harvard University Press, 1981.

Hraba, Joseph. *American Ethnicity*. Itasca, IL: Peacock, 1979.

Janowitz, Morris and Paul Hirsch (Eds.). *Reader in Public Opinion and Mass Communication*, 3rd ed. New York: Free Press, 1981.

Klapper, Joseph T. *The Effects of Mass Communication*. New York: Free Press, 1960.

Lemert, James B. *Does Mass Communication Change Public Opinion After All?* Chicago: Nelson-Hall, 1981.

McWilliams, Carey. *Brothers Under the Skin,* rev. ed. Boston: Little, Brown, 1964.

Morales, Armando. "The Collective Preconscious and Racism," *Social Casework,* May 1971, pp. 285-293.

Ringer, Benjamin B. *"We The People" and Others.* New York: Tavistock, 1983.

Rubin, Bernard (Ed.). *Small Voices and Great Trumpets: Minorities and the Media.* New York: Praeger, 1980.

Schwartz, Barry N. and Robert Disch (Eds.). *White Racism: Its History, Pathology and Practice.* New York: Dell, 1970.

Sowell, Thomas (Ed.). *Essays and Data on American Ethnic Groups.* Washington, DC: Urban Institute, 1978.

Steinfield, Melvin (Ed.). *Cracks in the Melting Pot,* 2nd ed. New York: Macmillan, 1973.

Sterritt, David. "Minorities in the Media," *Christian Science Monitor,* May 9, 1983, pp. 12-13; May 10, 1983, pp. 12-13.

Stroman, Carolyn and Lee Becker, "Racial Differences in Gratifications," *Journalism Quarterly,* 55 (Winter 1978), pp. 767-771.

"U.S. Population: Where We Are; Where We're Going," *Population Bulletin,* 37 (June 1982), pp. 3-45.

II

Entertainment Media Portrayals

"Virtually every minority characterization was designed to reinforce the attitude of White superiority. Given the low socioeconomic status of working-class Whites during the heyday of the industrial age, movie producers capitalized on audience insecurities by using minority stereotypes to bolster their self-esteem and reinforce racial attitudes."

3

FROM THE LIVE STAGE TO HOLLYWOOD BEFORE WORLD WAR II

ANY DISCUSSION OF minority-group portrayals in American entertainment must consider the concept of stereotyping. The *American Heritage Dictionary* defines stereotyping as "a conventional, formulaic, and usually oversimplified conception, opinion, or belief." In the broadest sense, stereotyping has been employed as a literary and dramatic device since the earliest beginnings of those art forms. It is a means of quickly bringing to the audience's collective consciousness a character's anticipated value system and/or behavioral expectations. Audience members are then able to assess the character against their own value systems and categorize the character as, for example, "the villain" or "the heroine." Stereotypes, therefore, are shortcuts to character development and form a basis for mass entertainment and literary fare.

Stereotyping can be a useful device when used without prejudice. A simplistic example would find a White villain brought to justice by a White hero in an entirely White social environment. The message transmitted to the audience would be that good overcomes evil. However, negative stereotyping of ethnic minorities in a White-dominated environment transmits a far different message when done historically and persistently with prejudice.

Because the concept of prejudice is central to our discussion, let's use the term as James M. Jones has defined it in his book *Prejudice and Racism*. Prejudice, he writes, "is a negative attitude toward a person or group based upon a social comparison process in which the individual's own group is taken as the positive point of reference."[1] In that context our example would transmit not only the notion that good (ethnic majority) overcomes evil (ethnic minority) but that the latter *is* evil. Thus, while stereotyping per se may have merit in popular literature and the arts, when combined with prejudice it poses a devastating obstacle to human development and understanding in a multicultural society.

Before examining ethnic minority portrayals in American mass entertainment, we should look at the social historic precedents and attitudes in which minority stereotypes were cultivated. This will provide insight into whether the stereotypes were prejudiced and help determine the degree to which social historical factors have been influential in their development and use. We shall consider the social historical experiences in the United States of four ethnic minority groups to determine whether a causal relationship existed between their experiences and their subsequent treatment in entertainment media.

NATIVE AMERICANS

Native Americans (Indians) were the first peoples of a different ethnicity to confront Anglo European settlers on the American continent. The settlers were at once faced with a dilemma of how to coexist with people they saw as primitive, but who also had some qualities they admired. Writings of early settlers referred to the natives' primitive innocence, their willingness to share food and other essentials of life freely in a communal environment, and their dark, handsome physical appearance. To the settlers these attributes were "noble." At the same time, White settlers also made observations about the natives' proclivity for nudity, open sexual relationships, and incidents of cannabalism. These traits were considered "savage." Thus emerged in colonial-era literature the concept of the "noble savage."

Initially the colonists decided to convert the natives to Christianity in an attempt to assimilate them while the task of creating an Anglo European society was under way. Religious conversion was eventually seen, however, as an impossibility, and the colonists easily rationalized that the natives had to be removed as a barrier to the "civilization" of the continent.

By the mid-1800s the policies for dealing with the "Indian problem" had found their justification in popular literature, which helped to establish the myth of the monolithic "Indian" without regard for the distinctions of more than 2000 different cultures, languages, and values systems the concept represented. The literary stereotype began as part of the western frontier writing formula developed after the Civil War. Writers of this genre included Bret Harte and Mark Twain. Readers of this fare were already conditioned to see the natives portrayed in a manner that justified their elimination as a barrier to western expansion. Twain, Harte, and others wrote of the picturesque scenery and romantic lifestyles of the frontier in contrast to the "savages" who occupied the land. In *Roughing It*, Twain described the Gosiute Indians as "scrawny creatures," "treacherous-looking," and "prideless beggars." It remained only for dime-novel author Edward S. Ellis to write during the 1880s and 1890s of the Indian as merely a prelude to a more enlightened White civilization.

Stories of actual and exaggerated atrocities by Indians upon White settlers, who pushed ever westward into the frontier, firmly established a hatred against them that clearly made them both an enemy in war and of the progress of civilization. Literature during the Indian wars is rife with tales of Indians burning, looting, raping, and scalping the pioneers who were fulfilling the fervor of "manifest destiny." It was against this backdrop that Frederick Jackson Turner's "Frontier Thesis," presented in 1893, argued that American (White) character had been molded by the experience of the western frontier. Jackson's ideas were accepted to the extent that they pervaded history textbooks into the middle of the twentieth century. Elimination or subjugation of the Native American was seen as merely an evolutionary step in the development of industrial America.

BLACK AMERICANS

In 1619, a year before the arrival of the *Mayflower* on the shores of the American continent, twenty Africans were brought to Jamestown aboard a Dutch pirate ship. The ship's captain offered to exchange his human cargo for a supply of foodstuffs. The young Black men and women with Spanish names such as Antony, Isabella, and Pedro were probably originally headed for the West Indies on a Spanish vessel before being intercepted by the Dutch ship.[2] The twenty Africans became the genesis of a Black population that was to have a major impact on the development of the future United States.

Although the fact of slavery in America and its legacy of human indignity have been well chronicled, the roots of its underlying psychosis have been less explored in popular literature. The popular notion regarding the treatment of Blacks and their African ancestors has tended to focus on slavery as a phenomenon of the southern White attitude based upon geographic and economic considerations. What is often overlooked is that slavery was a part of the northern experience from colonial times. It is clear that Black racism was a factor in English Calvinist and Puritan religious ideology before those influences were brought to the New World. This affected their attitudes toward Black people in two ways. First was the Anglo-Saxon belief that the color white represents things that are pure, clean, good, and reflect the spiritual light. Black, on the other hand, represents impurity, filth, evil, and the spiritual darkness. This concept persists to this day. Second, the Puritan concept of predestination relied on observation to distinguish the "elect" from the "damned." Those who seemed relatively prosperous and self-sufficient were deemed superior to those who were enslaved. Against this religiously seated and strongly held attitude, the reaction of the English colonists to Blacks in the New World even among inhabitants of the northern seaboard was predictable. In fact, on New York's famed Wall Street in 1711 slaves were the predominant commodity in trade, partly because Puritan law was ambiguous on the subject. One such law of 1641 is revealing:

> There shall never be any bond-slavery, villenage or captivitie amongst us; unlesse it be lawfully captives taken in just warrs, and such strangers as willingly sell themselves, or are sold to us: and such shall have the libertyes and Christian usuages which the law of God established in Israell concerning such persons doth morally require, provided this exempts none from servitude who shall be judged thereto by Authoritie.[3]

Whites in New England were first to establish what later would be called "Jim Crow" laws in the South as a means of codifying their prejudices against Blacks, although slavery never became a widespread practice there for economic reasons. In the South the mythology of the "happy slave" content to serve his or her master as the ultimate fulfillment of life grew as a justification for the exploitation of Blacks. Much of the post-Civil War literature paints a negative image of Blacks designed to reinforce institutional and social racism. Many of the accusations against Black integrity that emerged during Reconstruction are now too familiar: laziness, slow-wittedness, loose standards of morality, fondness for alcoholic beverages, and so on. Lynchings and other acts of violence against Blacks and those sympathetic to them are ample evidence of the attitudes held by White Americans toward them at the dawning of the twentieth century.

LATINOS

There is little mention of colonial Mexico in North American literature until the nineteenth century. Spain ruled Mexico for 300 years (1521-1821) before Mexico won its war for independence. In 1803, however, the Louisiana Purchase removed the vast buffer of territory between the United States and Mexico. The expansionist movement by U.S. settlers into the West and Southwest not only precipitated conflict with Native Americans, as discussed previously, but also led to war with Mexico in 1846.

Central to the development of relations between Mexico and the United States was the Santa Fe Trail, which was legally opened as a commercial trade route in 1821. The trail ran from Independence, Missouri, to Santa Fe, New Mexico, and became the focal point of friction between White settlers and Mexicans. When some inhabitants of the newly formed Republic of Mexico became disenchanted with their new government, Anglo-American settlers were there in significant numbers to spur the movement for independence by the mid-1830s. In fact, there is much to suggest that American literature of the period was primarily designed to stir up local sentiment for overthrow of the Mexican government in Texas and New Mexico. Thus Whites engaged in hostilities against Mexicans with Mexican allies during the war for Texas independence. At the same time, popular literature portrayed in vivid terms the perception of "cruel" General Antonio Lopez de Santa Anna's massacre of the "gallant" defenders of the Alamo (1836), which included folk heroes Davey Crockett and Jim Bowie. Americans were generally persuaded to visualize the Mexican as an inhuman enemy a decade before war with Mexico was officially declared.

Cruelty was not the only negative trait ascribed to Mexicans. Cecil Robinson, in his work, *Mexico and the Hispanic Southwest in American Literature*,[4] has chronicled the origins of several stereotypes that began to appear in Anglo writings before and during the U.S.-Mexican war. During that war, American naval Lieutenant H. A. Wise wrote that Mexicans were "beyond comparison the laziest and most ignorant set of vagabonds the world produces." George Wilkins Kendall penned: "Give them but tortillas, frijoles, and chile colorado to supply their animal wants for the day, and seven-tenths of the Mexicans are satisfied; and so they will continue to be until the race becomes extinct or amalgamated with Anglo-Saxon stock."

When Mexicans were not being portrayed in Anglo literature as lazy and indolent, they were assailed for uncleanliness. Texas romance writer Jeremiah Clemens gave his version of the origin of the term "greaser" and why he felt it was appropriate: "The people look greasy, their clothes are greasy, their dogs are greasy—everywhere grease and filth hold divided dominion, and the singular appropriateness of the name bestowed by the western settlers soon caused it to be universally adopted by the American army." In the short story "The Inroad of the Nabajo" by Albert Pike (1934), the women of Santa Fe are described as "scudding hither and thither, with their black hair flying, and their naked feet shaming the ground by their superior filth." It should be noted that several American writers found Mexican women quite charming and wrote at length about their feminine virtues, which contrasted sharply with puritanical customs of American women of the era in dress and social demeanor.

A major factor in the attitude of Whites toward Mexico and its people was the negativism toward Mexican ethnicity. Most of the population was either full-blooded native (Indian) or mestizo (mixture of Spanish ancestry and Indian). Anglo-American writers routinely referred with disdain to Mexicans as "these mixed races." But it was the sizable body of popular literature growing out of the lore of the Santa Fe Trail that set the tone for American imagery of Mexicans and the Southwest. Works such as *The Time of the Gringo* by Elliot Arnold, *Anthony Adverse* by Hervy Allen, and *Adventures in the Santa Fe Trade* by James Josiah Webb established the basic stereotypes by 1900.

ASIAN AMERICANS

Asian experience in America has a short history prior to 1900 because Chinese immigration didn't begin until the California gold rush in 1848. Japanese people didn't begin to arrive formally until after 1855, when the Japanese government passed laws enabling its citizens to emigrate. We are concerned in this discussion with the Chinese and Japanese, because other Asian and Pacific Island peoples were less a social factor in the United States before 1900 and because American attitudes toward the two groups were similar enough to be virtually indistinguishable. In fact, many Americans never bothered to take note of any differences between Chinese and Japanese people and later came to lump them together prejudiciously as simply the "Yellow Peril."

Since the overwhelming majority of Asian immigration was to California and other states on the West Coast, the social history of Asians in America during the nineteenth century is focused there. By 1870 there were more than 60,000 Chinese in California, who had settled into farming, mining, factory work, and domestic labor after railroad jobs became scarce. Whites, who had come West to seek quick wealth in the gold rush, came to resent the Chinese because they had jobs while many Whites were unemployed. Dennis Kearney, leader of the California Workingman's Party, orchestrated an anti-Chinese movement with the backing of the *San Francisco Chronicle*. Kearney ended every speech with the slogan "The Chinese Must Go." Kearney and his followers stirred a sentiment of prejudice against Chinese workers, who were highly visible because of their adherence to traditional customs of dress, pigtail hair style, and communal living. Suddenly, after twenty years of serving as a welcome source of cheap labor and enjoying a reputation for industry, honesty, thrift, and peaceful disposition, the Chinese became the object of scorn. They were now seen by Whites as debased, clannish, and deceitful. In the 1870s, a series of racially motivated incidents of violence occurred in several western towns, resulting in the deaths of numerous Chinese inhabitants.

Finally, in 1882, the first Chinese exclusion law was passed and in 1887 only ten Chinese immigrated to the United States. Ironically, the Chinese Exclusion Act of 1882 made possible the increase in Japanese immigration. The decline in Chinese immigrant labor proved the fact of White racism, because their jobs went unfilled and a serious farm labor shortage developed in California and other western states. Soon there was a demand for Japanese immigrants who had proven farming skills and were willing to work for low wages. Between 1899 and 1904 nearly 60,000 Japanese came to America to meet the labor demand.

History repeated itself when, between 1901 and 1906, the corrupt administration of San Francisco Mayor Eugene Schmitz and his political boss Abraham Ruef used the Japanese as scapegoats when public attention was turned on their own dubious activities. Schmitz's regime was backed by organized labor, which claimed the Japanese worked for lower wages and were driving Whites out of the job market. At the same time, Japan was quickly defeating the Russians in the Russo-Japanese War (1904) and moving to seize Korea. Japan's military successes created apprehension in America that Asians were a threat to Western civilization.

Once again it was the *San Francisco Chronicle* that crusaded in front-page articles against immigration, this time with the Japanese as objects. The *Chronicle* urged and supported a city-wide boycott of Japanese merchants in San Francisco. The paper charged the immigrants with maintaining loyalty to the emperor of Japan. Mass meetings were held denouncing Japanese immigrants, and acts of assault and other violence soon followed against them. The official reaction to what became known as the "Yellow Peril" was a series of laws restricting Japanese immigrant rights in America. This culminated with passage of the Immigration Act of 1924 banning entry to the United States for all aliens not eligible for citizenship, although the legislation was clearly targeted for the Japanese.

During the height of "Yellow Peril" hysteria, Chinese and Japanese persons were viewed as devious and vicious. Popular literature warned of the dangers of intermarriage with Asians and charged openly that Asian men purposefully sought White women. These attitudes found their way into entertainment media, as we shall see.

BEGINNINGS OF MASS ENTERTAINMENT: THE LIVE STAGE

Now that we have seen the historic social relationships between White Americans and ethnic minorities, it is clear White attitudes have been molded negatively toward each of the groups for specific purposes. In each case our definition of prejudice (a negative attitude toward the groups based upon a comparison process using White society as the positive point of reference) has been fulfilled. We have also seen these prejudicial attitudes reflected in popular literature and observed how they affected American political, economic, and social life. Our next task is to consider the relationship of these prejudicial attitudes to mass entertainment. To understand that relationship we must take a look at the developmental highlights of mass entertainment in America.

It is no accident that the rise of American mass entertainment coincided with the populist movement that began in the 1820s and 1830s. The election of Andrew Jackson to the presidency in 1828 marked the ascension of the "common man" to political and social prominence if not individual economic stature. Cities became population centers and laborers moved there from the farms to become wage earners. The genteel, socially elitist American with refined cultural tastes was inundated by the onrushing tide of the populist movement.

The pivotal year 1833 marked the beginning of the penny press newspaper ushered in by Benjamin Day's *New York Sun* and its symbolic motto "It Shines for ALL!" Just as Day's unsophisticated newspaper became the reading fare of an audience clamoring for "news" of gossip, sensationalism, and crime, so did live entertainment change to accommodate the tastes of the working class. It was also in 1833, in New York City's Bowery Theatre, that an uninhibited audience shouted down the orchestra's symphonic overture and hollered instead for a rendition of "Yankee Doodle"; the audience got its wish. Just as the penny press made newspapers affordable for the masses, ticket prices for live entertainment plummeted from several dollars to 25¢ or less.

From the middle of the nineteenth century to the 1920s, the live stage became the first major mass entertainment medium in America. People in the cities filled large, ornate theaters, and rural dwellers attended traveling shows housed in tents. Theatrical agents quickly came to understand the imperative of catering to the public's taste. Their reward was a full cash box and lusty cheers; those who failed suffered the wrath of hostile catcalls, hisses, and financial loss. Ethnic minorities played a figurative, if not literal, role in the development of mass entertainment because the populist audience demanded their inclusion in theatrical performances. The terms of that inclusion, however, were the accommodation of the attitudes and values of the masses. In general, the audience wanted plays with common people (themselves) portrayed as heroes. They wanted foot-tapping music and dance and maintained a strong desire to see anything that fulfilled their perceptions of Black American culture. Perhaps above all, they wanted comedy, and ethnic minorities were a convenient foil. "Leave 'em laughing" became an early show-business axiom.

One early favorite play had a Native American theme and was titled *The Original, Aboriginal, Erratic, Operatic, Semi-Civilized and Demi-Savage Extravaganza of Pocahontas*. Stereotypical myths of American Indians, which had been spread by writers such as James Fenimore Cooper and pulp novelists, easily made the transition to the stage. After the Civil War live entertainment took to the outdoor theater arena with "Buffalo Bill" Cody and his "Wild West" show leading the way. Cody played out the American myth of the taming of the West and its native Indian population to eastern audiences while the real Indian wars were being fought across the country. Cody legitimized himself by periodically returning to the West to serve as a scout and Indian fighter. His show played to packed audiences in the United States and Europe for several decades. Other traveling shows, including circuses and variety acts, spread ethnic stereotypes across America by 1900.

Minstrel shows featuring White actors in blackface makeup appeared in the 1830s after an itinerant White actor, Thomas Dartmouth Rice, borrowed a song and dance routine from a little Black slave boy he had seen perform on a street corner. Billing himself as "Daddy" Rice, he applied burnt cork to his face and dressed in tattered clothing to the delight of audiences from New York's Bowery Theatre to the London stage. He added other caricatures of Black personalities to his act and the minstrel show was born. For decades, Blacks could neither perform in nor attend these shows, which were based on their musical and dance traditions. Ironically, when Black minstrel troupes did become acceptable to White audiences, they were compelled to perform in blackface makeup.

For 80 years the minstrel show was the most popular form of live American entertainment. In its classic form the minstrel show consisted of two acts. Part one employed a minimum of 15 men on stage in a semicircular seating arrangement with gaudily dressed comedians at the end seats. A nattily attired "interlocutor" stood in the center and a comedic exchange took place between him and the comedians. Singers and banjo and tambourine players made up the rest of the troupe, and songs, dances, rapid-fire jokes, and gags came without pause. Part two of the show (often called the "olio") was composed of recitations, monologues, specialty songs, comedy skits, and burlesque routines. After minstrel shows faded in popularity the olio concept was expanded into a separate group of acts and became known as vaudeville. Vaudeville launched the careers of some of America's most honored performers, including George Burns, Bob Hope, Jack Benny, and Abbott and Costello. It remained only for Al Jolson to refine minstrel show affectations to indelibly stereotype an ethnic group in American entertainment. With renditions of "Mammy," "Rockabye Your Rockabye Baby to a Dixie Melody," "Swanee," and others, Jolson was being called "Mr. Show Business" as early as 1915 but he had been a popular fixture since the turn of the century. Jolson was unquestionably the most popular entertainer in America during the period. By the time motion pictures began to supplant the live stage show in popularity, the quintessential stage musical "Showboat" opened the Broadway season in 1927 with a favorite White American theme at its core: the interplay of Blacks and southern Whites set against an idyllic romantic background along the Mississippi River.

MINORITIES IN THE MOVIES

Thomas Edison is generally credited with the development of motion picture technology with his invention of the Kinetoscope in 1889. In 1903 one of his assistants produced the first motion picture with a story line, *The Great Train Robbery*. Movies were projected without sound until 1927, when Al Jolson starred in *The Jazz Singer*, the first "talking" (and, of course, "singing") movie.

Ethnic minority portrayals appeared very early in motion pictures. As early as 1894 one could view the *Sioux Ghost Dance* on one of Edison's contraptions and by 1898 Buffalo Bill's Wild West show had been committed to film complete with its imagery of the Native American Indian's collapse before White "civilization." Only a year after *The Great Train Robbery*, Biograph released a one-reel feature (*A Bucket of Cream Ale*) depicting a Black maid employed by a White man. The maid was played by a White actress in blackface makeup. Between 1910 and 1914 several films projected Mexican stereotypes, including a series of works with the term "greaser" in the titles. Consistent with the treatment of Asian immigrants at the turn of the century, Asians appeared stereotypically as diabolical personalities in film with the 1916 release of *The Yellow Menace*. Interestingly, in *The Yellow Menace* both Asians and Mexicans combine forces in a subversive plot against the United States.

Although there are many differences between and among the ethnic minority cultures under consideration here, a close examination of their treatment in American mass entertainment reveals remarkable similarity. Our review earlier in this chapter of the social historic experiences of minorities shows negative prejudicial attitudes against each group were held by Whites before those attitudes manifested themselves in popular media.

Generally, all ethnic minority characterizations in early films projected an attitudinal posture of White superiority. That attitude revealed itself on screen through the portrayal of minorities as inferior in two major capacities: intellect and morality. Virtually every minority characterization was designed to reinforce the attitude of White superiority. Given the low socioeconomic status of working-class Whites during the heyday of the industrial age, movie producers capitalized on audience insecurities by using minority stereotypes to bolster their self-esteem and reinforce racial attitudes. White insecurities, as reflected in the first 40 years of American popular cinema, were revealed to be a fear of miscegenation and the threat that minority cultures would have an impact on White social values. Thus, just as live stage producers and entertainers profited financially by giving the masses what they wanted, moviemakers quickly developed a symbiotic relationship with their patrons, often at the expense of ethnic minority Americans.

Several basic movie themes derived from the attitudinal premises of White intellectual and moral supremacy (see list, below) and were applied at various times to Indians, Blacks, Latinos, and Asian Americans alike.

Some Traits Commonly Applied to Minority Portrayals in Early Movies

Intellectual	*Moral*
preoccupied with simple ideas	low regard for human life
inferior strategy in warfare/ conflict situations	criminal activity
low or nonexistent occupational status	sexual promiscuity
poor speech patterns/dialect	drug/alcohol abuse
comedic foil	dishonesty

With the release of the technical epic *The Birth of a Nation* by D. W. Griffith (1915), movies began to institutionalize racial stereotypes. Griffith established a pattern, which would endure for decades, of portraying American Blacks as intellectually and morally inferior to Whites, and the film carried a strong message against sexual contact between the races. Perhaps the first film to openly proclaim the doctrine of White supremacy over native American Indians was William S. Hart's *The Aryan*, which was released in 1916. One of the titles projected across the screen of this silent movie also played to the fear of miscegenation and read in part "Our women shall be guarded." As was most commonly the practice in early movies, Whites portrayed all of the ethnic minority characters in both films. (It is interesting to note, however, that genuine Indians were sometimes employed to play minor roles, but the practice was not without problems. Directors found it difficult to teach them how to act "Indian," prompting one observer to write an article on "The Dangers of Employing Redskins as Movie Actors.") An exception was Japanese actor Sessue Hayakawa, who was involved in at least two early films in which he portrayed Asian characters. In *Typhoon* (1914), Hayakawa plays a young Japanese diplomat in Paris who, among other things, becomes romantically involved with a French actress. During the course of an argument the woman hurls racist epithets, including "whining yellow rat," at the diplomat and he kills her. In *The Cheat* (1915), Hayakawa is cast as a deceitful Asian who schemes

The Cheat (1915) featured the first Asian star in Hollywood, Sessue Hayakawa. In this scene he attempts to seduce a young White socialite (Fannie Ward) whom he has lured into his boudoir. Forty-two years later, Hayakawa starred in *Bridge on the River Kwai.* (Paramount Studios photo, courtesy of the Academy of Motion Picture Arts and Sciences)

to obtain the sexual favors of a naive, but married, White socialite. In both *Typhoon* and *The Cheat* the message is clear: Interracial love leads to tragedy.

Latinos fared no better in the first two decades of American cinema. A series of films denigrating Mexicans appeared, including *Tony the Greaser* (1911) and *The Greaser's Revenge* (1914). Mexicans in American film were the vilest of characters who indulged in banditry, pillage, plundering, rape, and murder. The portrayals were so severe that the Mexican government banned such films in 1922 after filing a written protest in 1919 that went unheeded. Hollywood's response was to transport the "greaser" role to other nations or to invent locales with psuedo-Latin names. In a perverse manner these films set the stage for the popularity of the mysterious, forbidden "Latin lover" roles that became a movie staple in the 1920s and 1930s. Rudolph Valentino was Hollywood's biggest star in that role.

HOLLYWOOD'S HEYDAY: 1930-1945

The fact that stereotypes can and do change is evidenced by shifts in minority portrayals during the 15-year period from 1930 to 1945. Although basic attitudes held by Whites toward ethnic minorities did not undergo significant change, the passage of time altered social relationships between Whites and minorities. The result was that Hollywood had to make changes to conform to new realities. Unfortunately, portrayals did not become more accurate and sensitive to minority experience but merely were adjusted to conform to more credible representations. For example, Blacks could not continue to be seen as only criminals and undesirables of various types (the primary theme of the years 1900-1920) because it was clear they had other dimensions of character that were easily observed in "real life." The movie industry response to social reality was simply to shift to new stereotypes still consistent with prejudicial notions.

Native American portrayals changed very little between 1930 and 1945, probably because of their unique place in American lore. They symbolized the fulfillment of the American dream—the immigrant's ability to conquer the obstacles presented by a new continent and its existing inhabitants and to harvest its seemingly endless riches as reward. Hollywood adopted the Indian as a living monument to the ideals of manifest destiny and created a stereotype that barely managed to be a facsimile of Indian culture. Examples include *Drums Along the Mohawk* (1939) and *Northwest Passage* (1940). No distinction was made in the movies among Indian cultures of the Northeast, the Plains, and the Southeast. Feathers, beads, fringed pants, pinto ponies, and halted English dialects were applied indiscriminately to represent the concept of "Indian" to movie audiences. The notion played well across the United States, as moviegoers seemingly could not get their fill of "cowboy and Indian" movies and serials. The Indian's role was to help audiences constantly relive his defeat at the hands of the U.S. Calvary and other assorted "good guys." Thus the major change in Native American movie portrayal from 1930 to World War II was the crystalization of an image. The Indian became an American cliché. Clichés die hard and the movie Indian remained throughout the heyday of Hollywood cinema.

In this scene from *Drums Along the Mohawk* (1939), Indians are depicted in a fierce battle with White settlers. The portrayal of Indians as savages was a common theme in motion pictures for decades. (20th Century Fox photo, courtesy of the Academy of Motion Picture Arts and Sciences)

A more pronounced stereotypical shift took place in the movie characterization of Blacks during the boom period. The venomous, hate-filled disparagement of Blacks epitomized in *Birth of a Nation* and other films of its era, such as *The Wooing and Wedding of a Coon* (1905), *The Masher* (1907), and *The Nigger* (1915), evolved into less threatening characterizations. The new stereotype played to White perceptions of Black personalities who, in the vernacular of the era, "knew their place" in American society. Blacks now appeared in movies for the purpose of entertaining White audiences within the context of social limitations. They had roles in musicals, where they could demonstrate their "rhythmic" talents as singers and dancers. Meanwhile, the supposed inferior mental capacities of Blacks made for hilarious comedy. When in movie character, Blacks were subservient to Whites as maids, mammies, domestics, and sidekicks. The pre-World War II era brought to the screen Stepin Fetchit, Mantan

Mantan Moreland provided comic relief in fifteen "Charlie Chan" movies as Chan's chauffer, Birmingham Brown. As shown in this publicity photograph, Moreland often froze in wide-eyed terror when faced with suspenseful situations, a common Hollywood portrayal of Blacks. (RKO photo, courtesy of the Academy of Motion Picture Arts and Sciences)

Moreland, and Willie Best. It also produced the *Our Gang* series, with the characters of Buckwheat, Farina, and Stymie. When the old days of the antebellum South were recalled by Hollywood, as in *Gone with the Wind*, Blacks played the happy, faithful, and sometimes lazy slaves. Hattie McDaniel received the first Oscar

Hattie McDaniel earned an Oscar for her portrayal of the faithful mammy to Vivien Leigh in *Gone with the Wind* (1939). Hollywood usually depicted Black slaves as being delighted with their servile roles. (MGM photo, courtesy of the Academy of Motion Picture Arts and Sciences)

awarded to a Black actor for her portrayal of the dutiful and protective mammy of Scarlett O'Hara in the screen classic. Her award as best supporting actress was, therefore, doubly symbolic.

Perhaps the primary reason for the change in Latino stereotyping during the 1930s was economics. The formal protest and subsequent banning of American moviemaking and distribution in Mexico by the Mexican government in 1922 did not go unnoticed in other Latin American countries. Although Hollywood intended the "greaser" stereotype to be its vision of Mexicans, Central and South American nations took equal offense when filmmakers began to create euphemisms for the roles in an attempt to placate Mexico. Film distribution sales in the affected countries were lucrative, so Hollywood eventually imported Latino actors and actresses to star in sizzling romantic features in an attempt to appeal to the foreign market.

It took the film industry a while to learn how to cope with the problem effectively. In the late 1920s and 1930s filmmakers promoted Latinos to a more sophisticated level of "greasery." The Latino male was yet to attain personal integrity and social acceptability but he did, in the words of one movie critic, at least dress well. At the same time it was non-Latino actors such as Noah Beery and Paul Muni who played the Latino roles in *The Dove* (1928) and *Bordertown* (1935), respectively. Alas, the "Latin lover" wasn't even Latino.

One of the traits Hollywood ascribed to Mexicans was a quick temper, and films of this era almost always allowed for a display of irrational Latino temperament. The concept was soon incorporated into female roles and by the mid-1930s and early 1940s Hollywood had recruited a number of sensuous, tempestuous leading ladies for the purpose. The idea was to appeal to both U.S. and Latin American audiences. Among the new female stars were Delores Del Rio (*The Red Dance*, 1928) and Lupe Velez (*Hot Pepper*, 1933; *Strictly Dynamite*, 1934; *Mexican Spitfire*, 1940). One concept in the tradition of Hollywood ethnic portrayals was unchanged, however; interracial movie romances between Latinos and their White lovers were virtually never successful.

By this time relations with Latin America were vital for political reasons, because the United States could ill afford to offend potential allies at a time when war was imminent. This circumstance paved the way for other Latino actors, who virtually flooded Hollywood shortly before the outbreak of World War II. The display of Hollywood goodwill and profit motive produced Carmen Miranda, Cesar Romero, and Desi Arnaz, and film titles began to reflect a Latin American flavor (*Down Argentine Way*, 1940; *A Weekend in Havana*, 1941). Concurrently, there was a conscious attempt to acquaint American audiences with Latin American history through movies on Benito Juarez and Simón Bolívar. Although political and economic pressures combined to accord Latinos the largest degree of change in stereotype among minorities between 1930 and 1945, certain prejudices lingered on screen. In general, Latinos were not seen as people with family values, stable romantic relationships, or interest in honorable careers. Moreover, Latino men still had an uncomfortable (for White American audiences) proclivity for romantic interest in White women.

With the passage of the anti-Japanese Immigration Act of 1924, the presence of Asians in popular films effectively ceased

Lupe Vélez, who was born in Mexico, was cast in a series of movies, including *Mexican Spitfire* (1940) as the sexy, tempestuous Latina. (Paramount Studios photo, courtesy of the Academy of Motion Picture Arts and Sciences)

until they were brought to the American conscience once again with the arrival of World War II. The "Yellow Peril," insofar as the Japanese were concerned, was no longer a threat to White American sensibilities during the 1930s. Instead, China and its people became the center of American attention in the Far East. China was in the midst of civil war and had been since 1911. Negative racial imagery had been popularly established with the appearance around 1910 of Sax Rohmer's fictional character, Dr. Fu Manchu, in several stories and novels. Fu Manchu soon became a diabolical movie villain and provided Hollywood with an entree into new stereotypes based on Chinese warlords. Movies of the genre proved to be highly successful. Among the most profitable of the films exploiting the "mysterious Orient" were *The Bitter Tea of General Yen* (1933), *Oil for the Lamps of China* (1935), and *The General Died at Dawn* (1936). In each of these films, the American audience was given the impression that Chinese people are prone to violence, anarchy, corruption, vice, and prostitution, although the central Chinese characters were portrayed in more complex tones. There was no attempt in the movies to explain either why the wars occurred or what the role of imperialism was in China. Perhaps the only countervailing view was given impetus by Pearl Buck's Pulitzer Prize-winning novel *The Good Earth*, which was published in 1931. The 1938 movie version retained Buck's sensitive account of Chinese peasants as hardworking, loving, family people. There was, however, a strong anticommunist flavor in films about China during the mid- to late 1930s, with communists depicted most often as the villains.

On the domestic front, the decade of the 1930s belonged to Charlie Chan, who was the Chinese-American's cinematic representative, although no Chinese or other Asian actor has portrayed him during the series (which now spans six decades with the 1981 release of a Peter Ustinov version). Other White actors who have portrayed the polite, bowing, proverb-spouting detective in the white suit include Warner Oland, Sidney Toler, Roland Winters, J. Carrol Naish, and Ross Martin. Charlie Chan movies were rife with stereotypical affectations. Although Chan seemed the most cerebral of the characters involved in his movie escapades, there were also the "Oriental" traits with which American audiences could identify. Chan was mysterious in his crime-solving techniques; one never knew what thought processes or logic he was employing until the critical moment at the movie's end. White America's memories of the diabolical Asian were readily recalled when Chan offered this advice to one of his many sons: "Keep eyes, ears open. Keep mouth shut." His slow gait, drowsy manner, and halting speech suggested that Chan may have spent private moments with an opium pipe. The character's immense popularity with American movie audiences throughout the 1930s and 1940s may have contributed to the pro-Chinese sentiment that existed then.

Whereas Hollywood tried to temper its stance toward Latinos as World War II approached, it revived and escalated its negative portrayals of the Japanese during that period. Because the Chinese peasant enjoyed favored status among Americans in the afterglow of Pearl Buck's *The Good Earth* and the subsequent movie based on it, Hollywood had little difficulty resurrecting the "Yellow Peril" theme against Japan as it became a threat to China. The attack on Pearl Harbor sealed the fate of the Japanese

Charlie Chan, here played by Sidney Toler, strikes a familiar pose in *The Chinese Cat* (1944). Chan epitomized several stereotypes but was, perhaps, the most popular Asian character Hollywood has produced. (Monogram Pictures photo, courtesy of the Academy of Motion Picture Arts and Sciences)

in American cinema, but the Japanese Americans who were soon shuttled to "relocation" camps felt the sting of attitudes long since implanted in the mass psyche and nurtered in movie houses. In films produced between 1942 and 1945 Hollywood dusted off the old images of Japanese duplicity, inhumanity, and lust for White women. Unlike the Germans, who were portrayed as a respectable but misguided people under the influence of the Nazi regime, the Japanese were seen in American theaters strafing Red Cross ships, bayoneting children, and delighting in applying torture techniques handed down from centuries of malevolent practice. Examples can be found in *Wake Island* (1942), *Guadalcanal Diary* (1943), and *Objective Burma* (1945).

ANALYSIS

Entertainment stereotypes of ethnic minorities in American mass media have historical roots in racist attitudes that existed for various social and political reasons against each of the groups prior to their inclusion in media. The stereotypes were based upon negative prejudicial characteristics that, when compared against the values of the majority White society, were deemed to be innately inferior traits. Because the economic success of mass entertainment media in the United States was predicated on their ability to meet audience demands, mass support for negative and inferior minority portrayals indicates that producers satisfied consumer desires. The stereotypes, then, were representative of popular attitudes.

We have also seen that although wide cultural differences exist among the minority groups under consideration, their portrayals in American mass media have been remarkably similar and are the result of the attitudinal premise of White intellectual and moral supremacy. The fundamental concepts of ethnic stereotyping were applied consistently in each of the American mass entertainment media forms discussed: popular literature, the live stage, and motion pictures. This was the dubious legacy upon which American entertainment media entered the post-World War II era and the age of commercial television.

NOTES

1. James M. Jones, *Prejudice and Racism* (Addison-Wesley, 1972), p. 3.
2. Lerone Bennett, *Before the Mayflower* (Penguin, 1966), p. 30.
3. W. D. Jordan, *White over Black: American Attitudes Toward the Negro, 1550-1812* (Penguin, 1969), p. 7.
4. Cecil Robinson, *Mexico and the Hispanic Southwest in American Literature* (University of Arizona Press, 1977).

4

TELEVISION AND MOVIES AFTER WORLD WAR II

FORCES OF WORLD HISTORY and technology combined to make their impact on the treatment of ethnic minorities in American mass media following World War II. During the next two decades there was a war in Korea and U.S. involvement in Vietnam began, signaling a major change in global politics. Domestically, McCarthyism came and went, as did the civil rights movement. The motion picture was in the process of being supplanted as the prime mass entertainment medium by television.

Although motion pictures were entering a transition period and seeking to redefine their niche in American mass entertainment, producers continued to release movies about or including minorities. Stereotypes continued to change in order to reflect the current political viewpoints, racial attitudes, and moods of the White majority audience. Native American Indians were used during the period as metaphors by filmmakers who wanted to make political or philosophical statements about other issues. For example, *Arrowhead* (1953) was seen by critics as an ultra-right-wing allegory of the McCarthy era, while *Cheyenne Autumn* (1964) spoke strongly against German extermination camps as well as Indian persecution. Later, both *Soldier Blue* and *Little Big Man* (1970) made statements about American involvement in Vietnam. At the same time, White America (in the midst of the Black-inspired civil rights movement) experienced a guilt complex over the historical and persistent mistreatment of Indians. The result was a series of

Hollywood productions designed to purge that guilt, including *Hombre* (1967), *Tell Them Willie Boy Is Here* (1969), and *Jeremiah Johnson* (1972). Taking matters further, Hollywood reversed itself in its portrayals of two Indian tamers it had immortalized in earlier films. In *Little Big Man* (1970), General George A. Custer is characterized as meeting a just ending at the Little Big Horn massacre as retribution for atrocities perpetrated against the Indians. Similarly, William Cody is portrayed as a mercenary eagerly exploiting Indians for the sake of showmanship in *Buffalo Bill and the Indians* (1976). The 1970s can generally be viewed as the decade when movie portrayals became pro-Indian. Although the image of the violent Indian remained into the 1980s, Hollywood tended to mitigate the violence by placing it in the context of survival, self-defense, or retribution.

Black Americans benefited from a shift in White attitudes following World War II when (under the prodding of the National Association for the Advancement of Colored People, other civil rights groups, and the Truman administration), Hollywood began to make films illustrating the folly and unfairness of racial discrimination against them. A catalyst in this movement was the manner in which Black military men had distinguished themselves during World War II in fighting for the cause of American freedom. The evils of prejudice against Blacks were denunciated in *Pinky, Lost Boundaries,* and *Home of the Brave* (all 1949), *No Way Out* (1950), *Blackboard Jungle* (1955), and *The Defiant Ones* (1958). The 1960s belonged to the imagery of the sophisticated Black, who was heroic in proportions. Actor Sidney Poitier epitomized the intelligent, cool Black American who harnessed his hidden rage in tolerance to prejudice and ignorance found in Whites of lesser stature in *Guess Who's Coming to Dinner* and *In the Heat of the Night* (both 1967). Poitier won the Oscar for best actor for his portrayal of a handyman who builds a chapel for White European nuns in a rural American community in *Lilies of the Field* (1963). Harry Belafonte and Sammy Davis, Jr., were two other Black actors who starred in films of the period in roles showing Blacks in nonthreatening circumstances.

The mid-1960s and early 1970s brought a definitely threatening Black image to the movies as the so-called blaxpoitation movies featuring nearly all-Black casts cavorted on screen with the assumption of a militant posture. The civil rights movement led by Dr. Martin Luther King, Jr., was at its zenith. Hollywood again purged its conscience as urban Blacks took revenge against Whites in such movies as *Sweet Sweetback's Baadasssss Song* (1971) and in two urban detective films featuring Richard Roundtree in *Shaft* (1971) and *Shaft's Big Score* (1972). Whites generally showed little box-office interest in blaxploitation movies and the genre soon lost its financial luster. The rest of the 1970s was marked by a trend toward films designed to attract mixed racial audiences. *Cooley High* (1975) and *Carwash* (1976) were examples. In the early 1980s, with the civil rights movement a distant memory, roles for Blacks in motion pictures became extremely scarce, a circumstance they shared with other ethnic minority film craftspeople.

The immediate post-World War II period saw a continuation of the relationship established before the war between Latinos and Hollywood that was built on economic considerations. During the war U.S. filmmakers could not distribute their wares to European markets. Latin American countries came to represent 20 percent of Hollywood's total foreign market business, resulting in the development of joint movie projects. Many movies were filmed in Latin American nations with writing and financing provided by Hollywood. Most of the supporting roles were played by Latino actors, and the alliance led to an overly positive image of Latino characters as evidenced by such films as *The Fugitive* (1948) and *Way of the Gaucho* (1952). In 1953, a precedent was established with the making of *Salt of the Earth*, in which all of the major roles were portrayed by Latino or Latin American actors.

By the 1960s, the Latin American market withered for Hollywood because those countries had developed their own film industries and screen personalities. The number of Hollywood movies using Latino themes dropped drastically and those that did reverted to old stereotypical form by reintroducing the "greaser" as an urban gang member. Puerto Ricans were singled out for updated "greaser" treatment in two 1961 films, *West Side Story* and *The Young Savages*. The emphasis was on gang violence in urban America. Hollywood continued the violent "greaser" trend with *Duck You Sucker* (1972), *Bring Me the Head of Alfredo Garcia* (1974), *The Warriors* (1978), and *Boulevard Nights* (1979). A distorted view of the Mexican family was presented in *Children of Sanchez* (1978), but the early 1980s have included movies produced and directed by Chicanos (*Seguin*, 1981, and *The Ballad of Gregorio Cortez*, 1982). The 1981 release of *Zoot Suit* followed the success of the play, which began its run in 1978. In *Zoot Suit*, the Mexican American is realistically portrayed during a World War II race riot in Los Angeles. A series of movies beginning in the 1970s featured the nonthreatening comedic adventures of Cheech and Chong in the Mexican American urban barrio. These films, however, were criticized for their perceived glorification of the drug culture, sexist orientation, and nontraditional lifestyle of the featured characters. In general, Hollywood offerings did little to portray Latinos as part of the social mainstream in the United States during the first half of the 1980s other than in bit parts.

Japanese portrayals continued to be negative immediately after World War II, when American audiences were offered more war movies. Japanese acts of cruelty and torture were seen in *Tokyo Joe* (1949) and *Three Came Home* (1950). An exception, perhaps inspired by a guilt response to the Japanese relocation camps, was *Go for Broke* (1951), which was a positive portrayal of the heroic Japanese-American military units that fought in Europe. A major reversal would soon take place, however, between Japanese and Chinese imagery in the movies.

With the coming of the Korean war, the "cold war," and McCarthyism, the issue of communism became the focal point of American fears and anxieties. Synonymous with communism were the Soviet Union and China. The same China whose people had been viewed so warmly by Americans only a decade earlier was once again seen as home of the "Yellow Peril." Japan, on the other hand, was a close ally and virtually a U.S. satellite by the late 1950s. Popular movies reflected both attitudes.

Initially, the Japanese were portrayed with much more sensitivity than at any time since the Immigration Law of 1924. *The Bridge on the River Kwai* and *Battle of the Coral Sea* (1959) are examples of the softer treatment given the Japanese by Hollywood. Even the touchy subject of Japanese-White romance was explored in *Sayonara* (1957) and *My Geisha* (1962). Although such romances did not have happy endings, they were nevertheless not treated as a basic violation of nature.

Meanwhile, China (by now commonly referred to as "Red China" or "Communist China") took on the movie depictions reminiscent of the early 1930s. The Chinese regime was seen as oppressive and exploitive of its own people in *Satan Never Sleeps* (1962) and as a devious threat to the American system in *The Manchurian Candidate* (1962). The same year also marked the release of two films, *55 Days at Peking* and *The Sand Pebbles*, which were set in early twentieth-century China but reinforced the image of drug addiction, prostitution, inhumanity, and deceit as staples of Chinese life. From the mid-1970s, following the reopening of diplomatic and trade ties with China, the pendulum swung again in China's favor and Hollywood curtailed its negative portrayals after several fantasy characterizations such as *Dr. No* (1962) and others in the James Bond spy thriller series. A surge of American interest in Oriental martial arts, however, spurred the creation of a series of films featuring almost nonstop violent action scenes showing villains and heroes employing kung fu, karate, and other combative techniques. Chinese-American actor Bruce Lee, an acrobatic master of the martial arts, became the catalyst for that motion picture genre that portrayed the Chinese as sadistically violent. Generally, however, the films depicted Chinese characters in both heroic and villainous roles.

In the post-Vietnam era, American film producers seem ready to make the Vietnamese their next target of Asian stereotyping based on the same long-standing attitudes. They have been portrayed on screen as crafty, devious, guerilla warfare perpetrators of violence in *The Deer Hunter* (1978) and *Apocalypse Now* (1979), among others, into the 1980s.

MINORITIES IN THE TELEVISION AGE

Movies of both older and recent vintage did not cease to perpetrate their stereotypical images on either White audiences or people of color after their run in American theaters; many of them have continued to reach the masses via television and may do so for years to come. Commercial television became a major mass medium in 1948, the year Milton Berle's comedy and variety show spurred the purchase of TV sets in epidemic proportions. Minorities were quickly made a part of the new medium, appearing in the traditional roles to which they had been limited in theatrical movies.

Among the first minority TV characters was Tonto, the Lone Ranger's "faithful" Indian companion played throughout the series' eight-year run by Jay Silverheels, an actor of Mohawk tribal heritage. *The Lone Ranger* first aired on television in 1949, but had begun as a radio series in 1933. While the Lone Ranger's mask often made those he encountered in his western adventures apprehensive, the fact that he maintained a friendship with an Indian made him even more suspect. Tonto's image, however, was positive because he fought for justice in the highest tradition of American folklore. His role as a Native American perpetrated the established stereotypes, including the pinto pony, broken English dialect, fringed buckskin attire, and secondary status relative to the White hero.

Unfortunately, the historical portrayal of Indians on network television differs little from that experienced in Hollywood. The list of prime-time TV series featuring positive, accurate representations of Native Americans, in an examination of either past or present conditions, is extremely brief. Perhaps the only attempt to do so was made in the 1955-1956 TV season, when CBS aired *Brave Eagle*. The show sought to portray the Indian viewpoint of the White expansionist movement into his territory during the latter part of the nineteenth century. The program did feature actual Indian cast members but, ironically, a real Indian (Keena Nomkeena) played the foster son to White actor Keith Larsen, who played a Cheyenne tribal chief. A White actor also played an old sage who orally recited tribal history and events. Nevertheless, the series has not been equaled into the 1980s in its basic objective as a regularly aired network offering, although there have been documentaries and special TV movies that have infrequently appeared with sympathetic themes. *Brave Eagle* was followed by ABC's *Broken Arrow*, which appeared for five years (1956-1960). The series, however, featured an all-White cast and the story line centered around Indian and White cooperation in fighting frontier injustice. During the era when television was dominated by "westerns" (1960s), Indians were mostly relegated to their movie image, serving as either foils or backdrops to the stories of how the West was won.

Black Americans constitute the largest minority presence in network television. That fact, however, has not resulted in an altogether satisfactory TV portrayal of the realities of the diversified Black experience in the United States, but the more recent history shows improvement over earlier years. In 1950, three network shows went on the air featuring Blacks in their casts as regulars. They were *Beulah, The Jack Benny Show* and *The Stu Erwin Show*, and each portrayed Blacks in subservient domestic roles. The Beulah character was a maid and mammy figure in a White

Jay Silverheels was the first Native American to be featured in a network (ABC) TV series. He played Tonto, the companion of *the Lone Ranger*, complete with fringed buckskin attire and Indian pinto horse. (Photo by permission of Wrather Corporation)

household (played first by Ethel Waters and later by Louise Beavers) who had a scatterbrained girlfriend (Oriole, played by Butterfly McQueen) and a shiftless boyfriend. Eddie Anderson portrayed Jack Benny's valet Rochester on TV for 15 years, and Willie Best, who had played imitative Stepin Fetchit roles in numerous movies, brought the character to the Erwin show as the family handyman.

The first show with an all-Black cast made its television debut in 1951, although it had been immensely popular as a radio series since 1929 with its White creators playing the major roles. *Amos'n'Andy* was awaited with much anticipation across the nation because the show's creators, Freeman Gosden and Charles Correll, held a widely publicized four-year search for the Black actors who would bring the show to television. A special televised segment was arranged before a studio audience for Gosden and Correll to introduce the handpicked cast prior to the first show. In introducing the male actors, the creators occasionally referred to them as "boys," a term long despised by Blacks as a relic of slavery in the United States. The original series lasted two years but reruns continued into the mid-1960s, always in controversy over the images it projected about Blacks. Although the show was based mostly on characters with little intellectual capacity and otherwise lacking ethical values and employment, there were Black characters seen as attorneys, business owners, educators, and other professionals. Nevertheless, pressure from civil rights groups forced the program off the air entirely in 1966 when CBS withdrew it from sale.

The other significant program featuring Blacks prior to the civil rights movement of the 1960s was the musical variety show hosted by singer Nat "King" Cole from 1956 to 1957. Cole was the first Black to host a network show and NBC made considerable efforts to keep it afloat despite poor ratings throughout its 13-month history. Although Cole was an extremely popular vocalist and successful recording star, the majority audience did not watch his show even with big-name Black and White guest artists making appearances.

From the mid-1960s into the mid-1980s Blacks have been seen on numerous TV series, usually as comedy-variety show hosts or in situation comedies. Many shows employed what were seen by critics as a single "token" Black character, but from *Amos'n'Andy* to 1984 there have been only four other shows (all situation comedies) with predominantly Black casts that lasted more than one season in regular network television: *Sanford and Son* (1972), *Good Times* (1974), *The Jeffersons* (1975), and *What's Happening!* (1976). Of course, the TV ratings epic *Roots* aired as a prime-time "miniseries" special in 1977 and many believed it served as a catharsis of guilt for Whites over the historical treatment of Blacks in America. An estimated 100 million viewers watched the program over eight consecutive nights, beginning several trends in television programming.

By the mid-1980s the primary roles for Blacks in prime-time network television were still in situation comedies rather than serious dramatic programs. Critics maintained that network television in the 1980s was almost all situation comedies and prime-time "soap opera" serials. Actress Diahann Carroll, who became the first Black woman to star in a network comedy/dramatic series (*Julia*, 1968), made history again in 1984 when she joined the regular cast of ABC's prime-time soap opera *Dynasty*.

Latinos were also brought to the small screen early in television history when the romantic figure of *The Cisco Kid* rode into American homes in 1950. The series aired for seven years but only in syndication to independent stations. It was the first successful syndicated program and was among the first color filmed series. The Cisco Kid had been an entertainment fixture since his creation in the O. Henry short story, "The Caballero's Way." In the original story, Cisco was a bandito-type character who preyed on the rich to help the poor, a la Robin Hood. The character was brought to the movies in several productions with various leading men, including Duncan Renaldo, who brought the role to TV. Cisco and his sidekick, Pancho, delighted youngsters, who were the key to their popularity, as they enjoyed a jovial repartee while roaming the Southwest to fight injustice. Renaldo's portrayal was vintage "Latin lover," except he never got romantically involved with the love-stricken ladies because his audience was primarily children. Pancho, played by Leo Carillo, was a rotund, gregarious character who affected the stereotypical speech American audiences had come to expect from movie Mexicans who were not "Latin lovers." Often Pancho would urge his partner, "Hey Cees-ko, let's went!" The next Latino role appeared in 1951 when a White actor, Don Diamond, played El Toro, the Mexican sidekick to the lead in *Kit Carson*.

But the biggest Latino television personality of the early days of television was Desi Arnaz, who was Lucille Ball's actual and screen husband in the long-running show, *I Love Lucy*. Although Arnaz played a respectable husband who was a band leader, he also played straight man to Lucy's zany schemes. His Latin temperament, which exploded into a torrent of Spanish when Lucy's ill-fated activities were revealed, was classic stereotyped imagery.

The popular series came to television in 1951 and continued in original production until 1961. A swashbuckling adventure show, *Zorro*, debuted in 1957 and, although set in early California, it concerned the political struggles of Spanish settlers. Mexicans, however, served only as villains, buffoons, or backdrops to the affairs of the Spanish aristocracy.

In the 1960s three television programs stood out for their Latino portrayals. In *The Real McCoys* (1957-1963), Tony Martinez played farmhand Pepino Garcia, a role consistent with audience expectations. A non-Latino carried the TV image of the simple-minded Mexican when *The Bill Dana Show* appeared in 1963 for a two-year run. Dana's opening line with a thick Mexican accent became a virtual national catch-phrase because of his nightclub act and record sales: "My name, Jose Jimenez." In the show, Jimenez worked as a hotel bellhop whose ineptness constantly got him into comedic situations. Perhaps the most unusual prime-time TV show centering on Latino characters was *The High Chaparral* (1967-1971). It was one of the numerous "adult westerns" aired during the period and featured an interracial marriage between the daughter of a Mexican cattle baron and a wealthy White rancher. The characters portrayed by Latino actors, however, generally had roles as ranch hands.

In the 1970s two network situation comedies were based on the Mexican American barrio of East Los Angeles. More recognized and criticized of the two was *Chico and the Man*, starring Freddie Prinze, which aired for five seasons on NBC beginning in 1974. Chico was a young streetwise character who used his savvy to drum up business for the auto repair garage where he worked. The racial "humor" and image portrayed by Chico was the subject of controversy throughout the show's network existence. In 1976 another "sitcom" about an East Los Angeles family was brought to ABC, titled *Viva Valdez*. It lasted only four months. Two other series featuring Latino actors began in the 1970s and continued until 1983. NBC screened *CHIPS* for the first time in 1977, co-starring handsome Latino actor Erik Estrada as a California Highway Patrol officer with romance on his mind. *Fantasy Island* (1978) starred Ricardo Montalban as the romantic figure host on an idyllic isle. Neither portrayal was very distant from the Latin lover roles Hollywood had created decades earlier. In 1984 ABC made its second attempt at a sitcom centered on the life of an East Los Angeles barrio family with Paul Rodriguez in *a.k.a. Pablo*. Critics claimed the show was harmful because Rodriguez's jokes were seen as ridiculing Mexican American culture. The program lasted only six episodes and did not return in 1985.

Asian portrayals came to television in 1949 in an ABC crime show called *Mysteries of Chinatown*, starring White actor Marvin Miller as Dr. Yat Fu. The show was set in San Francisco's Chinatown, where Miller's character was a stereotype as owner of an herb and curio shop. The regular supporting cast was all White and, as evidenced by the show's title, was designed to exploit the old stereotype of the "mysterious" Asian. Next to surface was the TV version of *The Adventures of Fu Manchu* (1956), another crime drama with an all-White cast. The program was vintage "Yellow Peril" imagery, with Dr. Fu sending his agents on various missions designed to subvert the cause of Western civilization. The nefarious and wiley Dr. Fu was based in various cities in the Orient as the series dredged up the old Sax Rohmer stereotypes. In fact, the series was facilitated by Rohmer's sale of rights to his creation in 1955 to Republic Pictures. The show was a non-network syndicated production and aired for only one season. Ironically, the following year (1956) it was followed to television by the other venerable Chinese character, Charlie Chan. *The New Adventures of Charlie Chan* was also a syndicated series lasting only one year. Chan was played by J. Carrol Naish, but an Asian actor, James Hong, was cast in the role of Chan's "number-one son" as Barry Chan. The series was produced in Great Britain and the Chan character operated from London.

In the 1960s ABC aired an adventure series, *Hong Kong*, which reinforced the Chinese image of intrigue, sexy women, smuggling, and drug peddling. At least two Asian actors were cast as series regulars during its single year run (1960-61). The same network brought *The Green Hornet* to prime time TV for a one-year stay in 1966-67. The significance of the series was the casting of Bruce Lee as the Green Hornet's sidekick, Kato. Lee's weekly demonstration of martial arts skills as he fought crime helped launch the popularity of Oriental self-defense techniques in the United States. Interestingly, *The Green Hornet* was the creation of George Trendle, who also developed *The Lone Ranger*. In both concepts the hero is supported by a trusty ethnic minority sidekick, perhaps for the purpose of adding fantasy appeal for the mass audience. Sparked by the influence of Bruce Lee was another ABC series, *Kung Fu*, a western starring David Carradine and supporting Asian actors, including Keye Luke and Philip Ahn. Lee was a consultant to those who developed *Kung Fu* and labored under the impression he was to be their choice for the lead role. When Carradine was selected for the part, Lee confided to friends that he had been the victim of racism. *Kung Fu's* producers told Lee they didn't believe a Chinese actor could be seen as a hero in the eyes of the American television audience.[1] The show, which aired from 1972 to 1975, became a throwback to the "mysterious" Asian stereotype. With racism standing as a barrier to stardom in the United States, Bruce Lee went to Hong Kong, where he achieved superstardom throughout Asia as a film star.

The greatest Asian presence in television began in the 1960s and featured an array of supporting police and criminal characters in the long-running CBS series *Hawaii Five-O* (1968-1980). At least three Asian actors appeared as regulars on the show and the lead character, Detective Steve McGarrett, pursued an arch-enemy Asian character, Wo Fat, periodically throughout the show's 12-year tenure. Generally, Asian portrayals in *Hawaii Five-O* were varied and diverse, although definite stereotypes were projected. The show's vulnerability to stereotypical criticism was its portrayal of White superiority and leadership in a predominantly Asian environment.

There have been several prime-time shows throughout the history of American television that perpetuated the subservient, humble Asian image. Among them were *Bachelor Father* (1957-1962), with an Asian "houseboy" character played by Sammee Tong, and *Bonanza* (1959-1972), with Chinese cook Hop Sing played by Victor Sen Yung. In *The Courtship of Eddie's Father* (1969-1972), Miyoshi Umeki played a housekeeper who was often befuddled by situations that arose in the household. Umeki's character was apparently married to an American, because her role was that of "Mrs. Livingston," although her mannerisms and philosophy were clearly the Japanese stereotypes U.S. entertainment media have created over the years.

The early 1980s were characterized by a continuation of Asian supporting roles in various sitcoms and dramatic offerings. Two unique programs using Asian themes came to network TV in 1980. A week-long miniseries, *Shogun*, was based on the exploits of a White adventurer in feudal Japan. Although providing American audiences with some insight into Japanese culture, the program placed an emphasis upon the violence of samurai warriors and an aura of sexual mysticism surrounding Japanese women. NBC brought a variety show called *Pink Lady* to its schedule, featuring a Japanese singing duo of the same name. The two young ladies were attractive and spoke little English, so comic Jeff Altman served as facilitator. As an attempt to bring the demure, humble, and sexy image of the Japanese woman to network television, *Pink Lady* was canceled after less than two months on the air. That female image, however, returned to prominence in 1983, when actress Rosalind Chao took a costarring role in *After M*A*S*H*. In the CBS series, which aired until December 1984, her role was that of the Korean wife of a White ex-G.I. who had served in the Korean war.

ANALYSIS

The historical overview reveals that ethnic minority stereotyping is dependent upon the social, political, and economic realities of the moment, and changes accordingly. At any given historical period the nature of a specific minority group's portrayal may be much more positive than another's. Basic negative traits, however, have never been abandoned totally, although specific instances of mass guilt purging periodically appear in entertainment media.

Ethnically prejudicial stereotyping is debilitative to a society, especially one as culturally diverse as the United States. Not only does it work against common understanding and the recognition of the family of humankind, it provides succeeding generations of minorities and nonminorities alike with distorted self-images. The coupling of biased portrayals with the social and psychological power of mass entertainment threatens the maturation of American society. But the attitudinal change must begin with the masses, because producers of mass entertainment are, generally, motivated more by economic incentive than by social morality. If there is to be significant change it will occur when the masses demand it. History shows that the audience demanded and got "Yankee Doodle" in place of a symphony. If audiences demand a symphony of honest and realistic minority portrayals from their entertainment media, they will get them.

NOTE

1. See the account of Bruce Lee's encounter with the producers of *Kung Fu* in Kareem Abdul-Jabbar and Peter Knobler, *Giant Steps: The Autobiography of Kareem Abdul-Jabbar* (Bantam, 1983), pp. 188-189.

SUGGESTED READING

Allport, Gordon W. *The Nature of Prejudice*. Garden City, NY: Doubleday, 1958.

Bataille, Gretchen M. and Charles L. P. Silet (Eds.). *The Pretend Indians: Images in the Movies*. Ames: Iowa State University Press, 1980.

Berkhofer, Robert F., Jr. *The White Man's Indian: Images of the American Indian from Columbus to the Present*. New York: Knopf, 1978.

Bogle, Donald. *Toms, Coons, Mulattoes, Mammies and Bucks: An Interpretive History of Blacks in American Films*. New York: Viking, 1973.

Brooks, Tim and Earle Marsh. *The Complete Directory to Prime Time Network TV Shows, 1946 - Present*. New York: Ballantine, 1981.

Churchill, Ward, Norbert Hill, and Mary Ann Hill. "Media Stereotyping and Native Response: An Historical Overview," *Indian Historian, 11* (December 1978), pp. 45-56, 63.

Cripps, Thomas. "The Death of Rastus: Negroes in American Films Since 1945." *Phylon*, 28 (Fall 1967), pp. 267-275.

Cripps, Thomas. *Slow Fade to Black: The Negro in American Film, 1900-1942*. New York: Oxford University Press, 1977.

Friar, Ralph and Natasha Friar. *The Only Good Indian . . . : The Hollywood Gospel*. New York: Drama Book Specialists, 1972.

Hsu, Francis L.K. *The Challenge of the American Dream: The Chinese in the United States*. Belmont, CA: Wadsworth, 1971.

Hughes, Langston and Milton Meltzer. *Black Magic*. Englewood Cliffs, NJ: Prentice-Hall, 1967.

Ichihashi, Yamato. *Japanese in the United States*. Palo Alto, CA: Stanford University Press, 1932.

Isaacs, Harold. *Scratches on Our Minds: American Images of China and India*. New York: John Day, 1958.

King, Stephen W. *Communication and Social Influence*. Reading, MA: Addison-Wesley, 1975.

MacDonald, J. Fred. *Blacks and White TV*. Chicago: Nelson-Hall, 1983.

McWilliams, Carey. *Prejudice; Japanese Americans: Symbol of Racial Intolerance*. Boston: Little, Brown, 1944.

Miller, Randall. *The Kaleidoscopic Lens: How Hollywood Views Ethnic Groups*. Englewood, NJ: Ozer, 1980.

Pearce, Roy Harvey. *Savagism and Civilization: A Study of the Indian and the American Mind*. Baltimore: Johns Hopkins University Press, 1965.

Shien-woo Kung. *Chinese in American Life: Some Aspects of Their History, Status Problems and Contributions*. Seattle: University of Washington Press, 1962.

Toll, Robert C. *The Entertainment Machine*. New York: Oxford University Press, 1982.

Woll, Allen L. *The Latin Image in American Film*. Los Angeles: UCLA Latin American Series, 1977.

III

Nonentertainment Media Portrayals

"News media have offered an image of ethnics as 'problem people,' which means they are projected as people who either *have* problems or *cause* problems for society."

5

ADVERTISING: THE MEDIA'S NOT-SO-SILENT PARTNER

IN THE LATE 1960s a lovable cartoon character appeared on television screens and in magazines across the United States. Named the Frito Bandito, the cartoon figure of a mustachioed Mexican bandit with six-gun, broad sombrero, and a sinister smile went around houses sneaking Fritos corn chips from unsuspecting mothers. "Bullet"-riddled "wanted" posters produced as part of an advertising campaign for the snack food advised housewives to buy two bags of the corn chips, because "he loves cronchy Fritos corn chips so much he'll stop at nothing to get yours. What's more he's cunning, clever—and sneaky."[1] Television commercials featured youngsters sneaking corn chips from the family supply, then biting into the crunchy chips as "Mexican"-style mustaches appeared on their faces.

The Frito Bandito was a lovable, and successful, salesman for the Frito-Lay Corporation, maker of the corn chips. He was described by the director of advertising for the company as a "simple character, which is intended to make you laugh; in turn, we hope that this laughter will leave our trademark implanted in your memory."[2] But many Latinos, particularly Chicano activist and civic groups, did not react to the Frito Bandito with laughter. They pointed out that the cartoon character was nothing more than a humorous version of the stereotype Mexican bandit, one who perpetuated and reinforced the stereotype of Mexicans as mustachioed thieves. Protests were organized against Frito-Lay and boycotts threatened against television stations airing the commercials. After some local television stations were persuaded in 1970 that the cartoon character was racially offensive and agreed not to air the advertisement, Frito-Lay announced it would cancel what had been a highly successful advertising campaign.

A little more than ten years later, Frito-Lay launched yet another advertising campaign playing on the Anglo perceptions of Latinos and Latin America. But this time the approach was very different. The product was Tostitos, another corn chip produced by the company, but one that was touted as being authentically Mexican. Rather than featuring a gun-toting mustachioed bandit under a broad sombrero, the campaign was centered on a tall, distinguished Latino, reminiscent of the "Latin lovers" who populated earlier generations of Hollywood movies. He spoke with a Spanish accent, but this time it was a lilting, cultured accent that resounded with careful pronunciations of consonants and vowels that highlighted the correct pronunciation of the company's product.

In each commercial the stately spokesman told viewers about his fond memories of his growing up as a young boy in his Latin American homeland. Among his fondest memories were coming home from school and play to finding warm corn chips that had just been prepared. He told viewers how good they tasted and how much he missed them. But, he continued, now corn chips with that same authentic taste and shape were now available in the United States to everyone, not just those fortunate enough to come from Latin America. He praised the Tostito corn chips available in plastic bags at local stores and attested to their authenticity.

This time there were no protests against the commercials from Latino organizations, no threats of boycotts against the product, and no angry letters to the regulatory agencies overseeing broadcasting or advertising. This time Frito-Lay had struck the right chord with Latinos and non-Latinos. The company played on the accepted imagery of Latinos and Latin America, but instead of reinforcing the image of the sneaky Mexican bandit, the company played on the romantic image of the distinguished, cultured Latino, perhaps more a product of Spain than of Mexico. The campaign, which also ran in media directed to Latinos in the United States, represented a change in the thinking at Frito-Lay, from seeing Latinos as the object of humorous stereotypes to portraying them as people with a romantic past that could be brought into your home through the purchase of Tostitos. It was a transition that illustrated an evolution in advertising, an industry that has been identified as essential to the American character in the United States.

ADVERTISING AND MEDIA IN THE LAND OF PLENTY

In 1950 historian David M. Potter was invited by the Wahlgreen Foundation to prepare six lectures on the American character and the impact of economic abundance on shaping the character of the people living in the United States. In these lectures, which were later published in a revised form in a book titled *People of Plenty*, Potter identified advertising as the "institution of abundance," that unique part of the society "that was brought into being by abundance, without previous existence in any form, and, moreover, an institution which is peculiarly identified with American abundance."[3] He also noted that media scholars up to that time had not recognized the central role that advertising has placed in shaping and developing media in the United States.

As Potter and subsequent scholars have noted, the development of advertising as a revenue source for print and, later, broadcast media required media managers to develop news and entertainment content that would attract the largest possible number of people. This gave birth to the term "mass media," which describes the ability of the media to attract the large audience to which advertisers wanted to transmit their commercial messages. The circulation and rating figures are the bread and butter of the media, since they translate into increased advertising insertions and higher advertising rates. The media attract the mass audience by developing content with a broad appeal that often is directed at the lowest common denominator of culture in the audience. The advertising, like the editorial and entertainment material it supports in newspapers, magazines, radio, and television, is also geared to appeal to a mass audience that might produce buyers. This mass appeal by both advertisers and the media they support is targeted to the audience in the majority, not to racial or other minorities who might happen to pick up a newspaper or listen to a radio program.

Far from being an appendage to the media industry, Potter described advertising as a force that dictates the editorial and entertainment content of the media, which depend on advertising dollars for their revenues. Mass media charge artificially low subscription fees to boost their circulation, which force the media to depend on advertisers even more for their revenues. This, in turn, is accompanied by editorial or programming philosophies that place a priority on attracting the largest possible audience. Media content, wrote Potter, is nothing more than the bait to attract the audience and hold its attention between the commercial messages:

> What this means, in functional terms, it seems to me, is that the newspaper feature, the magazine article, the radio program, do not attain the dignity of being ends in themselves. They are rather means to an end: that end, of course, is to catch the reader's attention so that he will then read the advertisement or hear the commercial, and to hold his interest until these essential messages have been delivered. The program or the article becomes a kind of advertisement in itself—becomes the "pitch," in the telling language of the circus barker. Its function is to induce people to accept the commercial, just as the commercial's function is to induce them to accept the product."[4]

According to Potter, the development of content as bait for the mass audience means that the mass media include material that will attract the most people and, at the same time, delete material with the potential of offending or leaving out any potential members of the audience. This places some rigid constraints on media editorial and entertainment content.

> First, a message must not deal with subjects of special or out-of-the-way interest, since such subjects a by definition have no appeal for the majority of the audience. Second, it must not deal with any subject at a high level of maturity, since many people are immature, chronologically or otherwise, and a mature level is one which, by definition, leaves such people out. Third, it must not deal with matters which are controversial or even unpleasant or dis-

tressing, since such matters may, by definition, antagonize or offend some members of the audience.[5]

ADVERTISING AND MINORITIES

Given the social and legal restrictions on the participation of racial minorities in the society of the United States during much of this country's history, it is not hard to see how the desire to cater to the perceived views of the mass audience desired by advertisers has resulted in entertainment and news content that largely ignores minorities, treats them stereotypically when they were recognized, and largely avoids grappling with such issues as segregation, discriminatory immigration laws, land rights, and other controversies that affected certain minority groups more than they do the White majority. While the portrayal of racial minorities is amply analyzed in other chapters of this book, it is important to recognize that those portrayals have been, to a large extent, supported by a system of advertising that requires the media to cater to the perceived attitudes and prejudices of the White majority and that also reinforces such images in its own commercial messages. For years, advertisers in the United States have reflected the place of racial minorities in the social fabric of the nation by either ignoring them or, when they have been included in advertisements for the mass audience, by processing and presenting them so as to make them palatable salespersons for the products being advertised. These portrayals have largely mirrored the stereotyped images of minorities in the entertainment media, which, in turn, were designed to reflect the perceived values and norms of the White majority society. In this way, minority portrayals in advertising have paralleled and reinforced the images of minorities in other media.

The history of advertising in the United States is replete with minority images that, like the Frito Bandito, respond to and reinforce the preconceived image that many White Americans apparently have of Blacks, Latinos, Asians, and Native Americans. Over the years advertisers have employed Latin spitfires such as

Chiquita Banana, Black mammies such as Aunt Jemima, and noble savages such as the Santa Fe Railroad's Super Chief to pitch their products to a predominantly White mass audience of consumers. In 1984 the Balch Institute for Ethnic Studies in Philadelphia sponsored an exhibit of more than 300 examples of racial and ethnic images used by corporations in magazines, posters, trade cards, and story boards. In an interview with the advertising trade magazine *Advertising Age*, institute director Mark Stolarik quoted the catalog for the exhibit, which capsulized the evolution of minority images and how they have changed.

> Some of these advertisements were based on stereotypes of various ethnic groups. In the early years, they were usually crude and condescending images that appealed to largely Anglo-American audiences who found it difficult to reconcile their own visions of beauty, order and behavior with that of non-Anglo-Americans. Later, these images were softened because of complaints from the ethnic groups involved and the growing sophistication of the advertising industry.[6]

The advertising examples in the exhibit include positive White ethnic stereotypes, such as the wholesome and pure image of Quakers in an early Quaker Oats advertisement and the cleanliness of the Dutch in a turn-of-the-century advertisement for Colgate soaps. But they also featured a late-nineteenth-century advertisement showing an Irish matron threatening to hit her husband over the head with a rolling pin because he didn't smoke the right brand of tobacco. Like Quaker Oats, some products even incorporated a racial stereotype image on the package or product line being advertised, such as Red Man Chewing Tobacco.

"Lawsee! Folks sho' whoops with joy over AUNT JEMIMA PANCAKES," shouted a bandanna-wearing Black mammy in a magazine advertisement for Aunt Jemima pancake mix, which featured a plump Aunt Jemima on the box. Over the years Aunt Jemima has lost some weight, but the stereotyped face of the Black servant continues to be featured on the box. Earlier advertisements for Cream of Wheat featured Rastus, the Black servant on the box, in a series of magazine cartoons with a group of cute but ill-dressed Black children. Some of the advertisements played on the stereotypes ridiculing Blacks. In one, a Black schoolteacher, standing behind a makeshift lectern made out of a boldly lettered Cream of Wheat box, asks the class, "How do you spell Cream of Wheat?" Others appeared to promote racial integration, such as a magazine advertisement captioned "Putting It Down in Black and White," which showed Rastus serving bowls of the breakfast cereal to Black and White youngsters sitting at the same table.

Racial imagery was also integrated into the naming of trains by the Santa Fe railroad, which called one of its passenger lines the Super Chief and featured highly detailed portraits of the noble Indian in promoting its service through the southwestern United States. In another series of advertisements, the railroad used cartoons of Native American children to show the service and sights passengers could expect when they traveled the Santa Fe line. General Motors advertised its Pontiac automobile with the slogan "Pontiac Heap Fine Car."

These and other portrayals catered to the mass audience mentality by either neutralizing or making humor of the negative perceptions that many Whites may have had of racial minorities. The advertising images, rather than showing minorities as they really were, portrayed minorities as filtered through Anglo eyes. This presented an out-of-focus image of racial minorities, but one that was palatable, and even persuasive, to the White majority to which it was directed. In the mid-1960s Black civil rights groups targeted the advertising industry for special attention, protesting both the lack of integrated advertisements and the stereotyped images that the advertisers continued to use. The effort, accompanied by support from federal officials, resulted in the overnight inclusion of Blacks as models in television advertising in 1967 and a downplaying of the images that many Blacks found objectionable. "Black America is becoming visible in America's biggest national advertising medium," reported the *New York Times* in 1968. "Not in a big way yet, but it is a beginning and men in high places give assurances that there will be a lot more visibility."[7]

But the advertising industry did not generalize the concerns of Blacks, or the concessions made in response to them, to other groups. At the same time that some Black concerns were being addressed with integrated advertising, other groups were being ignored or singled out for continued stereotyped treatment in such commercials as those featuring the Frito Bandito.

Among the Latino advertising stereotypes cited in a 1969 article by sociologist Tomás Martínez[8] were commercials for Granny Goose chips featuring fat gun-toting Mexicans; an advertisement for Arrid underarm deodorant showing a dusty Mexican bandito

Chinese Stereotypes in Advertising. **This 1880s advertisement for Celluloid Waterproof collars, cuffs, and shirt fronts reflects not only the styles of dress during the period but also attitudes toward Chinese. Unlike ordinary shirt adornments, which required starch and ironing, the Celluloid products did not need laundering, a feature that threatened to drive the pigtailed Chinese laundrymen featured in the advertisement out of business.**

spraying his underarms after a hard ride as the announcer intoned, "If it works for him it will work for you"; and a magazine advertisement featuring a stereotypical Mexican sleeping under his sombrero as he leans against a Philco television set. Especially offensive to Martínez was a Liggett & Meyers commercial for L&M cigarettes that featured Paco, a lazy Latino who never "feenishes" anything, not even the revolution he is supposed to be fighting. In response to a letter complaining about the commercial, the director of public relations for the tobacco firm defended the commercial's use of Latino stereotypes:

> "Paco" is a warm, sympathetic and lovable character with whom most of us can identify because he has a little of all of us in him, that is, our tendency to procrastinate at times. He seeks to escape the violence of war and to enjoy the pleasure of the moment, in this case, the good flavor of an L&M cigarette.[9]

Although the company spokesman claimed that the character had been tested without negative reactions from Latinos (a similar claim was made by Frito-Lay regarding the Frito Bandito), Martínez roundly criticized the advertising images and contrasted them to what he saw as the gains Blacks were then making in the advertising field:

> Today, no major advertiser would attempt to display a black man or woman over the media in a prejudiced, stereotyped fashion. Complaints would be forthcoming from black associations and perhaps the FCC. Yet, these same advertisers, who dare not show "step'n fetch it" characters, uninhibitedly depict a Mexican counterpart, with additional traits of stinking and stealing. Perhaps the white hatred for blacks, which cannot find adequate expression in today's ads, is being transferred upon their brown brothers.[10]

In 1970 a Brown Position Paper prepared by Latino media activists Armando Rendon and Domingo Nick Reyes charged that the media had transferred the negative stereotypes it once reserved for Blacks to Latinos, who had become "the media's new nigger."[11] The protests of Latinos soon made the nation's advertisers more conscious of the portrayals that Latinos found offensive. But, as in the case of the Blacks, the advertising industry failed to apply the lessons learned from one group to other racial minorities.

Although national advertisers withdrew much of the advertising that negatively stereotyped Blacks and Latinos, sometimes replacing them with images of affluent, successful images that were as far removed from reality as the portrayals of the past, the advances made by those groups were not shared with Native Americans and Asians. Native Americans, no longer depicted as either noble savage or cute cartoon characters, have all but disappeared from broadcast commercials and print media advertising.

On the other hand, Asians, particularly Japanese, have been dealt more than their share of commercials depicting them in stereotypes that cater to the fears and stereotypes of White America. As was the case with Blacks and Latinos, it has taken organized protests from Asian-American groups to get the message across to the corporations and their advertising agencies.

In the mid-1970s a Southern California supermarket chain agreed to remove a television campaign in which a young Asian karate-chopped his way down the stores aisles cutting prices for customers. Nationally, several firms whose industries have been hard-hit by Japanese imports fought back through commercials, if not in the quality or prices of their products. One automobile company featured an Asian family carefully looking over a new car and commenting on its attributes in heavily accented English. Only after they bought it did they learn it was from the United States, not Japan. Another automobile company that markets cars manufactured in Japan under an English-language name showed a parking lot attendant opening the doors of the car, only to find the car speaking to him in Japanese. For several years Sylvania television ran a commercial boasting that its television picture had been selected repeatedly over competing brands as an off-screen voice with a Japanese accent repeatedly asked, "What about Sony?" When the announcer responded that the Sylvania picture had also been selected over Sony's, the off-screen voice faded away, shouting what sounded like a string of Japanese expletives. A 1982 *Newsweek* article observed that "attacking Japan has become something of a fashion in corporate ads" because of resentment over Japanese trade policies and sales of Japanese products in the United States, but quoted Motorola's advertising manager as saying, "We've been as careful as we can be" not to be racially offensive.[12]

But many of the television and print advertisements including Asians featured images that are racially insensitive, if not offensive. A commercial for a laundry product showed a Chinese family that used an "ancient Chinese laundry secret" to get their customers' clothes clean. Naturally, the Chinese secret turned out to be the packaged product paying for the advertisement. Companies pitching everything from pantyhose to airlines featured Asian women coiffed and costumed as seductive China dolls to promote their products, some of them draped in a Chinese setting and others attentively caring for the needs of the Anglo men in the advertisement. One airline boasted that those who flew with it would be under the care of the "Singapore girl."

Asian women appearing in commercials are often featured as China dolls, with the small, darkened eyes, straight hair with bangs, and a narrow slit skirt. Another common portrayal features the exotic, tropical Pacific Islands look, complete with flowers in the hair, a sarong or grass skirt, and shell ornamentation. Asian women hoping to become models have sometimes found that they must conform to these stereotypes or lose assignments. One Asian American model was told to cut her hair with bangs when she auditioned for a beer advertisement. When she refused, the beer company decided to hire another model with shorter hair cut in bangs.[13]

The lack of a sizable Asian community or market in the United States is sometimes cited as the reason that Asians are still stereotyped in advertising and, except for children's advertising, are rarely presented in integrated settings. However the growth rate and income of Asians living in the United States would seem to indicate Asians have the potential for overcoming the stereotyping and lack of visibility that Blacks and Latinos have already challenged. By the mid-1980s there are a few signs that advertising is beginning to integrate Asian Americans into crossover advertisements that, like the Tostitos campaign, are designed to have a broad appeal. In one commercial, television actor Robert Ito was featured telling how he loves to call his relatives in Japan because the calls make them think that he is rich, as well as successful, in the United States. Of course, he adds, it is only because the long-distance rates of the AT&T are so low that he is able to call Japan so often.

In the 1970s, mass-audience advertising in the United States became more racially integrated than in any time in the nation's history. Blacks, and to a much lesser extent Latinos and Asians, could be seen in television commercials spread across the broadcast week and in major magazines. In fact, the advertisements on network television often appeared to be more fully integrated than the television programs they supported. Like television, general-circulation magazines also experienced an increase in the use of Blacks, although studies of both media showed that most of the percentage increase had come by the early 1970s. By that time the percentage of prime-time television commercials featuring Blacks had apparently leveled off at about 10 percent. Blacks were featured in only between 2 and 3 percent of magazine advertisements as late as 1978. That percentage, however small, was a sharp increase from the .06 percent of news magazine advertisements reported in 1960.[14]

The gains were also socially significant, since they demonstrated that Blacks could be integrated into advertisements without triggering a backlash among potential customers in the White majority. Both sales figures and research conducted since the late 1960s have shown that the integration of Black models into television and print advertising does not adversely affect sales or the image of the product. Instead, a study by the American Newspaper Publishers Association showed, the most important influences on sales are the merchandise and the advertisement itself. In fact, while triggering no adverse affect among the majority of Whites, integrated advertisements were found to be useful in swaying Black consumers, who respond favorably to positive Black role models in print advertisements. [15] Studies conducted in the early 1970s also showed that White consumers did not respond negatively to advertising featuring Black models, although their response was more often neutral than positive.[16] However, one 1972 study examining White backlash did show that an advertisement prominently featuring darker-skinned Blacks was less acceptable to Whites than those featuring lighter-skinned Blacks as background models.[17] Perhaps such findings help explain why research conducted later in the 1970s revealed that, for the most part, Blacks appearing in magazine and television advertisements were often featured as part of an integrated group.[18]

Although research findings have showed that integrated advertisements do not adversely affect sales, the percentage of Blacks and other minorities in general-audience advertising has not increased significantly since the numerical gains made through the mid-1970s. Those minorities who do appear in advertisements are often depicted in upscale or integrated settings, an image that the Balch Institute's Stolarik criticized as taking advertising "too far in the other direction and created stereotypes of 'successful' ethnic group members that are as unrealistic as those of the past." Equally unwise, from a business standpoint, was the low numbers of Blacks appearing in advertisements. At the conclusion of a 1983 study, marketing professor Lawrence Solely wrote:

> Advertisers and their ad agencies must evaluate the direct economic consequences of alternative strategies on the firm. If it is be-

> lieved that the presence of Black models in advertisements decreases the effectiveness of advertising messages, only token numbers of Black models will be used. Previous studies have found that advertisements portraying Black models do not elicit negative affective or conative responses from consumers. Given the consistency of the research findings, more Blacks should be portrayed in advertisements. If Blacks continue to be underrepresented in advertising portrayals, it can be said that this is an indication of prejudice on the part of the advertising industry, not consumers.[20]

ADVERTISERS' COURTSHIP OF SPANISH GOLD AND THE BLACK MARKET

While Solely stopped short of accusing corporate executives of racial prejudice, he contended that a "counterpressure" to full integration of Blacks into mainstream media portrayals was that "advertising professionals are businessmen first and moralists second."[21] If so, then it was the business mentality of advertising and corporate professionals that led them into increasingly aggressive advertising and marketing campaigns to capture minority consumers, particularly Blacks and Latinos, in the 1970s and 1980s. Long depicted as low-end consumers with little disposable income, Black and Latino customers became more important to national and regional advertisers of mainstream goods who took a closer look at the size, composition, and projected growth of those groups. Asians, who experienced a sharp percentage growth in the 1970s and were generally more affluent than Blacks and Latinos, were not targeted to the same extent, probably because of their relatively small numbers and differences in national languages between the groups. And, except in regions in which they constituted a sizable portion of the population, Native Americans were largely ignored as potential consumers of mainstream products.

One part of the courtship of Blacks and Latinos grew out of the civil rights movements of the 1960s, in which both groups effectively used consumer boycotts to push issues ranging from ending segregation to organizing farmworkers. Boycotts had long been threatened and used by minority consumers as economic leverage on social issues. But in the 1960s Black ministers organized the

Philadelphia Selective Patronage Program, in which Blacks did business with companies that supported their goals of more jobs for Blacks. This philosophy of repaying the corporations that invest in the minority communities through consumer purchases was replicated in other cities. It was followed by slick advertising campaigns directed at minority consumers. In 1984 the same line of thinking led Coors Beer to seek an end to disputes with Blacks and Latinos by signing controversial agreements with the National Association for the Advancement of Colored People (NAACP) and with five national Latino groups that committed the brewery to increase its financial support of the activities of those organizations as Blacks and Latinos increased their purchases of Coors.

A second, and more influential, element of the courtship has been the hard-selling job of advertising agencies and media specializing in the Black and Spanish-speaking Latinos. Spurred by the thinking of Black advertising executive D. Parke Gibson in his 1968 book *The $30 Billion Negro* and a steady stream of articles on Black and Latino consumers in media trade publications during the 1960s, national advertisers became aware of the fact that minorities were potential consumers for a wide range of products. The advertisers also were persuaded that the inattention they had previously received from mainstream products made Blacks and Latinos respond more favorably and with greater loyalty to those products that courted them through advertisements on billboards and in the publications and broadcast stations they used.

The third, and most far-reaching, element in the courtship was a fundamental change in the thinking of marketing and advertising executives that swayed them away from mass audience media. Witnessing the success they had in advertising on radio stations and magazines targeted to specific audience segments following the advent of television as the dominant mass medium in the 1950s, advertising agencies advised their clients to go after their potential customers identified with market segments, rather than the mass audience. Advertisers found that differences in race, like differences in sex, residence, family status, and age, were easy to target through advertising appeals in media in which the content was designed to attract men or women, young or old, suburban or rural, Black or White, Spanish or English speaking. These media, in turn, produced audience surveys to show they were effective in reaching and delivering specific segments of the mass audience. By the mid-1980s market audience segmentation had become so important to advertisers that the term "mass media" was becoming an anachronism. In a 1984 article in *Madison Avenue* (an advertising trade magazine), Caroline R. Jones, executive vice-president of Mingo-Jones Advertising, wrote:

> It is a basic tenet of marketing that you go after markets with rifles, not shotguns. It is foolhardy—and idealistic in the worst way—to try to sell the same thing to everyone in the same way. Good marketing involves breaking down potential markets into homogeneous segments; targeting the most desirable segments; and developing creative programs, tailored for each segment, that make your messages look different from your competitors'. All of that should be done with the guidance of thorough research on characteristics, beliefs and preferences of the people in the targeted markets.[22]

Like others who have pitched minority audiences to major corporations as ripe targets for slick advertisements, Jones advised advertising professionals to target advertising to Black consumers because "*there's money in it*." Among the factors she cited as making Blacks desirable customers was a reported disposable income of more than $150 million, a "high propensity for brand names and indulgence items," a high degree of "brand loyalty," a young and growing population, growing education and income, concentration in the nation's largest 25 cities, and "its own growing media network."[23]

Much the same approach has been used to sell Latinos to advertising agencies as a target too good to be passed up. A 1965 article on Latino consumers in the advertising trade magazine *Sponsor* was headlined "America's Spanish Treasure"; a 1971 *Sales Management* article proclaimed "Brown Is Richer than Black"; and in 1972 *Television/Radio Age* told readers "The Spanish Market: Its Size, Income and Loyalties Make It a Rich Marketing Mine."[24] In addition to the characteristics cited as making Blacks an attractive market, Latinos have been depicted as being especially vulnerable to advertisements because their use of Spanish supposedly cuts them off from advertising in English-language media. Thus advertisers are advised to use the language and culture familiar to their target audience to give their messages the greatest delivery and impact.

"U.S. Hispanics are most receptive to media content in the Spanish language," wrote Antonio Guernica in a 1982 book titled

Reaching the Hispanic Market Effectively.[25] Guernica and others have counseled advertisers to package their commercial messages in settings that are reinforced by Latino culture and traditions. These appeals link the product being advertised with the language, heritage, and social system with which Latinos are most comfortable, thus creating the illusion that the product belongs in the Latino home.

"The language, the tradition, the kitchen utensils are different [in a Latino home]," said Shelly Perlman, media buyer for the Hispania division of the J. Walter Thompson advertising agency in a 1983 *Advertising Age* article. "There are ads one can run in general media that appeal to everyone but that contain unmistakable clues to Hispanics that they are being sought. It can be done with models, with scene and set design—a whole array of factors."[26] Corporations seeking the Latino dollar also have been told to picture their products with Latino foods, celebrities, cultural events, community events, and family traditions. The goal has been to adapt the product to make it appear to be a part of the Latino lifestyle in the United States, which often requires sensitivity to the language, food, and musical differences between Latinos in different parts of the nation and from different countries in Latin America.

For both Blacks and Latinos, the slick advertising approach often means selling high-priced, prestige products to low-income consumers who have not fully shared in the wealth of the country in which they live. But Blacks and Latinos, who have median family incomes well below national averages, have nonetheless been targeted as consumers for premium brand names in all product lines and particularly in liquor, beer, and cigarettes.

As a result, corporations making and marketing products ranging from beer to diapers try to show Blacks and Latinos that consumption of their goods is part of the good life in America. It may not be a life that they knew when they grew up in the ghetto, barrio, or a foreign country. It may not even be a life that they or their children will ever achieve, but it is a lifestyle they can share by purchasing the products used by the rich and famous. Of course, prestige appeals are used in advertising to all audiences, not just minorities, but it has a special impact on those who are so far down on the socioeconomic scale that they are especially hungry for anything that will add status to their lives and help them show others that they are "making it." According to Caroline Jones:

> The Black consumer is not unlike other consumers when it comes to the basic necessities of life—food, clothing and shelter. There is a difference, nevertheless, in the priority the Black consumer adopts in the pursuit of happiness; in other words, in how he structures the *quality* of his life. Some differences are by choice. And some differences are because of *lack* of choice. . . . The Black consumer must often react to what he has *not* been able to enjoy or choose, or what he must choose from among products that have not overtly invited him to use them . . . . in general the Black consumer all too often has learned to live with his feelings of being ignored altogether or excluded psychologically.[27]

"In the light of life's uncertainties, Blacks also seek instant gratification more than do Whites, who can enjoy 'the good life' earlier and longer," Jones adds, citing a successful advertising campaign for Polaroid cameras that courted Blacks with the line "Polaroid gives it to you now."[28] This means that advertisers can strike responsive chords at a different levels with minority groups than with the White majority.

Latinos, particularly recent immigrants or those who have moved up from the economic level of their parents, may also share these feelings. To both groups advertising is corporate America's welcome mat, the happy face that lets them know that they are important enough to be recognized. By recognizing elements of the Black or Latino experience that may have been ignored by White Americans, the advertisers also play on national or racial pride to boost sales of their products. In the 1970s, Anheuser-Busch commissioned a series of glossy advertisements commemorating the great kings of Africa and Schlitz produced a Chicano history calendar. These and similar advertising campaigns provided long-overdue recognition of Black and Latino heritage, but they also prominently displayed the corporate symbols of their sponsors and were designed to boost the sale of beer more than to recognize overlooked historical figures and events.

Since the goal of advertising is to promote sales and consumption of the products advertised, advertising agencies serve no moral code other than to promote the products as ethically as possible to stimulate consumption. Print and broadcast media penetrating the segments of the mass audience that the advertisers wish to cultivate have been the beneficiaries of the increased advertising emphasis on Blacks and Latinos. Most surveys show that Blacks and Latinos depend more on radio and television than on print media, a fact that is probably more related to their lower median level of education and the wide availability of Black and Spanish-language broadcasting than any innate racial differences between them and Whites. Accordingly, most of the millions of dollars that national advertisers spend to reach these minority audiences is spent on broadcast media.

The minority-formatted media are eager to promote themselves as the most effective way to reach minority consumers. In 1974 New York's Black newspaper, the *Amsterdam News*, vigorously attacked the credibility of a *New York Daily News* audience survey that indicated the *Daily News* reached more Black readers. In a 1979 *Advertising Age* advertisement, *La Opinión*, a Los Angeles Spanish-language daily newspaper, promised advertisers it could show them how to "wrap up the Spanish-language market." Advertising is the lifeblood of the print and broadcast media in the United States and the minority-oriented media have been quick to promote themselves as the most effective vehicles for penetrating and persuading the people in their communities to purchase the products advertised on their airwaves and in their pages.

ANALYSIS

The relationship between racial minorities and advertising has undergone dramatic changes since the early 1960s. Blacks have been the most visible in the changes that have occurred in both mainstream and segmented advertising, although Spanish-speaking Latinos also have become more important as a market segment. In spite of experiencing the greatest percentage growth of any racial group in the years between 1970 and 1980, Asian Americans still had not been recognized as a major consumer force by advertisers in the mid-1980s. But, given the projected growth figures for Asians in the United States, it appears inevitable that the group will be increasingly important as a market segment in the future, particularly if Asian Americans continue to demonstrate income and education levels above national norms and if they respond to racially sensitive advertising in media directed to Asian Americans. Native Americans, divided between the cities and rural areas, have become largely invisible in mainstream advertising. The noble Super Chief has gone the way of the passenger train he once advertised, as have the caricatures that once stereotyped Native Americans in advertising. The small percentage of the population in urban areas that Native Americans make up and their geographic dispersion in rural areas make them less attractive for mainstream advertisers looking at potential market segments. As far as advertising is concerned, it appears that Native Americans will continue to be treated as the most invisible minority.

National advertisers in mass-audience media appear to be reluctant to learn from the experiences with one group in dealing with others. Thus Blacks, Latinos, Asians, and Native Americans have all had to wage individual battles against stereotyping and racially offensive advertisements. Blacks, the most visible racial minority in network television and general-interest magazine advertising, still constitute only a very small percentage of the characters in those media. Asians and Latinos are still infrequently used in mainstream advertisements. Gains have been noted in the use of Black celebrities, such as Bill Cosby, the Jacksons, and Reggie Jackson, in advertising with a "crossover" appeal to both Blacks and non-Blacks. Given the use of different languages and the smaller sizes of the groups, it would appear that integration of Latinos and Asians into mainstream advertising will most likely follow the "crossover" model, such as the Tostitos commercial or the Robert Ito long-distance telephone spot. Such advertisements afford the advertiser the advantage of reaching the majority of potential consumers, including English-speaking Latinos and Asians.

Minority-formatted publications and broadcasters depend on advertising to support their media. They have benefited from the increased emphasis on market segmentation by promoting the consumption patterns of the audiences they reach and their own effectiveness in delivering persuasive commercial messages to their readers, listeners, and viewers. But advertising is also a two-edged sword; advertisers expect to take more money out of a market segment than they invests in advertising to that segment. Black and Spanish-language media will benefit from the advertising dollars of national corporations only as long as they are the most cost-effective way for advertisers to persuade Blacks and Latinos to use their products. This places the minority media in an exploitative relationship with their audience, who, because of language, educational, and economic differences sometimes, are exposed to a narrower range of media than Whites. Advertisers support the media that deliver the audience with the best consumer profile at the lowest cost, not necessarily the media that best meet the information and entertainment needs of their audience.

The slick, upscale lifestyle used by national advertisers is more a goal than a reality for most Blacks and Latinos. It is achieved through education, hard work, and equal opportunity. Yet advertisers promote consumption of their products as a shortcut to the good life, a quick fix for low-income consumers. The message to their low-income audience is clear: You may not be able to live in the best neighborhoods, wear the best clothes, or have the best job, but you can drink the same liquor, smoke the same cigarettes, and drive the same car as those who do. At the same time, advertising appeals playing on the cultural or historical heritage of Blacks and Latinos make the products appear to be "at home" with minority consumers. Recognizing the importance of national holidays and the forgotten minority history, they have joined with Blacks and Latinos in commemorating dates, events, and persons. But they also piggyback their commercial messages on the recognition of events, leaders, or heroes. Persons or events that in their time represented protest against slavery, oppression, or discrimination are now used to sell products.

Advertising, like mining, is an extractive industry. It enters the ghetto and barrio with a smiling face to convince all within its reach that they should purchase the products advertised and purchase them often. It has no goal other than to stimulate consumption of the product; the subsidization of the media is merely a by-product. But owners of minority-formatted media, having gained through the increased advertising investments of major corporations, now have greater opportunities to use those increased dollars to improve news and entertainment content and

Selling the Audience. **Like all advertiser-supported media in the United States, print and broadcast media serving minority audiences must convince advertisers that they are effective in delivering advertising messages. This 1979 advertisement for Los Angeles's Spanish-language daily newspaper *La Opinion* illustrates how one medium made the pitch.**

thus better meet their social responsibility to their audience. Unlike advertisers, who may support socially responsible activities for the purpose of promoting their own images, minority publishers and broadcasters have a long, though sometimes spotty, record of advocating the rights of the people they serve. Their growing dependence on major corporations and national advertising agencies should do nothing to blunt that edge as long as the audiences they serve continue to confront a system of inequality that keeps them below national norms in education, housing, income, health, and other social indicators.

NOTES

1. "Using ethnic images—An advertising retrospective," *Advertising Age*, June 14, 1984, p. 9.

2. Tomás Martínez, "How advertisers promote racism," *Civil Rights Digest*, Fall 1969, pp. 8-9.

3. David M. Potter, *People of Plenty* (University of Chicago Press, 1954), p. 166.

4. Ibid., pp. 181-182.

5. Ibid., pp. 184-185.

6. "Using ethnic images."

7. Cited in Philip H. Dougherty, "Frequency of blacks in TV ads," *New York Times*, May 27, 1982, p. D19.

8. Martínez, "How advertisers promote racism," p. 10.

9. Ibid., p. 11.

10. Ibid., pp. 9-10.

11. Domingo Nick Reyes and Armando Rendón, *Chicanos and the Mass Media* (National Mexican American Anti-Defamation Committee, 1971).

12. Joseph Treen, "Madison Ave. vs. Japan, Inc.," April 12, 1982, p. 69.

13. Ada Kan, "Asian models in the media," unpublished term paper, Journalism 466: Minority and the Media, University of Southern California, December 14, 1983, p. 5.

14. Studies on the increase of Blacks in magazine and television commercials cited in James D. Culley and Rex Bennett, "Selling Blacks, selling women," *Journal of Communication*, Autumn 1976, Vol. 26, No. 4, Autumn 1976, pp. 160-174; Lawrence Solely, "The effect of Black models on magazine ad readership," *Journalism Quarterly*, Vol. 60, No. 4, Winter 1983, p. 686; and Leonard N. Reid and Bruce G. Vanden Bergh, "Blacks in introductory ads," *Journalism Quarterly*, Vol. 57, No. 3, Autumn 1980, pp. 485-486.

15. Cited in D. Parke Gibson, *$70 billion in the black* (Macmillan, 1979), pp. 83-84.

16. Laboratory studies on White reactions to Blacks in advertising cited in Solely, "The effect of black models," pp. 585-587.

17. Carl E. Block, "White backlash to Negro ads: Fact or fantasy?" *Journalism Quarterly*, Vol. 49, No. 2, Summer 1972, pp. 258-262.

18. Culley and Bennett, "Selling Blacks, selling women."

19. "Using ethnic images," p. 9.

20. Solely, "The effect of black models," p. 690.

21. Ibid.

22. Caroline R. Jones, "Advertising in Black and White," *Madison Avenue*, May 1984, p. 53.

23. Ibid., p. 54.

24. Félix Frank Gutiérrez, "Spanish-language radio and Chicano internal colonialism," doctoral dissertation, Stanford University, 1976, pp. 312-314.

25. Antonio Guernica, *Reaching the Hispanic Market Effectively* (McGraw-Hill, 1982), p. 5.

26. Theodore J. Gage, "How to reach an enthusiastic market," *Advertising Age*, February 14, 1983, p. M-11.

27. Jones, "Advertising in Black and White," p. 56.

28. Ibid.

6

THE PRESS: MINORITIES IN AND OUT OF THE NEWS

NEWS, WHICH AMERICANS RECEIVE every day via newspapers, radio, television, and magazines, is a vital commodity. Researchers call news reporting in these media the "surveillance" function of mass communication, the task of surveying the trends and events occurring in society and reporting those that seem to be most important and consequential to its well-being. Without such information people would be seriously hindered in their ability to participate in the political affairs of the republic or to make business, professional, and personal decisions. Obviously, tens of thousands of events and activities take place daily in the United States and throughout the world, but only a miniscule fraction of them are reported through the major national or local news media.

The most important characteristic of news is "consequence" (importance).[1] In other words, those who make decisions about news media content first consider the importance of the event to the audience. This process is, of course, subjective, but the decision makers (theoretically, at least) stake their professional livelihood on their ability to provide the information most desired and needed by society.

Another, closely related, social role of news media is the "correlation" function, or the task of analyzing the selected news, offering analysis and opinion to the society concerning its potential impact, and/or suggesting what should be done about it. Often, social policies are formulated by opinion leaders with the assistance of news media as a forum.

Researchers have labeled the persons who are involved in the news selection process "gatekeepers" of information because they are in the position of either letting information pass through the system or stopping its progress. Performance of the gatekeeping function results in what some scholars have called "agenda-setting" for the society. The process of filtering out huge volumes of information while allowing only a few items to reach the mass audience is an act that by itself adds credence and importance (consequence) to the surviving events and issues. The extent to which gatekeepers bear responsibility for the flow of news information and set the agenda in the United States is a topic of discussion among social scientists. It is clear, however, that gatekeepers are vitally influential in the process. The perspective of American values, attitudes, and ambitions brought to the masses by mass communication have largely been those of gatekeepers and others with access to media.

Historically, and continuing to the present, ethnic minorities have not been gatekeepers in mainstream American mass media. Their exclusion from the process is the subject of the next chapter, but the effect of that exclusion is our present concern. Indian, Black, Latino, and Asian coverage in American news media has been and remains a reflection of the attitudes held by gatekeepers and those who influence them. The frequency and nature of minority coverage in news media, therefore, reveal the attitudes of the majority population throughout American history as much as do portrayals in entertainment media. News coverage may be more significant, however, because of its role and function in society: While entertainment is "make-believe," the news is "real." Since news reflects what is really important to a society, minority coverage in mainstream news reporting provides insight into the status of minorities. By their professional judgments, the gatekeepers of news reveal how consequential minorities are to American society and determine the ways in which they are interpreted to the majority audience.

North American newspaper press history began in 1690 with the publication of the ill-fated *Publick Occurrences*, which was banned after its first issue because editor Benjamin Harris failed to get approval from Boston colonial authorities. Significant here is the mention of Indians in at least two articles within the small four-page newspaper. Throughout the colonial period, references appeared in the press concerning both Indians and Blacks. Indians were of interest because of both the French and Indian War and the uneasy relationship between them and the White settlers. Blacks were the subject of advertisements for slave auctions and notices for runaway slaves. For most of the first 100 years after the founding of the republic, press coverage continued to focus on the "Indian problem," and the issue of abolition of slavery began to receive notice, along with Black runaways.

Newspapers, however, did not reach the vast majority of the population until the forces of technology, public education, and the political rise of the "common man" made the "Penny Press" in the 1830s the first truly "mass" medium in the United States. Since then, news about ethnic minorities in White news media has been characterized by developmental phases commonly experienced by each of the groups under consideration. Five stages can be identified historically: (1) exclusionary, (2) threatening issue, (3) confrontation, (4) stereotypical selection, and (5) integrated coverage phases. The first four phases were so uniformly practiced by news media as to become virtually established as covert policy. The final phase may be viewed as embryonic and possibly destined to become future professional news media policy.

Exclusionary Phase

The fact that each ethnic minority group had an initial social presence and contributed to the development of American life without any systematic inclusion in the reporting of public affairs reveals the status of minorities as inconsequential entities insofar as the gatekeepers of information were concerned. The inference to be drawn was that minorities were not an important consideration to the well-being of society. This is made clear in such a sacrosanct document as the Declaration of Independence, in which the phrase "all men are created equal" was understood to exclude Indians and Blacks. The point was so obvious that there was no need to insert the word "White" between "all" and "men." Furthermore, the U.S. Constitution specified (Article 1, Section 2) that for purposes of determining the number of members in the House of Representatives, a state could not count the Indian population, and each slave counted as only three-fifths of a person. Free Blacks were generally prevented from participating in political affairs by requirements of extensive property holdings as a qualification to vote.

Although the policy of virtual exclusion of ethnic minorities in news coverage may seem benign, it had a significant impact on the historical development of race relations in the United States. Its most immediate effect, as noted above, was to signal the status and role Whites accorded minorities in society. Lack of coverage of peoples of color in White news media had the effect of asserting their lack of status, a powerful social psychological message delivered to majority and minority groups alike. Ultimately, exclusion from news media coverage signified exclusion from American society, because the function of news is to reflect social reality. For that reason, minority exclusion in news set the course followed by the other phases of minority treatment in news. It was a course of alienation between Whites and ethnic minorities.

Threatening-Issue Phase

When ethnic minority groups first begin to appear as subjects of news media reports it is because they have been perceived as a threat to the existing social order. Threat is grounded in fear. As may be expected, Native Americans were the first to attract the attention of the news media because of the uneasy relationship between them and White settlers. The ambivalence manifested in the "noble savage" attitude of Whites toward Indians was the result of fear of Indian resistance to colonial expansion. Although the European settlers were intruders on the natives' soil, the colonial and early national press began to characterize their Indian hosts in the role of adversary with heavy use of the term "savages." Newspapers, therefore, made it easy to justify the displacement of Indians by focusing coverage on acts of Indian violence to reinforce the savagery theme. "Civilized" Whites were made to seem heroic for any actions, however extreme, resulting in the overthrow of savages. By the time the Penny Press era reached its zenith, the Indian wars of the West were in full hostilities.

Similarly, Blacks were the object of fears that set the press awash in a flood of articles speculating on the aftermath of emancipation. In the far West, Chinese laborers became the focus of fears they would displace Whites from the labor market, and the *San Francisco Chronicle* lead the press attack against them during the 1870s. More than 80 years later the same fear manifested itself in the California press, as headlines blared against the Mexican immigrant workers they labeled "wetbacks."

Confrontation Phase

When ethnic minority presence stimulates fear and apprehension in the majority population, the response is inevitably a social confrontation. News media, having already brought the threat to society's attention, then proceed to cover the response. The response is often violent in nature, such as the Indian wars of the westward expansion, the Mexican War, or the lynchings of Blacks in the South, Mexicans in the Southwest, and Asians in the West. At other times the response culminates in legislative action, such as segregation laws, peace treaties, immigration laws, or the creation of agencies such as the Bureau of Indian Affairs. On still other occasions, race riots dominate the news with a historical consistency that has involved virtually every ethnic minority group.

American news media generally approach confrontation coverage of minority-related issues from the perspective of "us versus them." It is a natural progression from the exclusionary phase: news people think of minorities as outside the American system, the actions of minorities must be reported as adversarial because they are seen as threats to the social order. Until the late 1960s, news headlines and text were filled with racial epithets in reporting on these social confrontations, thereby encouraging conflict instead of conciliation. When the Kerner Commission on civil disorders filed its report in 1967, it condemned this historical trend in news coverage by a press that "has too long basked in a White world, looking out of it, if at all, with White men's eyes and a White perspective."[2] More than during any other phase, it is during confrontation that news media have the opportunity to exhibit leadership in race relations; unfortunately, their historical track record has been poor.

Stereotypical Selection Phase

After society has met the minority threat via confrontation, social order must be restored and a transition must be made into a postconflict period. Although conflicts between Whites and ethnic minority groups have been numerous throughout American history, none of the conflict resolutions has resulted in the disappearance of minorities from the American social landscape. News media reportage, therefore, moves into another phase designed to neutralize White apprehension of minorities while accommodating the ethnic presence. Informational items that conform to existing White attitudes toward minorities are then selected for inclusion in news media and given repeated emphasis until they reach thematic proportions.

Examples include news stories that ostensibly appear to be favorable to minorities, as in the cases of "success stories," where a person has risen from the despair of (choose one) the reservation, the ghetto, the barrio, Chinatown, or Little Tokyo. These stories accomplish the two objectives of stereotypical selective reporting: (1) The majority audience is reassured that minorities are still "in their place" (that is, the reservation, ghetto, or whatever) and (2) those who escape their designated place are not a threat to society because they manifest the same values and ambitions of the majority. In the early 1980s, one of the nation's largest metropolitan newspapers headlined a story concerning a Black woman's appointment to the presidency of a major university with reference to her being the "granddaughter of [a] former slave." The headline fulfilled the objectives of stereotypical selection by invoking the image of Black slavery even though the issue had no relevance to the instant "news" event. At a moment of signal personal achievement, the newspaper came forth to put her "in her place" and thereby legitimize her accomplishment in the eyes of the majority. At the same time, such stories tangentially give credit to the social system that tolerates or praises minority upward mobility without facilitating it.

Other types of thematic stories also appear during the stereotypical selection phase of news coverage and, unfortunately, they are far more numerous. In the years since the 1967 issuance of the Kerner Commission report, the news media have responded to the call for better reporting of minority affairs with imbalanced coverage of minority problems. Minorities are more likely to pass the gatekeeper if they are involved in "hard news" events, such as those involving police action, or in the "colorful" soft news of holiday coverage, such as Chinese New Year, Cinco de Mayo, and Native American festivals. Other reporting in recent years has emphasized ethnic minorities on "welfare" who live in crime-infested neighborhoods; lack educational opportunity, job skills, and basic language skills; and, in the circumstance of Latinos and Southeast Asians, are probably not legitimate U.S. citizens.

The news media have served to reinforce existing stereotypes. The old stereotypes of ethnics as violent people who are too lazy to work and who indulge in drugs and sexual promiscuity are prominent. In fact, the preponderance of such reporting has lead some observers to say the news media have offered an image of ethnics as "problem people," which means they are projected as people who either *have* problems or *cause* problems for society. The legacy of news exclusion thus leads to the majority audience seeing minorities as a social burden—the "us versus them" syndrome carried to another dimension.

Integrated Coverage Phase

Integrated news coverage is the antithesis of exclusion. If it is to become the goal and policy of American news media, the last vestiges of prejudice and racism must be removed from the gatekeeper ranks. At present this phase is still largely a vision, but it is within the grasp of a society determined to include all Americans in the quest for social and economic equality. This does not mean that all news about minorities will be good news, but that minorities will be reflected in all types of news. News will be reported from the perspective that "us" represents all citizens. A major step in the process, of course, is the increased employment of minorities in news media professions. Equally important is an increased sensitivity among majority personnel to be attentive to untold stories from minority communities and the cultivation of news sources there.

The result should be a functional information surveillance system that promotes social understanding and alleviates unwarranted fears based on prejudices. In the meantime, major changes must be made in the training of journalists and in professional news philosophy if news reporting concerning ethnic minorities is to improve.

Obstacles to Integrated News

The issue of more equitable employment of minorities in news media professions represents an obvious opportunity to effect more accurate reporting of their role in society and merits detailed discussion, which is provided in the following chapter. For the moment, however, it is important to look at other factors currently working against the achievement of culturally integrated news reporting in the United States. Progress toward the integrated phase depends on the ability to overcome two major obstacles that have become matters of entrenched journalistic policy. Overcoming the first requires a renewed commitment to the ideals espoused by media owners and editors from the inception of professional news reporting standards; overcoming the second necessitates a change in the basic "news values" journalists apply to their work.

If news media reporting does expand to encompass wider minority representation, it will have to rededicate itself first to the principle that meeting the substantive communication needs of society is its first priority. The news media obligation to provide information and interpretation of issues and events to society is essential to the development and maintenance of an enlightened citizenry. A major barrier to integrated news coverage has been preoccupation with profit incentive, as media "marketing" of the news has led to, among other questionable practices, an increased emphasis on information targeted to high-economic-profile audiences. Among some major metropolitan daily newspapers, increased circulation among affluent readers has become the primary objective, while broadcast media seek higher audience ratings to attract major advertisers. Because minorities are vastly underrepresented in the upper-middle to upper-class income economic categories, they have been shortchanged in news media coverage.[3] This approach to news reporting has affected both the frequency and nature of minority coverage. Although news media, operating under the free enterprise system, have every right to pursue profits, they should not do so at the expense of their social responsibility to serve the informational needs of society. The surveillance function of mass communication requires that news media inform society about the perspectives, aspirations, and contributions of all its components.

As noted earlier, the Kerner Commission provided insight into the nature of a major news media problem: the values applied to news judgment. The commission noted that news was determined from "a White perspective." In other words, priorities of importance were based solely upon an event's significance to the White majority. This notion was instilled in future journalists at the very earliest stages of their training. News was virtually defined as being events of consequence to the majority audience, which meant Whites. This concept was easily made practicable because the social system ensured that news sources (persons of authority and social standing in the fields of politics, business, education, law enforcement, the military and so on) were White. Journalism educators taught their students that the essence of good news reporting was the attribution of facts gathered from authoritative sources. Those news sources, unfortunately, represented in disproportionate numbers White ideals and values held in common with the journalists and gatekeepers who reported on their activities. The ethnic and cultural minority view, therefore, was not "newsworthy." Even in reporting events about minorities, the news sources sought by reporters to interpret them were invariably White ones. This practice was a primary reason for the alienation and distrust of news media by minority citizens.

Because America's minority communities have not been reported on in the mainstream context by news media, their stories have not been told adequately. Numerous sources of information have yet to be tapped, and a lot of work remains before a semblance of balance is attained that will provide an accurate assessment of ethnic minority experience in the United States. In the 1970s and early 1980s, news media began to make inroads via special newspaper series and broadcast documentaries on specific minority issues. However, the task of integrating minorities into the news requires ongoing inclusion of their views regarding all major issues confronting society. To accomplish that objective, journalism educators and news professionals will have to redefine news values to include the perspectives of a wider spectrum of American citizens. One result may be a change in the composition and priorities of issues on the national agenda.

MINORITIES AND NEWSROOM POLICY

We have observed that ethnic minority misrepresentation in news media is partly the result of long-standing policies concerning news values and economic incentive. Although the Kerner Commission report was the watershed of national recognition of news media dereliction of responsibility, change has come slowly. Professional news organizations began to address the issues of minority training, employment, decision making, and coverage publicly in 1968. The nearly two decades since, however, can generally be characterized by an increase in stereotypical selection-phase reporting, notable exceptions notwithstanding. This suggests the difficulty of changing policy in news organizations. The nature of newsroom policy was set forth by sociologist Warren Breed in his work "Social Control in the Newsroom."[4] Among the major findings in Breed's study of daily newspapers was that every paper has policies that are covert and that often contravene ethical standards of professional journalism, including policies concerning issues of politics, business, and class considerations.

Because the policies are covert and, therefore, not written and codified for persons new to the staff, they must be learned by other means. Among the ways new reporters learn policy are by observing the content of the newspaper or news broadcasts, noting which material has been edited from one's work, conversing with staff members concerning the preferences and affiliations of superiors, and noting the priorities assigned to news story ideas discussed in planning conferences. A common complaint of ethnic minority reporters working in mainstream White newsrooms is the pressure of unwritten policy applied to their stories and "news angle" ideas. This is the manifestation of news being defined in terms of White majority perception. Both minority and White re-

Pulitzer Prize Winners. In 1984 15 Latino reporters, photographers and editors of the *Los Angeles Times* won the Pulitzer Prize Gold Medal for public service for their 27-part series on Latinos in Southern California. (Los Angeles Times/Larry Armstrong)

porters face sanctions when policy is violated. Sanctions include reprimand, loss of esteem among colleagues, and lessening of opportunity for upward mobility in the organization. A revealing look at how newsroom policy affects minority news coverage from the vantage point of a staff newcomer is presented below.

Content Observation

A contemporary reporter intent upon analyzing the news editorial product issued by his or her organization would find minority reportage ranging from the threatening issue to confrontation to stereotypical selection phases, depending on the historical moment and ethnicity of the minority group involved. The absence of a fully integrated approach to either individual reports or general coverage would be a strong indicator of organizational policy.

Conversely, stories about ethnic minorities focusing on special occasions—such as Cinco de Mayo, Chinese New Year, or Dr. Martin Luther King, Jr.'s, birthday—to the exclusion of more substantive reporting is likewise indicative of policy. Observation of minority views being included in reporting environmental issues, alternative energy sources, foreign policy, or the defense budget would signal the newcomer that such efforts on his or her part would be welcome. Past performance, therefore, becomes a policy statement as strong as any written or orally expressed edict—perhaps stronger. In certain contexts it is easier to challenge formal policies, because they are often accompanied by a procedure for making changes to them. It is difficult for the newcomer to counter the explanation that conditions exist "because that's the way we do things around here." It is more likely, however, that the force of content observation will not elicit inquiry from a newcomer anxious to accommodate him- or herself to the work environment. The compelling instinct is to conform in order to survive.

Editing by Superiors

A more direct means of conveying policy is the editing process. Newsroom editors are gatekeepers and enjoy professional superiority over staff reporters. The journalist who produces newspaper or broadcast material that is inconsistent with policy will be edited, either by alteration or by deletion of offending work. As such editing relates to news about minorities, the professional explanation—if any is given—is that the item lacks "newsworthiness" or that lack of space or time prevents its inclusion. Since it is the reporter's job to get work into print or on the air, the inability to achieve those objectives reflects upon professional competence. Editing is not necessarily a sanction against the newcomer, but it often denotes a policy infringement, and one or two applications are usually enough to complete indoctrination.

Informal Conversation

When staff members gather around the water cooler or have lunch together, the conversation often provides insight into policy.

Mention of political and/or civic affiliations and preferences maintained by executive superiors suggests to the astute newcomer issues and topics to emphasize or avoid. Attitudes held by peers toward ethnic minorities is evidenced by their informal conversation and comments about minority-related news stories. Policy facilitates a newsroom atmosphere and when consensus is apparent, whatever the issue may be, newcomers quickly get the message.

The informal conversation of newsroom colleagues, however, need not be supportive of the views and attitudes of superiors. For the newcomer's purposes, even negative conversation regarding the attitudes of superiors is sufficient to convey policy. Staff members aren't obliged to agree with policy, only to adhere to it.

News Planning Conferences

Journalists who become privy to news story-planning meetings can observe the hidden force of policy in action. The priority ranking of news events, activities, and ideas for future reporting assignments reflects the thinking of executives and editorial gatekeepers. The reception and "play" given to ethnic minority news as opposed to other comparable items reveals policy clearly. It is here where the relative consideration of values is weighed, where the perception of social consequence is manifest. Even the decision to do a special series on one minority group or another only highlights the ongoing neglect of established policy to provide the general audience with a complete surveillance of the social landscape. The news perspective is askew, but the newcomer accepts it as "standard operating procedure."

Sanctions for Policy Violations

Although organizational policy works subtly but effectively as a barrier to integrated news coverage, the sanctions for policy violations are equally subtle. There are four major sanctions that are self-motivated and psychologically self-imposed but nonetheless real. An important reason for newsroom conformity to policy is the reporter's desire to hold the esteem of peers. Few journalists, apart from those who attain national prestige, gain consistent recognition for performance. In the absence of letters or phone calls from the public, perhaps the greatest job satisfaction is the acknowledgment from fellow staff members of a job well done. Newcomers to a staff arrive with the desire to demonstrate quickly their right to "belong" by earning the respect of colleagues. Any violation of policy would cast the newcomer as incompetent or, worse, as a rebel.

As is true of most American professionals, journalists seek the rewards of career advancement. The fear of not getting the challenging assignments that lead to promotions and recognition by superiors is a strong motivation to learn and conform to policy. Because policy virtually defines the parameters of news value, breaches severely handicap a staff member competing with several peers for promotion.

A third major sanction is the desire of journalists to please superiors who have afforded them opportunity for employment. With that desire is a feeling of obligation to submit to policies and procedures (published or otherwise) established by management.

Finally, there is the ever-present possibility of job loss if policy is violated. Although it is rare for a reporter to be fired over misinterpretation of policy, journalists who violate policy may become subject to scrutiny. It is not difficult for an editor or management superior to find other reasons to terminate policy transgressors or to make them feel "uncomfortable" on the job. One example of the latter is the continued assignment of routine work that offers no prospect for personal satisfaction or peer recognition except to denote one's status "in the dog house."

It must be understood that newsroom policies and sanctions work against change in news coverage of minorities without regard for the ethnicity of reporters. Minority journalists lament the newsroom atmosphere that forces them to see their profession from a White perspective. They complain that colleagues and superiors, not overtly racist but insensitive or ignorant, evaluate their performance on culturally biased news criteria. To focus too heavily on minority-related issues jeopardizes peer esteem, and work on such issues rarely results in the kind of recognition that leads to promotion. Given the nature of the various factors supporting traditional newsroom policy, the slow progress made toward more equitable and accurate news reporting concerning minorities in American media becomes understandable but not excusable.

ANALYSIS

Mass communication, through its various media, makes up a vital social component that enables a social system to exist and function. The role of news transmission is to reflect the realities of the societal well-being by alerting it to dangers within and without and by providing an agenda of issues for consideration. Individuals involved in that process are termed "gatekeepers" of information. Because minorities began their American experience as social outsiders, they have, by long-standing tradition, been excluded from roles in mainstream news-gathering and -reporting institutions. Information concerning minorities that does get processed through the news media is filtered, almost entirely, through members of the social majority.

Historically, news media reporting of minorities can be viewed in characteristic phases, which, depending upon specific time and circumstances, have been experienced by Native Americans, Blacks, Latinos, and Asians alike. Initially, minorities are excluded from news reports because they are not deemed part of the social system. Their continuing presence, however, soon leads to their being reported as threats to society. Social response to the perceived threat leads to conflict with minorities and results in confrontation news reporting. Once the confrontation crisis subsides, news media begin reporting stereotypically selected items to reassure their audience that the minority group is no longer a threat. Socially integrated news reporting looms as a promise on the horizon as increased opportunity for minorities to participate in the information gatekeeping process becomes reality.

Obstacles remain, however, in the path leading to integrated news reporting. First is the placement of profit motivation before the responsibility to inform society accurately about the contributions, ambitions, frustrations, and issues important to all of its ethnic segments, a necessity for its most prosperous survival. The tendency for some media to cater to economically advantaged audiences at the expense of lower socioeconomic levels (where a disproportionate number of minorities are found) impedes news integration. Other media, under the guise of providing news, merely exploit prurient interests to attract the largest audience for profit. In both instances the result is inadequate and inaccurate reporting of essential information inclusive of majority and minority viewpoints.

A second obstacle to integrated news media reporting is the distorted sense of news values held by majority news professionals. Traditional reporting procedures have defined news from a White majority perspective. Although news media have been nationally cognizant of the need to change their approach since the Kerner Commission report of the late 1960s, progress toward integrated reporting has been extremely slow. Necessary reorientation of the reporting process has been inhibited because traditional prejudicial news values had become engrained as matters of newsroom policy.

Newsroom policy, evidenced by the work of sociologist Warren Breed, is a hidden phenomenon that is effective in maintaining philosophical control of the news-gathering and reporting process. Because professional journalistic mores preclude formal written policy curtailing freedom of expression among staff members, a covert system has evolved to teach and enforce policy. Newcomers learn policy by observing the organization's news content produced by peers, by noting which types of their own material are deleted in the editing process, by listening to informal conversation among peers concerning policy, or by participating in news content planning conferences.

Sanctions, which maintain enforcement of newsroom policy, are also subtle but effective. They include the desire of reporters to earn and maintain the esteem of peers, to advance up the organizational ladder, to fulfill obligations to employers, and to protect their jobs. These sanctions affect White and minority reporters alike.

American society will not achieve the goal of fully integrated news coverage that accurately reflects an image of itself until the concept of news is redefined to include minority perspectives. The consequences of failure to do so will result in a nation that falls short of its own vision and purpose for existence. Much of the responsibility for change must come from news media organizations, where dedicated, conscientious efforts must be made to examine whether outmoded and counterproductive policies are preventing progress toward integrated reporting.

NOTES

1. For a discussion of the definition of news and news values see any of several basic newswriting texts, including Curtis MacDougall, *Interpretative Reporting* (Macmillan, 1982) and William Metz, *Newswriting* (Prentice-Hall, 1985).

2. Kerner Commission, *Report of the National Advisory Commission on Civil Disorders*, (Bantam, 1968), p. 389.

3. See Félix Gutiérrez and Clint C. Wilson II, "The demographic dilemma," *Columbia Journalism Review*, January/February 1979, pp. 53-55, for a report on how socioeconomic factors affected news coverage strategies in the *Los Angeles Times*.

4. Warren Breed, "Social control in the newsroom," *Social Forces*, May 1955. Also reprinted in Wilbur Schramm, *Mass Communications*, 2nd ed. (University of Illinois Press, 1960).

SUGGESTED READING

"Double Jeopardy in the Newsroom," *Time*, November 29, 1982.

Durand, Richard M., Jesse E. Teel, Jr., and William O. Bearden. "Racial Differences in Perceptions of Media Advertising and Credibility," *Journalism Quarterly 55* (Autumn 1979), pp. 562-566.

Fisher, Paul L. and Ralph L. Lowenstein (Eds.). *Race and the News Media*. New York: Praeger, 1968.

Goldstein, Patrick. "Magazine Covers: Are Blacks Blacked Out?" *Ebony*, January 1984, pp. 65-69.

Gutiérrez, Félix. "The Latino Package," *The Journalist*, 1 (February 1983), pp. 14-19.

Jeffres, Leo W. and K. Kyoon Hur, "The Forgotten Media Consumer—The American Ethnic," *Journalism Quarterly*, 57 (Spring 1980), pp. 10-17.

Kassarjian, Harold H. "The Negro and American Advertising, 1945-65," *Journal of Marketing Research*, 6 (February 1969), pp. 29-39.

"Reaching Hispanic America," Magazine Special Report, *Advertising Age*, March 19, 1984, pp. M-9-M-41.

Reid, Leonard N. and Bruce G. Vanden Bergh, "Blacks in Introductory Ads," *Journalism Quarterly*, 57 (Autumn 1980), pp. 485-488.

Shopping Patterns Within Selected Ethnic Groups. Consumer Trend Analysis, Los Angeles Times Marketing Research Year 1979-1980.

IV

The Triple Threat of Minority Media Activism

"Faced with majority group mass media tainted by racism and insensitive to their needs, minorities in the United States have three options: (1) They may seek access into the majority media through employment; (2) they may develop and maintain their own communications media; and (3) they may apply pressure techniques of various forms to effect changes in majority media content as it relates to them."

7

ACCESS: MINORITY TRAINING AND EMPLOYMENT IN THE MEDIA

THERE IS AN OLD ADAGE that says, "Beauty is in the eye of the beholder." As an observation on American mass media, it is equally appropriate to say that stereotypical, distorted ethnic minority images are the visions of others. Media-industry employment data clearly reveal that minorities have virtually no influence in determining how they are represented. Resulting media images are, therefore, fashioned through the eyes of nonminority creators and decision makers.

Minorities had been very aware, of course, of discriminatory hiring practices in media professions and industries for generations. However, very little official attention was focused on minority media employment prior to the civil rights movement in the 1960s. By the late 1960s, U.S. governmental agencies had been formed to address the question of fair employment practices in American business and labor. Among those agencies were the Equal Employment Opportunities Commission (EEOC) and the U.S. Commission on Civil Rights. Upon publication of the Kerner Commission's strong indictment of mass media culpability in perpetuating discrimination, both the EEOC and the Commission on Civil Rights turned their attention to media hiring practices. At the same time, the Kerner report stimulated some news media professional associations to assess their hiring records. These efforts can be summarized by looking at minority employment in the two major categories of entertainment and news.

FILM AND TELEVISION ENTERTAINMENT INDUSTRIES

Chapters 3 and 4 discussed ethnic minority portrayals in Hollywood movies and television and the roles in which the actors were employed. Here we discover the nature of ethnic participation in behind-the-scenes stage crafts and in production management roles. In 1969 the EEOC held hearings in Los Angeles on minority employment in the film industry. The commission found Hollywood's minority employment rates well below even the average for other industries, which themselves had poor hiring records. Furthermore, the film industry data revealed discriminatory hiring practices in nearly every occupational category, whether white collar or blue collar.

The EEOC concluded:

> The motion picture industry reports approximately 19,000 employees, 13,000 of whom are white collar workers. But it is not the raw numbers of people employed that is significant, it is the fact that the industry plays a critical role in influencing public opinion and creating this country's image of itself. In order to portray accurately the nation's minority groups, the industry must employ minority personnel at all levels.
>
> The Equal Employment Opportunity Commission's analysis indicates that this is not happening.[1]

One studio official who testified before the commission said that of 81 management-level personnel, only 3 were members of ethnic minority groups. Of these, 2 were Latino and the single Black manager headed the janitorial department; there were no Asian or Native American managers. The studio executive also testified that his organization employed 184 workers classified as technicians. Of that number, only 5 belonged to ethnic minorities: 3 Latinos, 1 Black, and 1 Asian. Generally, the minority employment percentage among other industries in the Los Angeles metropolitan statistical area was twice that of the movie industry in the late 1960s. At that time minorities constituted approximately 40 percent of the Los Angeles metropolitan area population, but made up only 3 percent of the movie industry labor force.

In 1977 the U.S. Commission on Civil Rights conducted its investigation of the television entertainment industry and also convened a hearing in Los Angeles. Among those called to testify were officials of the various unions representing producers, directors, and writers, as well as minority craftsmen in the several theatrical trades. One witness, a Cherokee Indian, testified how a trade union "lost" the job application of a highly skilled Native American worker. When a union official was confronted about the incident, he replied, "No one tells us who we have to hire or anything of that matter. We decide that."[2] Other testimony revealed a union scheme to phase out Blacks who attained union membership systematically, by seeking their suspension without due process hearings. Additionally, experienced minority union members were overlooked for job promotion while young Whites who were sons of union journeymen obtained superior status directly out of high school without job experience. These examples of systematic discrimination and nepotism in the television industry were not countermanded by either network executives or union officials. The Commission on Civil Rights noted that the television entertainment industry had not assumed equal employment opportunity responsibilities in hiring practices.

Data were compiled over a three-year period (1974-1976) on union rosters representing the workers who produce the movies, situation comedies, and variety programs televised to millions of American viewers. Crafts represented in the trade union data included makeup artists, projectionists, prop workers, set designers, script supervisors, story analysts, and camera operators. Keeping in mind that eight years had elapsed since the EEOC had investigated the movie industry, the television trade union data presented at the hearing showed an average of only 8 percent minority employment for the period. More revealing was the fact that not even one minority person obtained work during the three years as either a script supervisor or a story analyst according to data supplied to the U.S. Commission on Civil Rights. Although the industry was (as was American society in general) experiencing the waning years of emphasis on affirmative action, only 50 percent of the minorities who applied for union rosters achieved their goal. Meanwhile, 62 percent of the White applicants were successful during the same period.

In August 1977, the Commission on Civil Rights published its findings on minority and female employment in television.[3] For historical perspective it must be noted that in 1969 the Federal Communications Commission (FCC) had adopted equal employment opportunity guidelines prohibiting job discrimination by broadcast licensees. The implied penalty was loss of license. It was during this period that the term "two-fer" became part of the lexicon of American broadcasting. A "two-fer" was any woman employed in broadcasting who happened also to be a member of an ethnic minority group. Broadcast executives were able to list such women in their hiring statistics twice, once under the sex category and again under the ethnic category—a "two-for-one" employee. The tabulated result padded the actual affirmative action employment total. The use of "two-fers" and other manipulative measures created some unusual employment data reported by American broadcasters. In an attempt to make the hiring and placement of minorities in upper-level job categories seem more equitable, the industry reported an astonishing 45 percent increase in ethnic managers between 1971 and 1975. At the same time, however, the *proportion* of all employees in those job categories increased by only 13 percent. A close look at the broadcasters' figures also revealed a dramatic decline in the number of clerical and service jobs listed. These data prompted a public-interest group to ask, "Do more executives need fewer clerks to serve them? Do larger staffs need less janitorial service?"[4] It was obvious that broadcasters had merely reclassified their minority employees into upper job categories while keeping them in the same old jobs with the same low salaries. Most minority "managers," particularly in television, held jobs with such titles as "community relations director" or "manager of community affairs." Almost without exception, even these persons (who were far removed from day-to-day programming decisions) reported to a White male department head.

Among the significant conclusions drawn by the U.S. Commission on Civil Rights regarding the employment of minorities in television were the following:

- Television executives used an underlying assumption that realistic representation of minorities would diminish the medium's ability to attract the largest possible audience.
- Broadcasters misrepresented to the FCC the actual employment status of minorities and women via reports on FCC Form 395.
- Minorities were not fully utilized at all levels of station management or at all levels of local station operations.

- White males held the overwhelming majority of decision-making positions.
- Minorities held subsidiary positions.
- Increased minority visibility as on-air talent belied lack of minority representation in managerial and other jobs off camera; in other words, ethnics were merely "window dressing."

Employment conditions had changed little in the 1980s. FCC statistics released in 1982 showed that minorities held about 17 percent of all jobs in broadcast television and about 14 percent in cable TV. Although the FCC reported the number of minority "officials and managers" to be 9 percent, it still included in that category low authoritative positions such as promotion directors and research directors, jobs most frequently held by minorities.[5] Those figures include the small and slowly growing number of minority-owned TV stations that have largely minority management staffs. Another round of hearings descended upon Hollywood and the television industry on June 1, 1983, when the House Subcommittee on Telecommunications, Consumer Protection, and Finance heard from a group of Black actors led by Sidney Poitier. Poitier, the first Black to win an Oscar for best actor, urged the committee to instigate a full-scale investigation of the "flagrant unfairness in the hiring practices of producers, the studios and the networks." Poitier's words seemed to echo the testimony of other witnesses who had appeared nearly fifteen years earlier before another federal committee. In the interim, new technologies had come to American mass entertainment, including cable and pay TV, satellite video transmission, and VCRs. But minority hiring in the film and television industries remained the same—slow and at minimal levels.

NEWS MEDIA

If minority hiring in the mass entertainment industries has been shameful, their record is matched by the press, America's "fourth estate." The newspaper industry began to count its minority participants in the early 1970s. The American Society of Newspaper Editors reported that fewer than 1 percent of daily newspaper professionals were members of ethnic minority groups when the decade began. By 1972, minorities constituted 1.6 percent of the total. Interestingly, in the same year minority hiring in broadcast news peaked and has remained basically constant into the mid-1980s, with about 14 percent in television news and 10 percent in radio news. The broadcasting industry moved much more quickly on the issue of minority hiring in news because radio and television frequencies are licensed through a governmental agency, the Federal Communications Commission. Newspapers, on the other hand, are private enterprises that have to be motivated by conscience or social pressure to improve their employment practices.

Although minority hiring in broadcasting lost momentum within five years after it began, the industry saw no such decline in its drive for sexual equality. The hiring of women and their advancement up to decision-making ranks far outstripped that of minorities. For example, in 1972 only 4 percent of the nation's radio news directors were women, but by 1982 the figure had risen to 18 percent. In contrast, minorities made up only 4 percent of radio news directors in 1982. In 1972, 57 percent of the nation's television stations had at least one woman on the news staff, but by 1982 virtually every station (97 percent) had at least one female journalist. By comparison, ethnic minorities were in 60 percent of all TV newsrooms in 1972, but the figure had grown to only 72 percent by 1982.

Daily newspapers lag far behind radio and television news organizations in minority hiring. In 1984 there was only 5.8 percent minority representation among the nearly 1750 daily newspapers in the nation. The newspaper industry recently experienced a 4-year decline in its minority employment growth rate. According to the American Society of Newspaper Editors, the rate of minority hiring decreased each year from 1979 to 1983 and increased only two-tenths of a percent in 1984 (Table 7.1). About three-fifths of the daily newspapers in the United States have no minority journalists on their staffs. Moreover, about half of the editors who reported they employed no minority journalists said they had made no efforts to do so. One such editor commented that the purpose of his newspaper "is to inform the readers and to serve the community, not to embark on social engineering." Some editors openly admitted that racial prejudices in their communities would make a minority reporter resented and unwelcome. A California

TABLE 7.1 **Minority Employment Growth Rate in Daily Newspapers, 1978-1984**

Year	*Minority Percentage*	*Percentage Increase*
1978	4.0	–
1979	4.5	.50
1980	4.95	.45
1981	5.3	.35
1982	5.5	.20
1983	5.6	.10
1984	5.8	.20

SOURCE: Based on research data compiled by the American Society of Newspaper Editors.

TABLE 7.2 **Minority News Editorial Employment in White-Owned Daily Newspapers and Commercial Broadcasting Stations, 1982**

News Medium	*Estimated Total Employment*	*Percentage Blacks*	*Percentage Latinos*	*Percentage Asians*	*Percentage Indians*	*Total Percentage Minority*
Newspapers	50,000	3.1	1.4	0.8	0.2	5.5
Radio	10,000	7.0	2.1	0.3	0.6	10.0
Television	15,000	9.6	3.0	1.2	0.4	14.2

SOURCE: Compiled from "Minorities and newspapers: A report by the Committee on Minorities," American Society of Newspaper Editors, May 1982; and Vernon A. Stone, "Women gain but minorities barely hold their own in their share of broadcast news jobs," *RTNDA Communicator* (Radio-Television News Directors Association), April 1983, pp. 18-21.

editor said employing a minority reporter on his staff would create "suspicions among the higher echelons that we are becoming subversive."

A comparison of minority journalist employment in newspapers, radio, and television (Table 7.2) reveals television as the leader, although, as noted earlier, the figure has remained statistically constant for nearly fifteen years in both radio and television. In fact, television suffered a slight decline in minority hiring, from a high of 16 percent in 1977 to about 14 percent in 1982. In 1980 U.S. Census data placed minorities at about 17 percent of the population. Against that standard none of the news media industries has achieved statistical parity in minority hiring. Table 7.2 shows that in 1982 Blacks found news media employment in greater numbers than Latino, Asian, or Native American journalists. The numerical ranking of the four ethnic groups has been constant since such records have been kept. Latinos have been

TABLE 7.3 **Percentage of Each Minority Group of All Minorities Employed in White-Owned Daily Newspapers and Commercial Broadcasting Stations, 1982**

	Newspapers	*Radio*	*Television*
Blacks	56	70	69
Latinos	24	21	20
Asians	16	3	8
Indians	4	6	3
Total	100	100	100

SOURCE: See Table 7.2.

the second-largest minority group employed in news media professions and Asians third. Native Americans traditionally have been the least represented of the four groups, except in radio where they have slightly outnumbered Asians.

Table 7.3 provides a breakdown of minority news media employment by ethnic group in each medium in 1982. Blacks, as noted earlier, were the most represented group, but in somewhat smaller proportions in daily newspapers than in broadcasting. Latinos, Asians, and Indians, however, fared better in obtaining newspaper employment than they did in broadcasting as a percentage of all minority hiring.

It is important to note, once again, that minorities are extremely scarce in news department decision-making positions. Vernon Stone, chairman of the Radio-Television News Directors Association research committee, estimated that only 12 to 15 of the nation's TV news directors were members of minority groups in 1982, approximately 2 percent. Even more distressing to minorities who work in newsrooms is the lack of ethnics in the "pipeline" positions that lead to management levels.

Employment data for daily newspapers and radio and television outlets nationally indicate that the South and Far West regions have the best minority hiring records. The Midwest and Northeast sections of the United States have lagged significantly in hiring minority journalists in every medium. In 1982 nearly 75 percent of daily newspapers in the midwestern states of the Dakotas, Illinois, Indiana, Iowa, Kansas, Michigan, Minnesota, Missouri, Nebraska, Ohio, and Wisconsin had no minority journalists. A 1979 study found 84 percent of midwestern radio stations without a single minority journalist, although the television figure was better, at 62 percent. Those states contain several large urban metropolitan cities with significant Black, Latino, or Indian population centers.

RECRUITMENT AND TRAINING

Since the news professions are well aware of the shortage of minority employees, the issue of their efforts to recruit and train a more ethnically diverse work force deserves attention. We have noted earlier the attitudes of some newspaper editors who have no minority staff members regarding the hiring issue. Others who responded to the American Society of Newspaper Editors survey said they believed hiring minorities would lower the standards of their newspaper. "Generally, hiring minorities means reducing standards temporarily. Except for one reporter and one news editor, every minority person we've hired in 10 years was less qualified than a concurrently available White," said the editor of one of the largest midwestern daily newspapers.[6] However, there was disagreement over the notion that minorities were less qualified than Whites as journalists. The claim that minority staff members result in lower standards was labeled "hogwash" by another midwestern editor: "I can show non-minority employees who are less than qualified."[7]

The debate over whether minorities are less qualified or the victims of racism has not been confined to the newspaper industry. A trade magazine article on Black and other minority-group hiring reported that an angry exchange on the issue took place during a press coverage forum in New York City. In a confrontation reminiscent of Breed's study of newsroom policy (Chapter 6), WNBC-TV news correspondent Gabe Pressman responded to the charge of professional racism by invoking the importance of traditional standards of quality in reporting. J. J. Gonzalez, a reporter for WCBS-TV, rose from the audience to proclaim, "Who passes . . . judgment on competency? Come on, now! Don't tell me 'competency.' . . . When you get the competent person in, he is not allowed [to do the job]. So stop your bull!"[8] Randy Daniels, a Black journalist who left his job as a CBS correspondent after nearly ten years because he saw no career advancement opportunities in the network, echoed Gonzalez.

> I met with every level of management at CBS News . . . over issues that specifically relate to Blacks and other minorities. . . . When it became clear to me that such meetings accomplished nothing, I chose to leave and work where my ideas were wanted and needed. . . . I have found my race an impediment to being assigned major stories across the entire spectrum of news.[9]

Daniels also questioned the importance of training and qualifications for minorities in the work place: "Whites of equal training and ability, entering at the same level, somehow did not require a special training program and seemed to move up the ladder more quickly."[10]

The discussion about qualifications of minorities to perform as journalists has been a sensitive one on a number of fronts. Even the Kerner report noted that news media officials complained that too few "qualified" minorities were available for hire. The implications raised the ire of many minorities, who observed that people of color have found success in fields ranging from medicine to engineering to law and the arts, but somehow are not "qualified" to be writers, reporters, and editors for news media. On that issue one White newspaper editor agreed: "The business isn't magic. Mostly, it's trial-and-error training. If the word skills are adequate, any minority can be trained to do any newsroom task that any non-minority can do."[11]

In 1978 the major academic journalism organization, the Association for Education in Journalism (now the Association for Education in Journalism and Mass Communication) adopted a "Resolution on Minorities." Eight years earlier, AEJ had created a Minorities and Communication division with a multiracial membership base, but by the time the resolution was adopted the division's membership was almost entirely made up of ethnic minority academicians. More significantly, very little integration had taken place within AEJ itself, reflecting the fact that ethnic minorities constituted fewer than 2 percent of faculty members nationally teaching journalism and mass communication courses.[12] Among the failings of the journalism education establishment in facilitating newsroom and classroom integration are the following:

- continued use of curricula that fail to address and rectify historic and current inequities of mass media toward ethnic minorities

- failure to encourage the research, writing, and adaptation of textbooks that would lead to the development of more ethnically aware nonminority journalism students and professionals
- failure to hire, train, and develop minority journalism faculty
- failure to implement affirmative action criteria for accreditation of college journalism programs (In late 1984, efforts began to recruit minorities for service on accreditation teams.)

A number of training programs have been established by media organizations and professional groups to circumvent the shortcomings of the journalism education establishment. Several of them owe their impetus to the Kerner Commission report. Perhaps most well known is the Summer Program for Minority Journalists, housed at the University of California, Berkeley. The program's history parallels the interest level and commitment afforded the minority issue by major media corporations and other interested parties. In the wake of the Kerner report, the Ford Foundation supported creation of a training program at Columbia University known as the Michelle Clark Program for Minority Journalists. The project trained and placed 70 minority newspersons for print and broadcasting jobs from 1968 to 1974. When it lost its funding support in 1974, the program had been responsible for 20 percent of all minority journalists employed in daily newspapers nationally. Although the program was effective, the loss of financial support reflected the short-term commitment of the nation to the cause of news media integration. During the same period (1972 to 1978), the amount of scholarship money allocated for the education of minority journalists dropped 54 percent and the number of scholarships declined by 30 percent. Fortunately, with seed money from the Gannett Foundation, the program was revived in Berkeley as a newspaper-only training project under the auspices of the Institute for Journalism Education (IJE). IJE was formed by a dedicated group of minority and nonminority professionals to continue the struggle for ethnic parity in journalism. In 1978, IJE began a similar program to train minority editors at the University of Arizona, also using professionals as instructors.

Several news organizations instituted and maintained "in-house" training programs for minorities, but such efforts are few in number. Among the primarily newspaper-oriented programs are those sponsored by Capital Cities Communications, Gannett Newspapers, Knight-Ridder, and the Times-Mirror Co. None of the television networks has a systematic recruiting or training program, except for a modest effort at CBS. Much of the network television attitude on the subject was reflected in the remarks of an NBC executive who admitted that minorities are underrepresented in television and that the circumstance is "wrong, but we're not rectifying it by training or recruiting. It's a natural process that will rectify itself."[13]

ANALYSIS

The minority hiring records of the motion picture and television entertainment industries is poor, according to federal agencies that have conducted investigations since the late 1960s. Minorities continue to be scarce as workers in Hollywood trade unions. Broadcasters, particularly in television, were the first to react to federal pressures because of the licensing power of the FCC. Although their hiring rate far exceeded those of companion media industries, they were caught cheating in reporting minority hiring statistics because most were hired into low job-category levels. One example was the ploy of counting female minorities twice, as "two-fers," in an effort to pad minority hiring figures. In television, minorities were found primarily in visible "on-air" positions but were generally not found in decision-making management jobs.

Meanwhile, in the nation's newsrooms, daily newspapers were the most grudging ethnic employers and have by far the lowest minority employment rate of any mass media industry. In 1970 less than 1 percent of newspaper journalists were minority-group members and in 1985 the industry was still short of 6 percent and losing ground. Perhaps indicative of why daily newspapers lag in minority hiring is the attitude openly expressed by some editors that they have neither the desire nor the responsibility to integrate the profession. Broadcast news hiring of minorities took a back seat to that of women in the late 1970s and 1980s. As ethnic hiring slowed, women were making rapid progress in assuming positions in both management and other job categories.

The most common reason given by media executives for their poor minority hiring record has been that they can't find "qualified" minorities. Whatever the merits of that claim (there is considerable disagreement among news executives over qualifications of minority journalists), the record shows that industry commitment to ethnic recruitment and training has been spotty. At the same time, efforts of college and university journalism educators have been far less than the "intense" endeavor urged by the Kerner Commission in 1967. Curriculum, textbooks, and minority faculty hiring have changed little in academic journalism and mass communication departments.

The trends of minority employment in mass media industries since the mid-1970s reflect a slow rate of integration, with virtually no penetration into power management levels. Predictably, the result is media product in the mid-1980s that continues to distort the reality of the multiracial society in the United States today.

NOTES

1. U.S. Equal Employment Opportunity Commission, "Hearings before the Equal Employment Opportunity Commission on utilization of minority and women workers in certain major industries," Los Angeles, March 12-14, 1969, p. 352.

2. U.S. Commission on Civil Rights, "Hearing before the United States Commission on Civil Rights," Los Angeles, March 16, 1977.

3. U.S. Commission on Civil Rights, "Window dressing on the set: Women and minorities in television," August 1977.

4. Jennings and Jefferson, "Television station employment practices: The status of minorities and women, 1974," United Church of Christ, Office of Communications, New York, December 1975, p. 11.

5. Cynthia Alperowitz, *Fighting TV stereotypes: an ACT handbook* (Action for Children's Television, 1983).

6. American Society of Newspaper Editors, "Minorities and newspapers: A report by the Committee on Minorities," May 1982, p. 34.

7. Ibid., p. 35.

8. Michael Massing, "Blackout in television," *Columbia Journalism Review*, November/December 1982, p. 38.

9. Ibid., p. 39.

10. Ibid., p. 38.

11. "Minorities and newspapers," p. 35.

12. See annual reports on college and university journalism student enrollment by Paul Peterson in *Journalism Educator*, 1978-1984.

13. Paul Peterson, "Survey indicates no change in '83 journalism enrollment," *Journalism Educator*, Vol. 39, No. 1, Spring 1984.

8

ALTERNATIVES: THE DEEP ROOTS OF MINORITY MEDIA

WHEN MOST PEOPLE THINK about the beginnings of media in the United States, they often look to Europe as the foundation of both the technology and the system of media. Journalism history is often told in terms that emphasize the English-speaking traditions of media but ignore the historical past of other peoples. Although it may be useful to look to Europe to find some of the roots of media in the United States, a scholar looking there and nowhere else will get only a partial view of the media's rich history. Communication is a basic human activity, and people of all races and cultures have taken part in it. Journalism historians Edwin and Michael Emery describe some of the earliest forms of communication:

> Around 3500 B.C. the Sumerians of the Middle East devised a system of preserving records by inscribing signs and symbols in wet clay tablets using cylinder seals and then baking them in the sun. They also devised a cuneiform system of writing, using bones to mark signs in wet clay. Pictographs or ideographs—drawing of animals, commonly recognized objects, and humans—were popular in the Mediterranean area, China, India, what is now Mexico, and Egypt, where they became known as hieroglyphs. There is evidence that a system of movable type was devised in Asia Minor prior to 1700 B.C., the date of a flat clay disk found in Crete. The

> disk contained forty-five different signs that had been carved on individual pieces of type and then pressed into the clay.[1]

The Phoenicians created an alphabet in 1500 B.C. and used colored fluids to outline its symbols to produce the pictographs. About 1000 years later the Egyptians began using reeds from the Nile River to make papyrus, on which scribes using brushes or quills would mark hieroglyphics. The different sheets of papyrus were then joined to form scrolls, which were stored in centers of learning. Around A.D. 100 parchment made from animal skins was used for special manuscripts or scrolls. But it was the Chinese who made the greatest two inventions leading to modern communication, paper and printing. Emery and Emery describe their contributions:

> At about this same time [A.D. 100] the Chinese invented a smooth, white paper from wood pulp and fibres and also discovered a way to transfer an ideograph from stone to paper after inking the surface. Wang Chieh published what is considered the world's oldest preserved book from wood blocks in A.D. 868. Large blocks could be carved so that one sheet of paper, printed on both sides, could be folded into thirty-two pages of book size. Feng Tao printed the Confucian classics between 932 and 953 and in about 1045 the artisan Pi Sheng was inspired to devise a set of movable clay carvings—a sort of earthenware "type"—that could be reused.[2]

The technology of wood-block printing was not introduced in Europe until Marco Polo returned from China in 1295, but the Asian technology sped ahead, according to Emery and Emery. Movable metal type of copper or bronze came into use in Korea in 1241.

Record keeping and communication were also important in what was to become Latin America before the arrival of the Spanish in 1492. The native Incas, Aztecs, and Mayans all had elaborate systems of people involved in recording, transferring, and storing records, including scribes who wrote on bark tablets and artisans who recorded information and pictures on stone carvings. The Incas, governing a territory that rose precipitously from the ocean to the mountains, used an elaborate network of runners to transmit messages of importance throughout their empire. The Aztecs, who developed both a university and libraries, used an early form of mass communication by hanging colored banners on the main public square of their capital city of Tenochitlán, which is now known as Mexico City.

Although Hollywood movies have popularized the image of North American natives communicating through tom-toms, war drums, and smoke signals, the intertribal communication systems were actually more complex and systematic. A network of trails and footpaths spanned the continent and was traversed by specially trained couriers authorized to carry messages between tribes. James E. Murphy and Sharon M. Murphy describe communication between tribes before the arrival of the Europeans:

> A complex system of native communications covered most of North America before White contact. It was a unique network of trails and footpaths that crisscrossed the continent, passing through dense forests, over rivers and streams, across mountains and meadows. Traversing these trails were Indian runners, known as tribal messengers, who were officially recognized by governing systems such as those of the Iroquois in the East, the Cherokees in the South and Southeast, the Yuroks in the Northwest, and the Eskimos in present-day Alaska. Other tribes, having less complex tribal governing structures, named and trained young men, and sometimes young women, to act as messenger communicators carrying news from tribe to tribe. Their extraordinary strength and endurance, their fleetness of foot, and their intimate knowledge of the land amazed early European immigrants.[3]

Africans south of the Sahara Desert, divided into three chief groups and many tribes, also developed systems for recording and communicating information. Like the natives of North America, they also used "talking drums" to communicate from village to village and transferred information between tribes and other parts of the world along land and water trade routes. Rock painting was a key activity for the ancient residents of the Kalahari Desert near the southern tip of Africa, as well as people in the Sahara Desert in the north. Literature, often in the form of folk tales performed with music, passed along stories and important events from generation to generation. In some tribes special persons known as *griots* memorized the history of the tribe and passed it along to younger members, who would carry on the telling of history after they died.

EARLY PRINTING IN THE AMERICAS

Like the history of communication and printing in the world, the history of printed media in the Americas starts with a group other the English-speaking colonist. The first printing press to come to the Americas was brought from Spain to what is now Mexico in 1535, more than 100 years before the English colonists brought their first printing press to Harvard University in 1638. The earliest printing in the Americas, licensed by the Spanish royalty to printer Juan Cromberger of Seville, was built on the native languages and alphabets of the native peoples. The Spanish saw the main use of the press as printing government notices and proclamations, as well as catechisms to be used in converting the Aztecs and neighboring tribes to Catholicism. Therefore, the first booklets produced on the printing press were bilingual, using a European language such as Spanish or Latin in one column next to the same text in a native language, such as Nahuatl or Tarascan, in the next column. Armed with this bilingual format, the Spanish continued on their mission of conquering and converting the native tribes.

But the press was used for more than printing government documents and religious texts. In 1541 a terrible storm and earthquake struck Guatemala City, south of Mexico City. After the storm a notary public named Juan Rodríguez wrote what has been identified as the first printed news reporting on the American continent. Rodríguez's story of the storm and its destruction of the city was taken to Mexico City, where it was printed in an eight-page booklet by the operator of Cromberger's printing house, Juan Pablos; his pressman, Gil Barbero; and a Black slave whose name was not recorded. The front page of the booklet, giving the reader a foretaste of the news media that would follow it, began with an attention-getting headline.

"Report of the Terrifying Earthquake Which Has Reoccurred In the Indies in a City Called Guatemala," the news report blared in large type. "It is an event of great astonishment and great example so that we all repent from our sins and so that we will be ready when God calls us."[4] The actual report began on an inside page that began with a dateline and gave Rodríguez's first-person account of what had happened.

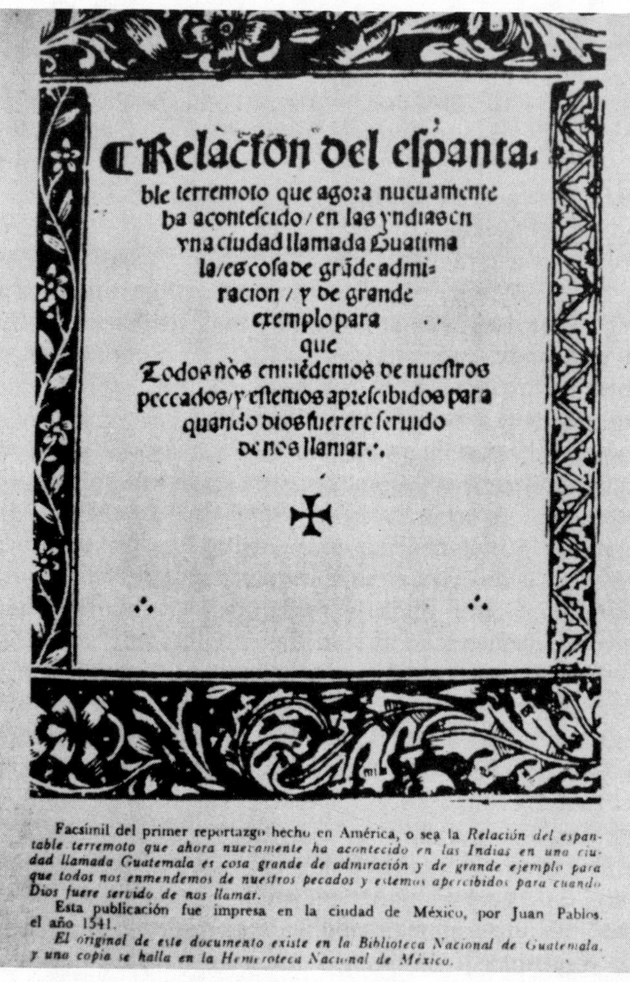

Relaciõn del eſpanta-
ble terremoto que agora nueuamente
ha aconteſcido / en las yndias en
vna ciudad llamada Guatima
la / es coſa de grãde admi-
racion / y de grande
exemplo para
que
Todos nos enmẽdemos de nueſtros
peccados / y eſtemos apreſcibidos para
quando dios fuere ſeruido
de nos llamar.

Facsímil del primer reportazgo hecho en América, o sea la *Relación del espantable terremoto que ahora nuevamente ha acontecido en las Indias en una ciudad llamada Guatemala es cosa grande de admiración y de grande ejemplo para que todos nos enmendemos de nuestros pecados y estemos apercibidos para cuando Dios fuere servido de nos llamar.*

Esta publicación fue impresa en la ciudad de México, por Juan Pablos, el año 1541.

El original de este documento existe en la Biblioteca Nacional de Guatemala, y una copia se halla en la Hemeroteca Nacional de México.

First Printed News Report in America. **The first use of printing to disseminate news in America was this 1541 account of an earthquake and storm that destroyed Guatemala City, written by Juan Rodriguez and published by Juan Pablos in Mexico City. (Journalism History)**

The news report, which was distributed in Mexico City, was the forerunner of what was to become a popular form of news reporting in New Spain, as the Spanish colonies were then called. Based on a European model, they were called *hojas volantes* (literally, flying pages or bulletins) and *relaciones* (reports), which were issued when major news occurred, when the government had a major announcement, or when ships bearing news of world events docked at Veracruz. As more presses arrived in New Spain, more printers took up the practice of printing and selling these irregularly issued news booklets. Mexican historian Julio Jiménez Rueda wrote that it was through the *hojas volantes* that "people knew of the death and coronation of kings, wars in Europe, earthquakes and calamities."[5]

By 1600, nearly 40 years before a printing press had even arrived in the English colonies, the presses of New Spain had produced at least 174 books. An additional 60 books have been identified without dates or verification.[6] The booklet format was also used in the first regularly issued printed news reports in America, the four volumes of the *Mercurio Volante*, published by Carlos de Siguenza y Gongora in Mexico City in 1693. Among the news covered in one of the issues of the *Mercurio Volante* was an account of the unsuccessful attempts of the Spanish to conquer and colonize the native inhabitants of what is now New Mexico.

Although the Latino roots of communication media were long overlooked or ignored by media historians, it has not always been that way. In 1810 Isaiah Thomas began the first history ever written of American journalism, the *History of Printing in America*, with a ten-page chapter on printing in Spanish America, but that chapter was deleted when the book was reprinted in 1874. Journalism historian Frank Luther Mott mentioned the 1541 Mexico City news report in a footnote reference to his 1941 journalism history text, but claimed that "no regularly published newspaper on the continent antedated the earliest Boston papers."[7] However, in 1984 the fifth edition of Emery and Emery's *The Press and America* included a new two-page section on the Spanish influence in American journalism, including a reproduction of the 1541 news report. In addition, in 1977 and 1979 *Journalism History* devoted the cover and several articles to the contribution of Latinos and the Latino press to the evolution of news media on the American continent. These Latin American roots have influenced the development of the press in the United States as well. Newspapers were published for the Spanish-speaking residents of Texas and New Mexico in the years before those territories were acquired by the United States in the 1840s.

As important as the contributions of Blacks, Latinos, Asians, and Native Americans have been in creating and developing their communication systems and media in other civilizations and countries, the focus of this book is to examine these groups as they have interacted with communication media in the United States, with an emphasis on commonalities and differences between the groups. All groups have had active media addressing the needs and interests of their communities in this country for more than a century.

The first newspapers for Latinos, Blacks, Native Americans, and Asian Americans all began in the nineteenth century. They were preceded by other media targeted to minority groups, most notably the Polish- and German-speaking residents of the English colonies and the new nation. They developed in the same era as the first mass-circulation press pioneered by Benjamin Day, the *New York Sun* in 1833. Despite their common chronological beginnings, there is another, more meaningful, commonality drawing together these different newspapers started at different times in different cities for four different racial groups: They were all started as a response to a crisis. The four newspapers (in chronological order) are the first Latino newspaper, *El Misisipí*, founded in New Orleans in 1808; the first Black newspaper, *Freedom's Journal*, founded in New York City in 1827; the first Native American newspaper, *Cherokee Phoenix*, founded in New Echota, Georgia, in 1828; and what apparently is the first Asian American newspaper, *Kim-Shan Jit San-Luk, The Golden Hills News*, founded in San Francisco in 1851 or 1854.

The First Latino Newspaper: *El Misisipí (1808)*

El Misisipí was founded in the midst of the Napoleonic Wars in Europe, when France had conquered much of the European continent, including parts of Spain. New Orleans, a major seaport where the Mississippi River flows into the Gulf of Mexico, was the port of passage for commerce and travelers coming in and out of the United States from Europe, as well as the Spanish colonies in the Caribbean Sea, Central America, and South America. The newspaper was a four-page publication printed primarily in Spanish, but with English translations of many of the articles and almost all of the advertising. It was started by an Anglo firm, William H. Johnson and Company, and was printed on the press of the *Louisiana Gazette*. Although the newspaper is cited in a

EL MISISIPI.

Vol. I.) MIERCOLES 12 DE OCTUBRE DE 1808. (No. 10.

Condiciones.

I. Se publicarà los MIERCOLES y SABADOS de cada semana.

II. Se pagaràn OCHO PESOS al año adelantando la mitad.

III. Los avisos se publicaràn en ambas lenguas ó en la que se quiera en los terminos regulares.

Del Diario de New-York.

Breve noticia de lo acaecido en Madrid el Lunes 2 de Mayo de 1808 por un Ingles que se hallò presente.

Jamas ha estado el público en perfecta tranquilidad desde que en mediados de Marzo se sospechó por la primera vez la intencion del Rey Càrlos IV de trasladarse à Sevilla con toda la familia Real.

La deposicion del Pricipe de la Paz el 18: su prision el 19 con la abdicacion del Rey Càrlos y exâltacion de su hijo Fernando verificadas en el mismo dia, cuyos eventos causaron gran satisfaccion por los felices efectos que podrian producir: la llegado de las tropas francesas à Madrid: la entrega de la espada de Francisco I à Murat; monumento que se conservaba en la Armeria del Rey como trofeo de la batalla de Pavia: la salida del Rey para Burgos: la entrega del Principe de la Paz à la Francia; y por ultimo la determinacion del Rey de pasarse á las fronteras y ponerse en manos de los Franceses en Bayona, fueron circunstancias que animaron la fermentacion y la subieron por grados à tal punto, que cada momento se temia alguna formidable explosion por la junta de Gobierno de la qual habia quedado Presidente el Infante Don Antonio para aquietar los alarmas del pueblo y evitar que hiciesen algunos actos de violencia contra los Franceses.

Un parte ó correo extraordinario acostumbraba venir todas las tardes de Bayona con las noticias de las transacciones: estas jamas se publicaban en la gaceta sino que circulaban en forma de extractos de cartas privadas de la comitiva del Rey: los primeros causaron una satisfaccion momentànea como que consistian unicamente en la descripcion de los honores hechos al Principe Fernando con motivo de su llegada, y en el cordial recibimiento de Bonaparte. Las noticias siguientes se hicieron ménos satisfactorias: primero se dieron unos indicios obscuros de que no iba bien todo, y luego se dixo mas claramente que la intencion del àrbitro de la Francia era forzar à Fernando à que renunciase su corona.

El parte del Sàbado 30 de Abril no llegó. Lo mismo avino al del Domingo 1° de Mayo en cuya espera estaban ansiosas millaradas de gentes en la puerta del Sol y en las calles de la cercania del Correo.

La guarnicion francesa de Madrid estuvo toda la noche sobre las armas, y al otro dia, 2 de Mayo, se levantó el Sol sobre muchos infelices destinados à no ver mas auroras. Este dia fué notable por la salida de la Reyna de Etruria y su hermano el Infante Don Francisco de Paula para Bayona.

La curiosidad llevó à muchisimos à la plaza del palacio para ser testigos de aquella escena; y muchas mugeres y familias fueron tambien para decir à Dios à sus maridos y parientes, y para lamentar su dura suerte en quedar sin ninguna prevision cierta. Quando salio à las puertas la primera carroza, creyeron muchos del populacho que el Infante Don Antonio Presidente de la Junta ó Gobernador interino iba tambien à dexarlos y con esta falsa idea comenzaron à alborotarse.

Cortaron los tirantes de la carroza y la metieron à empujones en el patio del palacio, pero asegurados de que Dn. Antonio quedaba en Madrid, dexaron que guarnecieran y que salieran. El General Murat mandó un Edecan para que se informase del caso: el populacho parecia animado à tratarlo con aspereza, pero habiendo promediado algunos oficiales esples. quedó libre y pudo volver à su Comandante.

Al irse, pues, los coches con la Reyna de Etruria y su hermano, manifestó este tal sentimiento y animo lo expresó con tan amargos gritos que enternecieron é irritaron al pueblo: entonces volvio el Edecan con una parte de las tropas francesas y comenzó la horrible y sanguinaria escena.

No es fácil atinar si los soldados franceses ó el populacho fueron los primeros agresores, pero es cierto que los franceses comenzaron à descargar su mosqueteria contra los que se le oponian, y que caian muchos inocentes espectadores: uno de estos fué un hermoso joven de 18 años que se hallaba en una ventana; cincuenta eran las once del dia. Las noticias de aquellas barbaras descargas se esparcieron por toda la villa y en ménos de una hora todos los de la baxa clase que tuvieron proporciones se presentaron armados en las calles.

Al principio tuvieron ventajas los españoles en muchas partes de la ciudad, à pesar de que no se les permitió à las tropas tomar partido por haberlas encerrado sus oficiales en los quarteles. Cayeron muchas tropas francesas, cuyas armas sirvieron al populacho que no tenia ningunas; pero luego que comenzaron à tener efecto las disposiciones del General Murat, se decidió la preponderancia por parte de los Franceses, que hicieron salir sus tropas y formadas en columna en los campos inmediatos entraron por las diferentes puertas, acompañado cada tozo de una ó mas piezas de artilleria volante que barrian las calles à medida qee avanzaban, las quales fueron colocadas en los lugares que les parecieron mas oportunos. Ademas de esto la infanteria hacia descargas en las encrucijadas sobre quantos pasaban y gustaba tirar particularmente à todas las ventanas y balcones en que veian gentes.

[illegible] defensas de los Es[illegible] pa[illegible] en el [illegible] donde estuvo hospedado Sir Benjamin King quando estuvo de Embaxador en esta Corte, y donde yacen las reliquias de este respetable Ministro.

(Se Continuarà.)

AVISO.

Dn. Juan Rodriguez, Abogado

TIENE el honor de avisar al público y á sus amigos, que desde hoy su demora y residencia ordinaria será en su habitacion à una legua poco mas de la Ciudad hàcia abajo del rio y del mismo lado, entre las habitaciones del Sr. Brown Coletor de rentas de los Estados y de Don Edemon Macarty; pero que mantendrà su estudio en la ciudad en casa del Doctor Deveze, calle de Maine ó de los Almacenes No. 16, donde se empleará en servicio del público segun su profesion desde las diez de la mañana hasta las quatro de la tarde. Octubre 8. [illegible]

Dn. JOHN RODRIGUEZ,

Attorney at Law,

HAS the honor to inform his friends and the public in general that from this date he will reside at his plantation, better than a league below the city and on the same side of the river, between the plantation of Wm. Brown, Esq. and that of Mr Edmond Macarty; but that he will still continue to keep his office in town, in the house of Doctor Deveze, No. 16, Main street, where he will execute any business in the line of his profession, from ten o'clock A. M till four PM. October 1. [illegible]

Pasage para Vera-Cruz o la Havana.

LAS personas que desearen pasar à estos puertos lo conseguiran acudiendo à casa de Dn. Leandro Muxo, ó a los cuartos de esta gaceta.

Septiembre 16.

Blanks for sale at this Office.

El Misisipí (1808), the first Latino newspaper in the United States, used both Spanish and English, including a bilingual advertisement for Don Juan Rodriguez, Attorney-at-Law, in the lower right-hand corner, as this 1808 edition shows. (Wisconsin State Historical Society) number of journalism history sources, not much is known about its founders, and only two copies remain from its two-year printing run.

However, a translation of the one copy remaining in the United States reveals the crisis under which the newspaper's readers were living. With Napoleon campaigning in Europe and attempting to establish a puppet regime in Spain, *El Misisipí* was filled with reports, from other newspapers and from sea captains, of events in Europe, including a story on the uprising of citizens in Madrid against Napoleon's forces. The newspaper also speculates on the possibility of England ending its hostilities with Russia and entering the war against France on the side of Spain. All the news was from outside of New Orleans and almost all of it concerned the war in Europe, including a long commentary on the events. Because there was no wire or electronic dissemination of news, most of the stories the newspaper published were several months old and, at times, differed with each other. In a separate column the editor commented on the different reports and their possible implications on Spain. The newspaper was also distinctly pro-Spanish, denigrating officials of the puppet regime established by Napoleon and speculating on the possibility of England entering the war against France on the side of Spain.

El Misisipí relied heavily on news reports taken from other newspapers, a common practice at that time, and reports of sea captains and sailors arriving from foreign ports. Among the articles in the only surviving issue of the newspaper in the United States, published October 12, 1808, are articles from the *Boston Chronicle* and a newspaper identified as the *Diario de New York (New York Daily)*. Since the editors did not translate the title of the Boston newspaper to the Spanish word *Cronica* and used the Spanish word *Diario* in the New York newspaper, there is some possibility that the *Diario de New York* may have also been a Spanish-language newspaper. However, no listings of a newspaper called the *Diario de New York* or the *New York Daily* are found in the accepted newspaper references for New York at that time, although there is a was a newspaper named the *New York Daily Advertiser* published in 1808.

The front page of the October 12, 1808, edition carried the report of the Madrid uprising on all of its three columns, adding only a brief notice of its publication schedule (Wednesdays and Saturdays), subscription rates ($8 a year, half payable in advance), and language policy ("in both languages or in the one wanted"), and a bilingual advertisement for Don Juan Rodríguez, Abogado (lawyer), with the Spanish version on top of an English translation of the same message. Rodríguez took the advertising space "to inform his friends and the public in general that from this date he will reside at his plantation, better than a league below the city," but added that he would "still continue to keep his office in town, in the house of Doctor Deveze, No. 16 Main Street, where he will execute any business in the line of his profession from ten o'clock a.m. till four p.m."

Inside the paper, the second page offered the report "of a correspondent" on the problem of separating facts from the official news, private reports, and rumors emanating from war-torn Europe. *El Misisipí* summarized what its editors felt was the latest factual information, naming the *Bayonne Gazette* as their source and calling that periodical "an official organ of the usurpers of the thrones of France and Spain." The newspaper then engaged in some of its own interpretation of the news:

> Madrid has long been in the possession of the French and the patriots of Spain are not to be duped by the mockeries of Bonaparte, however solemnized by a recreant minister of religion.

Citing victories against the French in Spain and Portugal, *El Misisipí* continued:

> We think therefore that nothing has yet appeared to discourage the friends of freedom. To hold their own ground is much for the patriots at the commencement of the struggle. Their armies will increase and improve in a far greater degree than those of the enemy.

The fourth page was devoted entirely to advertising, almost all in a bilingual format in which the Spanish copy ran in a space above the English text. Everything from ships to hardwood to supplies for sailors was advertised in the bilingual format. The advertising revealed something of the commerce and trade taking place in the sea and river port of New Orleans, which had been acquired by the United States from France only five years earlier and had briefly been part of the Spanish empire. One company, A. & J. M'Ilvain, Grocers, No. 43, on the Levee, offered sugar, coffee, tea, and a "general assortment of groceries" along with "2500 lbs. James River Chewing Tobacco, 1000 bushels Indian Corn, 2000 feet Walnut plank." The firm advised ships' captains preparing to sail, "SEA STORES Put up at the shortest notice." Another advertisement advised readers that "five or six gentlemen may be accommodated with Genteel Boarding in a private family, at the rate of 20 Dollars per month."

The largest advertisements, taking up nearly all of the second and third columns, were for Mrs. Zacharie, who offered "a handsome assortment of DRY GOODS" and *La Rionda*, apparently a dealer offering for sale two brigantines, the Sophia and the Minerve, both "with all her tackle," two houses on St. Phillip Street, and a long list of goods such as 800 tons of Campeachy Logwood, 40 bales of sarsaparilla, and 22 trunks of "Callicoes."[8]

Even though it was the first Latino newspaper in the United States, *El Misisipí* exhibited many of the characteristics that were to be found in the other Latino publications that were to follow it. For one, it was apparently directed toward a Spanish-speaking audience that had come to the United States because of warfare and political turmoil in their homeland, a consistent theme in immigration from Latin America and the Caribbean. Second, it was bilingual, recognizing the importance of both the English and Spanish languages to the Latino community. Third, its news content was heavily influenced by events elsewhere, just much of the content of Latino media over the years has been dependent on news from Latin America. And, fourth, like many of the Latino publications that were to follow, it apparently was operated as a business venture, devoting one-fourth of its space to advertising in both Spanish and English.

The First Black Newspaper: *Freedom's Journal* (1827)

A different kind of crisis triggered the founding of *Freedom's Journal* on March 16, 1827, by the Rev. Samuel E. Cornish and John Brown Russwurm. The crisis was slavery, which kept Blacks as property in much of the United States. White abolitionists favored the ending of slavery and had campaigned against it in the press, printing accounts of slavery written by freed Black slaves. After an attack on the abolitionists and Black leaders in the *New York Enquirer*, Cornish and Russwurm (who was the first Black person to graduate from a college in the United States) decided it was time for Blacks to start their own weekly newspaper. In the first edition of the four-page newspaper, the editors eloquently stated their reasons for starting the first Black newspaper:

> We wish to plead our own cause. Too long have others spoken for us. Too long has the public been deceived by misrepresentation in things which concern us dearly, though in the estimation of some mere trifles; for although there are many in society who exercise toward us benevolent feelings, still (with some sorrow we confess it) there are others who enlarge upon that which tends to discredit any person of color.[9]

Freedom's Journal is often described as an aggressive newspaper that agitated forcefully against slavery and for the rights of free Blacks in the North. But the newspaper was not just an abolitionist or Black civil rights periodical. It also built a sense of Black consciousness and community identity among Blacks throughout the United States. It was able to do this because the newspaper reflected the broad interests of Blacks, some of which continue to the present time. In addition to news and hard-hitting editorials, the newspaper offered information, features, culture, and entertainment to its Black readers. Its first issue reflected the broad interests of its editors and readers, carrying news from Haiti and Sierra Leone; the first part of a serial on Captain Paul Cuffee, a Black Boston shipper; a poem entitled "The African Chief"; and advertising for the B. F. Hughes School of Colored Children of Both Sexes. Throughout its years *Freedom's Journal* ran regular columns entitled "Foreign News," "Domestic News," and "Summary." These columns, which were based on news taken from other newspapers, were highly sensational. The "Summary" column was especially noted for its exploitation of the staples of sensational reporting: blood and sex.[10]

However, the newspaper was virulent in its opposition to slavery and in its advocacy of the rights of freed Blacks. Its editors also did not hesitate to attack the mainstream media in order to reinforce the importance of the alternative viewpoint that *Freedom's Journal* presented on these issues. Walter C. Daniel wrote of *Freedom's Journal* in his guide to the Black press:

> The editor of the *New York Enquirer* was attacked in a subsequent issue as one "whose object is to keep alive the prejudice of the whites against the coloured communities of New York City." Other articles disagreed with the platform of the American Colonization

FREEDOM'S JOURNAL.

" RIGHTEOUSNESS EXALTETH A NATION."

CORNISH & RUSSWURM, Editors & Proprietors | NEW-YORK, FRIDAY. MARCH 30, 1827. | [VOL. I. No. 3.

MEMOIRS OF CAPT. PAUL CUFFEE.

Being now master of a small covered boat of about 12 tons burthen, he hired a person to assist as a seaman, and made many advantageous voyages to different parts of the state of Connecticut and when about 25 years old married a native of the country, a descendant of the tribe to which his mother belonged.—For some time after his marriage he attended chiefly to his agricultural concerns, but from an increase of family he at length deemed it necessary to pursue his commercial plans more extensively than he had before done.—He arranged his affairs for a new expedition and hired a small house on West-Port river to which he removed his family. A boat of 18 tons was now procured in which he sailed to the banks of St. George in quest of Codfish and returned home with a valuable cargo. This important adventure was the foundation of an extensive & profitable fishing establishment from Westport river, which continued for a considerable time and was the source of an honest and comfortable living to many of the inhabitants of that district.

At this period Paul formed a connexion with his brother-in law Michael Warner, who had several sons well qualified for the sea service, four of whom have since laudably filled responsible situations as Captains and first mates. A vessel of 25 tons was built, and in two voyages to the Straits of Belisle and Newfoundland he met with such success as enabled him, in conjunction with another person, to build another vessel of 41 tons burthen in which he made several profitable voyages. Paul had experienced too many disadvantages of his very limited education, and he resolved, as far as it was practicable, to relieve his children from similar embarrassments. The neighborhood had neither a tutor nor a school-house. Many of the citizens were desirous that a school-house should be erected. About 1797 Paul proposed a meeting of the inhabitants for the purpose of making such arrangements as should accomplish the desired object. The collision of opinion respecting mode and place occasioned the meeting to separate without coming to a conclusion; several meetings of the same nature were held, but all were unsuccessful in their issue. Perceiving that all efforts to procure a union of sentiment were fruitless, Paul set himself to work in earnest and had a suitable house built on his own ground, which he freely gave up to the use of the public, and the school was open to all who pleased to send their children. How gratifying to humanity is this anecdote! and who that justly appreciates the human character would not prefer Paul Cuffee, the offspring of an African slave, to the proudest statesman, that ever dealt out destruction among mankind?—About this time Paul proceeded on a whaling voyage to the straits of Belisle, where he found four other vessels completely equipped with boats and harpoons, for catching whales. Paul discovered that he had not made proper preparations for the business, having only ten hands on board and two boats one of which was old and almost useless. When the masters of the other vessels found his situation they withdrew from the customary practice of such voyages and refused to mate with his crew. In this emergency, Paul resolved to prosecute his undertaking alone till at length two other masters thought it most prudent to accede to the usual practices as they apprehended his crew, by their ignorance might alarm and drive the whales from their reach and thus defeat their voyage. During the season they took seven whales: the circumstance which had taken place roused the ambition of Paul, and his crew they were diligent and enterprising and had the honor of killing six of the seven whales; two of these fell by Paul's own hands.

(To be Continued.)

PEOPLE OF COLOUR.

I have had three objects in view in thus going into the examination of the nature of slavery as a legal institution. In the first place I wish it to appear that the relation between the master and slave is a proper subject of legislation. It is a conventional right and depends entirely upon the laws.—as the laws create it they may modify, enlarge, restrain, or destroy it, without any other limitation than is imposed by the general good. It is not so much a right of property, as it is a legal relation; and it ought to be treated as such.

The second object was, to relieve slave-holders from a charge, or an apprehension of criminality, where in fact, there is no offence. There can be no palliation for the conduct of those who first brought the curse of slavery upon poor Africa, and poor America too.—But the body of the present generation are not liable to this charge. Posterity are not answerable for the sins of their fathers, unless they approve, their deeds. They found the blacks among them, in a degraded state, incapable either of appreciating or enjoying liberty. They have, therefore, nothing to answer for on this score, because they have no other alternative, *at present*, but to keep them in subjection. There is nothing so de-[illegible] by our principles, to the acknowledgment of guilt, in that which we at the same time believe to be absolutely unavoidable, and in which therefore, it is impossible really to feel self-reproach. Our southern brethren have high ideas of liberty.

There is nothing so calculated to make men restive under command, as a habit and love of commanding others. Upon their own principles, they have been forced to acknowledge even the existence of slavery, in any shape, as criminal. They have therefore concluded that as heavy a curse hung over the present generation for continuing slavery, even when it is plainly unavoidable, as over the last for introducing it. The consequence has been, that those who seriously bewailed the evil, have folded their arms in despair; and those who regarded only their own gratification, expecting to bear the curse at any rate, have taken the desperate resolution, "Let us eat and drink, for to-morrow we die." But the principle is preposterous, and the conclusion incorrect. A Christian may hold slaves, and exact their services, without any occasion to feel a pang of self-reproach *merely on account* of his holding slaves.

The third object aimed at, was to fasten the charge of criminality on the very spot where such a charge will be; and where it ought to be felt; and where alone reformation is practicable. There are no duties, without corresponding rights, and no rights without corresponding duties. While it is the duty of the slave to submit himself to his own master, so long as the laws of his country make him a slave, it is his right to be protected, *by the laws* in the enjoyment of life, health, chastity, good name, and every blessing which he can enjoy consistently with the public welfare.—And on the other hand, masters and legislators should feel, that subjection itself, in the best circumstances, is a sufficient calamity; and that the yoke ought to be made as light as possible. Christianity enforces this dictate of sound reason.* "Thou shalt love thy neighbor as thyself," is as much the law between master and slave, as between any other members of the human family. This is so obvious, as to appear almost like a truism. And yet this is the very thing that has always been lost sight of, among slave-holders. It has been wholly disregarded, in our own nation. Here is the point to be debated, and settled. This is the ground for fastening the charge upon our whole nation. The law of God requires that all the provision should be made *by law* which the public welfare will admit, for the protection and improvement of colored subjects, as well as white subjects. *And this has not been done.* We cannot free ourselves from this charge by pointing to the comfortable mud or even *brick* cabins, the warm jackets and shoes and the abundance of corn and salt with which the slaves are furnished.—We are travelling out of the record, by comparing their situation as regards food and lodging, labour and health, with that of the labouring peasantry in the old despotisms of Europe. We do not answer to this indictment, unless we either plead guilty, or show that our *laws*, our customs our modes of thinking and acting, recognize the humanity of the blacks'. We must show that their rights are acknowledged, their protection secured, their welfare promoted: and that, in every particular, excepting that of involuntary servitude and its necessary attendants, the stand upon the same ground with their masters.—When this is done' we shall feel no guilt on the subject. We shall fear no divine vengeance. We may hope to enjoy the favor of our merciful heavenly Father. But this is not done. I think I may venture to assert, that most of the slave-holding states, neither the laws, nor public opinion, secure to the slaves any of the privileges of humanity. Nothing more is done for them, in *kind*, than is done for the domestic beasts; and nothing more in *degree*, except as they are a more valuable species of property, and are recognised, to some extent, as possessing rational faculties. Let the contrary be shown. I say that of all that kind of provision, which goes to purify and elevate the character, and to create in the subject affection and confidence towards the government, every trace and track is completely excluded. The culture of their minds, the preservation of their morals, their instruction in the only religion which can make them good servants, happy neighbors, and hopeful heirs of eternal life, every thing of the kind is guarded against, by the *laws* at least, even more studiously than the abuse of their persons, and the destruction of their lives. Whatever is attempted for their improvement, is done by individual effort, and in direct violation of the laws. Here is our guilt; our full, dark, unmitigated guilt. It is the guilt of our nation. We in the non-slave holding states, do not feel it as we ought. But we cannot wash our hands, until we can safely declare, that we have done every thing we can, by public and private efforts, to remove the injustice. We have not done this. Comparatively speaking nothing has been done. The Colonization Society has indeed made a beginning, and done as well as could be expected. But I ask how long it will probably be, before that institution can dispose of 30,000 blacks in a year, which is only the *present* annual increase? Until they can do this, the number must be continually increasing. Indeed, I do not believe our southern brethren, in general, intend to do any thing more than to provide a sort of *safety valve*, by this Society, to serve as an outlet for their free blacks and supernumeraries. In our country, acts of the legislature are to be taken as to the expression of the public feeling, on all great subjects.—Towards the blacks, the language of each successive legislature has been, "Our fathers made your yoke heavy, but we will add thereto; our fathers chastised you with whips but we will chastise you with scorpions." Something must be done, to avert the fearful consequences.

We cannot expect any *efficient* measures to be adopted spontaneously in the slave holding states. The natural effects of slavery, upon the morals, industry, population, strength, and elevation of character, of a state, are so destructive, and it produces so much vexation, trouble and danger; the necessity of it is so very questionable; and its advantages are so trifling, compared with its evils, that we should naturally expect that those who are embarrassed with it would be solicitous about nothing else, than how to be delivered from the curse. But it is not so. The people are so wedded to their habits, and so fond of exercising unlimited power, and so many of their comforts seem to depend upon slavery, that we cease to wonder, at not finding any thing done by them towards improvement. I quote the language of Mr. Clarkson, the great friend of the blacks. "Their *prejudices* against the slaves are too great to allow them to become either impartial or willing actors in the case. The term *slave* being synonimous according to their estimation and usage, with the term *brute*, they have fixed a stigma upon their blacks, such as we who live in Europe could not have conceived, unless we had irrefragable evidence upon the point.—What evils has not this cruel association of terms produced? The West Indian master looks down upon his slave with disdain. He hates the sight of his features, and of his color; nay, he marks with distinctive opprobrium the very blood in his veins, attaching different names, of more or less infamy to those who have it in them, according to the quantity which they have of it in consequence of their pedigree, or of their greater or less degree of consanguinity with the whites.—Hence the West Indian feels an unwillingness to elevate the condition of the black, or to do any thing for him as a human being. I have no doubt, that this prejudice has been one of the great causes why the improvement of our slave population *by law* has been so long retarded; and that the same prejudice will continue to have a similar operation, so long as it shall continue to exist. Not that there are wanting men of humanity among our West Indian legislators. Their humanity is discernable enough when it is to be applied to the *whites*; but such is the system of slavery, and the degradation attached to slavery, that their humanity seems to be lost or gone, when it is to be applied to the *blacks*. Not again that there are wanting men of sense among the same body. They are shrewd and clever enough in the affairs of life, where they maintain an intercourse with the *whites*; but in their intercourse with the *blacks* their sense appears to be shrivelled and not of its ordinary size. Look at the laws of their own making, as far as the blacks are concerned, and they are a collection of any thing but—wisdom."† If these remarks are not applicable to the slave laws of our own states, let the contrary be shown.

* See Ep. vi. 5, 9. Col. iii. 22 iv. 1.

† "Thoughts on the necessity of improving the condition of the slaves, &c. with a view to their ultimate emancipation," p. 10, 11.

(To be Continued.)

CURE FOR DRUNKENNESS.

In speaking, on a former occasion, of the remedy for Intemperance proposed by Dr. Chambers of this city we expressed ourselves with a considerable degree of caution. As it is a subject of great importance to the community, and one on which they ought to be explicitly and accurately informed, we have within the past week spent more than one whole day in making a personal investigation into cases where the remedy has been applied, and into the nature of the medicine, in the hope of coming to a full and satisfactory conclusion. The result of our enquiries will be seen in the sequel.—*N. Y. Obs.*

The remedy is not the same with that proposed by Dr. Loiseau of New-Orleans: or if it is, the coincidence is unknown to Dr. Chambers. They have had no manner of intercourse on the subject, and are entire strangers to each other. Dr. C. has been in possession of the secret, in its essential principles, for a number of years.

The medicine is taken in liquor:—that of which the patient is most fond, is usually preferred. It is not unpleasant to the taste, as we have ascertained from those who have taken it, and still more accurately, from having tasted it ourselves.

In its operation it is powerful, but not dangerous. It usually operates as a cathartic, and also as an emetic; but not always in both respects. In all cases nausea is produced.

There are three modifications of the medicine; adapted to the peculiar habits of the patient and inveteracy of the disease. Of course it is important, in making application for persons at a distance, to state these particulars as definitely as possible. In the mildest form, we are told by Dr. C. that it fails of curing in about four cases out of twenty. Resort is then had to the other modifications.

In almost every instance, more than one dose is necessary. The greatest number of doses which have been taken in any case which we have examined, is seven or eight. The cure is generally complete in the course of a single week.

Before being mingled with the liquor in which it is to be taken, the medicine subsists in two forms—as a liquid and as a powder. The former is of a red color, the latter of a light brown, in this form it can be forwarded through the PostOffice, in letters containing the proper directions.

Dr. C. has had the generosity to offer it to the poor of this city who are unable to make any compensation, gratis. To others the price is not extravagant considering the nature of the remedy, and is varied in some measure according to the circumstances of the individual.

It has already been applied in a large number of cases; in only two of which so far as known to Dr. C. has it failed of effecting a cure, unless prematurely relinquished.

We have conversed with two respectable gentlemen, entirely disinterested, which have had opportunity to witness its effects on a large number of individuals, and it is their decided opinion that it is a real remedy.

Several persons of good standing in society

Freedom's Journal (1827), the first Black newspaper in the United States, carried news of general interest to Blacks, as well as strident opposition to slavery and calls to protect the rights of free Blacks in the northern states. (Journalism History)

Society which advocated returning Afro-Americans to Africa and reported on lynching. Russwurm believed in universal education as a critical need for Blacks who would be respected by White Americans.[11]

Russwurm left the newspaper in 1828 to become an editor and official in Liberia, a part of Africa that the abolitionist movement had established to return freed slaves to Africa. The newspaper continued to be published by Cornish under the title *Rights of All* until it apparently folded in 1829. In a 1977 article, Lionel C. Barrow, Jr., noted the important role of *Freedom's Journal* in establishing an important precedent as an alternative to the mainstream press. The article closed with the following passage:

> *Freedom's Journal* gave Blacks a voice of their own and an opportunity not only to answer the attacks printed in the White press but to read articles on Black accomplishments, marriages, deaths that the White press of the day ignored. Slavery is no longer here, but its vestiges are and today's reporters and publishers—Black and White—could do well to study the *Journal*, adopt its objectives and emulate its content. Blacks still need to "plead our own causes," and will need to do so for sometime to come.[12]

Like many of the Black and other minority newspapers that were to follow it, *Freedom's Journal* filled an important void. It did more than take issue with the coverage and editorial positions that were found in the White press and present an alternative to them. It also reported events of interest to Blacks with dignity and pride, demonstrating that its Black readers, though victims of racism, had a broader range of activities and interests than the mainstream press of the era presented. Over the years the Black press has continued to fulfill this dual role for its readers. On one side, it has raised the concerns and protests of Blacks when confronted with slavery, segregation, and discrimination. On the other, it has reported on the organizational, social, religious, and other activities and interests within the Black communities that have too often been ignored by the White media.

The First Native American Newspaper: *Cherokee Phoenix* (1828)

Like the first Latino and Black newspapers, the first Native American newspaper was born of a crisis, in this case the federal

CHEROKEE  PHŒNIX.

VOL. I. NEW ECHOTA, THURSDAY MARCH 13, 1828. NO. 4.

EDITED BY ELIAS BOUDINOTT.
PRINTED WEEKLY BY
ISAAC H. HARRIS,
FOR THE CHEROKEE NATION.

At $2 50 if paid in advance, $3 in six months, or $3 50 if paid at the end of the year.

To subscribers who can read only the Cherokee language the price will be $2,00 in advance, or $2,50 to be paid within the year.

Every subscription will be considered as continued unless subscribers give notice to the contrary before the commencement of a new year.

The Phœnix will be printed on a Super-Royal sheet, with type entirely new procured for the purpose. Any person procuring six subscribers, and becoming responsible for the payment, shall receive a seventh gratis.

Advertisements will be inserted at seventy-five cents per square for the first insertion, and thirty-seven and a half cents for each continuance; longer ones in proportion.

☞All letters addressed to the Editor, post paid, will receive due attention.

CHEROKEE LAWS.

The following laws of the Cherokee Nation we publish as we find them in print, [illegible], except what we suppose may be typographical errors. They have already been circulated in this Nation in a pamphlet form.—Our readers at a distance will perhaps be gratified to see the first commencement of written laws among the Cherokees. We publish some that are not now in force. The repealing laws will appear in the order of time they were passed.

LAWS.

Resolved by the Chiefs and Warriors in a national council assembled. That it shall be, and is hereby authorized, for regulating parties to be organized to consist of six men in each company; one captain, one lieutenant and four privates, to continue in service for the term of one year, whose duties it shall be to suppress horse stealing and the robbery of other property within their respective bounds, who shall be paid out of the national annuity, at the rates of fifty dollars to each captain, forty to the lieutenant, and thirty dollars to each of the privates and to give their protection to children as heirs to their fathers' property, and to the widow's share whom he may have had children by, or cohabited with, as his wife, at the time of his decease; and in case a father shall leave or will any property to a child at the time of his decease which he may have had by another woman, then, his present wife shall be entitled to receive any such property as may be left by him or them, when substantiated by one or two disinterested witnesses.

Be it resolved by the Council aforesaid, When any person or persons which may or shall be charged with stealing a horse and upon conviction by one or two witnesses, he, she or they shall be punished with one hundred stripes on the bare back, and the

Be it known, That this day, the various clans or tribes which compose the Cherokee Nation, have unanimously passed an act of oblivion for all lives for which they may have been indebted, one to the other, and have mutually agreed that after this evening the aforesaid act shall become binding upon every clan, or tribe; and the aforesaid clans or tribes have also agreed that if in future, any life should be lost without malice intended, the innocent aggressor shall not be accounted guilty.

Be it known also, That should it so happen that a brother, forgetting his natural affection, should raise his hand in anger and kill his brother, he shall be accounted guilty of murder and suffer accordingly. And if a man has a horse stolen, and overtakes the thief, and should his anger be so great as to cause him to kill him, let his blood remain on his own conscience, but no satisfaction shall be demanded for his life from his relatives or the clan he may belong to.

By order of the seven clans.
TURTLE AT HOME,
Speaker of Council.

Approved.
BLACK FOX, Principal Chief.
PATH KILLER, Sec'd.
TOOCHALAR.

CHARLES HICKS, Sec'y to the Council.
Oostanallah, April 10, 1810.

WHEREAS, fifty-four towns and villages having convened in order to deliberate and consider on the situation of our nation, in the disposition of our common property of lands without the unanimous consent of the members of the Council, and in order to obviate the evil consequences resulting in such course, we have unanimously adopted the following form for the future government of our nation.

ARTICLE 1st. It is unanimously agreed, that there shall be thirteen members elected as a Standing Committee for the term of two years, at the end of which term they shall be either re-elected or others; and in consequence of the death or resignation of any of said Committee, our head Chiefs shall elect another to fill the vacancy.

ARTICLE 2d. The affairs of the Cherokee Nation shall be committed to the care of the Standing Committee: but the acts of this body shall not be binding on the Nation in our common property, without the unanimous consent of the members and Chiefs of the Council, which they shall present for their acceptance or dissent.

ARTICLE 3d. The authority and claim of our common property shall cease with the person or persons who shall think proper to remove themselves without the limits of the Cherokee Nation.

ARTICLE 4th. The improvements and labors of our people by the mother's side shall be inviolate during the time of their occupancy.

ARTICLE 5th. This Committee shall settle with the Agency for our annual stipend, and report their proceedings to the members and Chiefs in council; but the friendly communication between our head Chiefs and the Agency shall remain free and open.

ARTICLE 6th. The above articles for our government, may be amended at our electional term, and the Committee is hereby required to be governed by the above articles, and the Chiefs and Warriors in Council

1817.

SCANDAL.

'There are people,' continued the corporal, 'who can't even breathe, without slandering a neighbor.'

'You judge too severely,' replied my aunt Prudy, 'no one is slandered who does not deserve it.'

'That may be,' retorted the corporal, 'but I have heard very slight things said of you.'

The face of my aunt kindled with anger. '*Me!*' she exclaimed, '*me!*—slight things of me! what can any body say of me?'

'They say,' answered the corporal gravely, and drawing his words to keep her in suspense, 'that—that you are no better than you ought to be.'

Fury flashed from the eyes of my aunt,

'Who are the wretches?'

'I hope they slander no one who does not deserve it,' remarked the corporal jeeringly, as he left the room.

The feelings of my aunt may well be conceived. She was sensibly injured. True she had her foibles.—She was peevish and fretful. But she was rigidly moral and virtuous.—The purest ice was not more chaste. The Pope himself could not boast more piety. Conscious of the correctness of her conduct, she was wounded at the remark of the corporal. Why should her neighbors slander her? She could not conjecture.

Let my aunt be consoled. A person who can live in this world without suffering slander, must be too stupid or insignificant to claim attention.

Cannibalism.—Extract of a letter from Messrs. Tyerman and Bennett, to Mr. Loomis, of the Sandwhich Island mission, dated Canton, Nov. 1825:

"We touched at New Zealand; and owing to the imprudence of our captain, the natives rose upon us, took us, and our vessel—and both were in their hands about an hour and a half. They stood over us with uplifted axes and weapons of destruction, as if waiting till some signal should be given;—and we expected every moment to be our last, and to be eaten as soon as killed.

The Cherokee Phoenix **(1828) carried articles in both English and the Cherokee syllabary developed by Sequoyah. (Journalism History)**

government's efforts to displace the Cherokee Nation from the millions of acres of lands it held in North Carolina, Georgia, and Tennessee. It was because of this crisis that the first Native American newspaper, the *Cherokee Phoenix*, was born to unify and express the opinion of the Cherokee people.[13]

The *Cherokee Phoenix* was established by the Cherokee Nation near the current site of Calhoun, Georgia, and printed its first edition on February 21, 1828. It appeared weekly, with a few gaps, for six years until 1834, when it folded. Like *El Misisipí* it was printed in a bilingual format, making use of both English and the 86-character Cherokee alphabet that had been introduced by Sequoyah (also known as George Gist) after 12 years of work in 1821. James and Sharon Murphy write that the newspaper was started out of two needs: the desire of missionaries to use print media to spread Christianity among the Cherokees and the desire of the leaders of the Cherokee Nation to unify Cherokees and others in support of the fight to keep their homelands.[14]

The first editor of the *Cherokee Phoenix* was Cherokee schoolteacher Elias Boudinot, who also was clerk of the Cherokee National Council. To raise funds for the new newspaper, he traveled along the East Coast speaking to philanthropic and religious groups. Financial support for the newspaper came both from Cherokee tribal leaders, who allocated $1500 to help purchase a press and type before Boudinet began his fund-raising trip, and from the American Board of Commissioners for Foreign Missions in New England, which helped support the casting of Sequoyah's alphabet into metal type. The missionary funds were requested by Samuel Worcester, a missionary among the Cherokees, who encouraged Boudinot's effort to start the first Native American newspaper. The Cherokees later repaid the missions board for its help.

Boudinot's vision, like that of the editors of *Freedom's Journal*, was of a newspaper that would accurately reflect the lives of his people and help mobilize public opinion in support of their struggle. In an 1826 speech entitled "Address to Whites" presented at the First Presbyterian Church in Philadelphia, he outlined the goals of the new newspaper as

> comprising a summary of religious and political events, etc., on the one hand; and on the other, exhibiting the feelings, dispositions, improvements, and prospects of the Indians: their traditions, their true character, as it once was, as it now is, and the ways and means

most likely to throw the mantle of civilization over all tribes; and such other matters as will tend to diffuse proper and correct impressions in regard to their condition—such a paper could not fail to create much interest in the American Community, favorable to the aborigines, and to have a powerful influence on the advancement of the Indians themselves.[15]

In its first issue the newspaper reprinted its prospectus, prepared by Worcester, which promised that in addition to local news the *Cherokee Phoenix* would report Cherokee laws and customs; cover their progress in education, religion, and culture; print news about other tribes; and include "interesting articles calculated to promote Literature, Civilization, and Religion among the Cherokees."[16] Subscriptions came from as far away as Germany and the newspaper was circulated widely among the Cherokees, although sometimes only one copy was allocated for each village. In the fourth issue the newspaper carried the first written laws of the Cherokees, with Boudinot's comments that he hoped "our readers will perhaps be gratified to see the first commencement of written laws among the Cherokees."[17] Although the newspaper printed articles in both languages, it was only on rare occasions that the same article was published in both. There were generally three columns in English for every two in Cherokee, since the structure of Sequoyah's alphabet devised characters for whole syllables and it took less space to write in Cherokee than in English.

Boudinot has been credited with building the *Cherokee Phoenix* "into a strong and loud voice of the Cherokee people as they struggled against increasingly insurmountable government opposition."[18] His voice was not always strident. In the first issue he promised the paper "will not return railing for railing, but consult mildness." But he made it clear that the newspaper would advocate the Cherokee position on those issues that brought them into conflict with the encroaching Whites and their governments. In the first issue he wrote:

In regard the controversy with Georgia, and the present policy of the Central Government, in removing, and concentrating the Indians, out of the limits of any state, which, by the way, appears to be gaining strength, we will invariably and faithfully state the feelings of the majority of our people. Our views, as a people, on this subject, have been most sadly misrepresented. These views we do not wish to conceal, but are willing that the public should know what we think of this policy, which, in our opinion, if carried into effect, will prove pernicious to us.

At the end of the column he explained how he chose the name Phoenix for the newspaper and looked forward to a time when all tribes would rise up and put an end to both the physical oppression and negative language to which they had been subjected. He wrote:

> We would now commit our feeble efforts to the good will and indulgence of the public, praying that God will attend them with his blessings, and hoping for that happy period, when all the Indian tribes of America shall rise, Phoenix like, from their ashes, and when the terms "Indian depredation," "war whoop," "scalping knife" and the like, shall become obsolete, and for ever be "buried deep underground."[19]

As Murphy and Murphy point out, in subsequent issues Boudinot used the press to protest attempts by the state of Georgia to include the Cherokee Nation within its criminal laws and fought against federal appropriations to remove the Cherokees from their mineral-laden lands. But, as with *Freedom's Journal*, it is unfair to describe the *Cherokee Phoenix* as a newspaper that was concerned solely with the struggles confronting the Cherokees. The newspaper also carried advertising for merchants, a boarding school, and other businesses catering to the needs of its readers. The newspaper also campaigned against alcoholism among the Cherokees and the slavery in which Blacks were held, even though Cherokee law permitted the owning of slaves and had other provisions discriminating against Black slaves. The newspaper also ran advertisements by owners of runaway slaves and occasionally ran anecdotes in Black dialect.[20]

A year after it was founded the newspaper enlarged its title to become the *Cherokee Phoenix and Indian Advocate*, indicating its activist role in Native American struggles. Over the years the editor and staff continued to protest encroachment of Cherokee legal and civil rights by Whites, including the harassment, arrests, and threats directed toward the newspaper's staff by Georgia officials. As the Cherokees came under intense pressure to move from their ancestral lands, the leaders of the nation itself became divided on the issue. Boudinot resigned the editorship in 1832, after he had been ordered by Cherokee Principal Chief John

Ross not to publish reports of the division among the leaders. The new editor was Ross's brother-in-law, John Hicks, who continued to fight against the land grabbing and harassment confronting the Cherokees. But the newspaper appeared less regularly and finally ceased publication on May 31, 1834.

The *Cherokee Phoenix*, like the other Native American newspapers that were to follow it, found the bilingual format to be an effective way of communicating with both its Native American and immigrant audience. Although the bilingual format is diminishing among Native American newspapers today, it remained a characteristic of Native American publications for a number of years. Like the *Cherokee Phoenix* many of the newspapers that followed devoted the majority of their space to news of specific interest to Native Americans, with less attention to national and international events without a specific impact on the Native American population. And, like the *Cherokee Phoenix*, those Native American newspapers that appear to have had the greatest success have been those that are affiliated with and receive a portion of their financial support from a specific tribe.

The First Asian American Newspaper: the *Golden Hills' News* (1851?)

Although journalism historians point with certainty to *Freedom's Journal* as the first Black newspaper, *Cherokee Phoenix* as the first Native American newspaper, and (with near certainty) *El Misisipí* as the first Latino newspaper, it is with less confidence that the first Asian American newspaper is identified in this book.[21] There is little doubt that travelers and settlers from Asia were in the territories that now make up the United States for a long time before what appears to be the first newspaper appeared. There are documented, though disputed, reports of Hui Shên, a Chinese Buddhist priest, sailing down the coast of what is now California following his arrival in what is now British Columbia, Canada, in 458 A.D., about a thousand years before Christopher Columbus first landed in the Americas. Spanish explorers on the California coast in 1774 reported finding the wreck of a ship of what is believed to be of Asian construction. People from Asia have been reported in the United States since at least 1785, when several Chinese sailors became stranded in Baltimore. The first enumeration of Chinese by the United States census was in 1820.[22]

But it was the need for cheap, hard-working labor in California, both before and during the Gold Rush, that brought the first in a series of waves of immigration from Asian countries to the United States. The *Alta California*, a leading English-language newspaper in San Francisco, made what one scholar has called "editorial humor" of the Chinese, including its own "Chinese letters" to ridicule Chinese literature. On a more serious and commercially lucrative side, English-language newspapers made use of lithography to insert Chinese characters into advertisements and in reports on the inscriptions on Chinese graves.[23] It is in the time, place, and context of the 1849 California Gold Rush that what is apparently the first Asian American newspaper is found.

Although there is some disagreement about the date of its founding, the first reported Asian American newspaper in the United States appears to have been a Chinese-language newspaper, *Kim-Shan Jit San-Luk*, the *Golden Hills' News*, reported as beginning publication in San Francisco as early as 1851 and being printed on an irregular schedule. The newspaper took its title from the phrase "golden hills," which was used by Chinese workers coming to the California during the Gold Rush, and was a religious publication. Another early newspaper, the *Oriental*, is reported as having begun publication as a weekly in 1853, also with a religious slant. These founding dates were cited in a 1939 federal report on the history of foreign journalism in San Francisco,[24] but pioneer California editor Edward Kemble cited a founding date of 1854 for the *Golden Hills' News* and 1855 for the *Oriental* in his history of California newspapers written in 1858.[25]

But whatever its starting date, the *Golden Hills' News*, like the racial minority newspapers that preceded it, was born in crisis. In this case it was the trauma faced by Chinese workers as they left their homeland, crossed an ocean, and came to the United States with hopes of making their fortune in the gold fields of California. Instead, they not only found a country that was vastly different than their own in language and culture, but often learned that they would have to do the hardest labor at little or no wage to repay the cost of their passage. Perhaps worst of all, they found themselves treated as outcasts in a state newly populated by immigrants, subject to legal, economic, and social discrimination in a strange land. Both the *Golden Hills' News* and the *Oriental* had their foun-

THE GOLDEN HILLS' NEWS

金山日新錄

The golden Hills' News.

SAN FRANCISCO, Saturday [illegible] 27, 1854.

The Chinese Exodus.

The people of San Francisco are a great people —great in the rapidity of their growth, great in the aspect of enterprise and determination, which their cities, villages and Institutions present, and in the original characteristics of their inhabitants. They are great by origin—they have no origin—they are **sui generis**—they are a comminglement based on Liberty, which fuses all into **oneness**. They are great by their love of freedom. They hold no seven by nine creed, which, like that of some of the Press, would cry privelege for themselves and despotism for others. They are great in their "Constitution," which declares, that all men are free and equal. The people and escutchon of California are things to rejoice over—they are DEMOCRACY.

But the California picture is **unique**—their **tout ensemble** is the history of Civilization. The "Eastern States" have their Irish exodus, their German exodus, and hordes of Saxons, Danes, Celts, Gauls and Scandinavians, but we have **all** these, and the most wonderfull of all a CHINESE EXODUS! The great wonder of the century is the astonishing flight of the hitherto immobile Chinamen across the Pacific ocean, to seek refuge and liberty in the bosom of "The Golden Hills". It actually tickles the fancy to even think of Chinamen quitting the celestial empire—the paradise of earth—the garden of green Hyson—the Flowery Land, beyond which was supposed to lay outer darkness, and to come and mingle [illegible] for yellow gold, instead of at home to fight and struggle for the "yellow [illegible] of office".

Yes, John Chinaman disregarding the threats of the bastinado, and the tortures said to await his return to the "Flowery abode", for having forsaken the habits of his forefathers, joins the tide of Progress, and the Rubicon once passed, where sl all his exodus end! The days of Chinese exclusion, small feet, and stand-still-ism, are ending–Chinese are no longer **rare avis in terris**—to see them is no longer to see "the Elephant". They are fast assisting to colonize California and various islands in Polynesia.

Statistics show. that the principle emigration of the Chinese is from the Canton river, and the rising port of Shanghai. The reverends Charles Taylor and M. P. Yates, both Missionaries at Shanghai, say that the latter port is thrown open, without restriction to the Foreigner, that Americans wander unmolested 40 miles into the interior, and that the Natives instead of calling Americans "outside barbarians," look up to them with profound respect. No Chinaman sneers at you in the streets; there is no hindrance whatever to your study of their character and habits; they always look at you with an expression of good will," says Bayard Taylor. Is it too much to ask of a Christian population "to do unto them," at least, what it seems "they do to us," in their own land! Is it too much to ask of this Cosmopolitan state, in the veins of whose population flows the blood of a thousand tribes, to give freedom of growth and fair play to the Mongol element! Is it too much to ask of a Commercial People to give a generous aid and liberal encouragement to any means, that assist the Chinese to a knowledge of our laws and habits, and a sympathy with our interests! Surely not. Therefore Merchants, Manufacturers, Miners and Agriculturists, come forward as friends, not scorners of the Chinese, so that they may mingle in the march of the world, and help to open for America an endless vista of future commerce.

Published by HOWARD & HUDSON,
163 Clay St., betw Montgomery & Kearny.

Printed by F. KUHL

The Golden Hills' News (1851?) apparently the first Asian American newspaper in the United States, used a bilingual front-page format with commercial notices in lithographed Chinese characters in the left-hand columns and a call for better treatment of Chinese immigrants in an English-language right-hand column, as this 1854 edition shows. (Journalism History) dation among the Christian groups with missionaries in China and outposts in the Chinatown then developing in San Franciso. The groups offered support to Chinese immigrants in the hostile land, hoping to convert them to Christianity in the process.

In his history of the Chinese in the United States from 1850 to 1870, Gunther Barth notes that the first issue of the *Golden Hills' News*, which he says appeared in April 1854, stated the paper would appear twice weekly and that it was published by William Howard, with Chinese characters lithographed by F. Kuhl. But by July of that year it had begun weekly publication. In an article the day after the first edition appeared, the *San Francisco Herald* compared appearance of the typography in Chinese newspapers to a spider crawling out of an ink bottle and onto a white sheet of paper. The paper sold for 25¢ a copy, with a monthly subscription costing 75¢. Charges for advertising were $1 for fewer than 25 characters, $2 for between 25 and 50, and 3¢ apiece for more than 50 characters. Barth describes most of the content as being in colloquial Cantonese, with most of the news coming from California and advertising coming from sales and auctions.[26] But, like *El Misisipi* and the *Cherokee Advocate*, the newspaper also used a bilingual format.

The front page of the May 27, 1854, edition features Chinese characters on the left-hand two-thirds of the page, with an English-language column apparently addressed to the Whites of San Francisco on the right-hand side. The Chinese characters reported news of interest to its Asian immigrant readers. One story described conditions for Chinese in San Franciso, including treatment by Whites. Another announced a church meeting. There were reports on relations between China and Japan, a sea battle pitting Russia against France and Britain, and a notice of a ship departing for Japan. One story told of the plight of poor Chinese families in other parts of the United States. The material in English called for better treatment of Chinese in California, noting that the Chinese were among many groups coming to California:

> But the California picture is **unique**—their **tout ensemble** is the history of Civilization. The "Eastern States" have their Irish exodus, their German exodus, and hordes of Saxons, Danes, Celts, Gauls and Scandanavians, but we have **all** of these, and the most wonderful of all a CHINESE EXODUS! The great wonder of the century is the astonishing flight of the hitherto immobile Chinamen across the Pacific ocean, to seek refuge and liberty in the bosom of "The Golden Hills."

The writer quoted missionaries in Shanghai who wrote that Americans could "wander unmolested" 40 miles into the Chinese interior and claimed that Chinese who saw Americans would "look up to them with profound respect." That behavior was compared with the treatment that Chinese immigrants were subjected to in San Francisco. An appeal for better treatment of Chinese was made to the English-speaking readers:

> "No Chinaman sneers at you in the streets; there is no hindrance whatever to your study of their character and habits; they always look to at you with an expression of good will," says Bayard Taylor. Is it too much to ask of a Christian population "to do unto them," at least what it seems "they do to us," in their own land? Is it too much to ask of this Cosmopolitan state, in the veins of whose population flows the blood of a thousand tribes, to give freedom of growth and fair play to the Mongol element? Is it too much to ask of a Commercial People to give a generous aid and liberal encouragement to any means, that assist the Chinese to a knowledge of our laws and habits, and a sympathy with our interests? Surely not. Therefore Merchants, Manufacturers, Miners and Agriculturists, come forward as friends, not scorners of the Chinese, so that they may mingle in the march of the world and help to open for America an endless vista of future commerce.[27]

The English-language editorial was incorporated into the newspaper's format. Later issues continue to advocate the rights of Chinese in California and demonstrate the willingness of Chinese to take part in the traditions of their new country. Two July editorials were headed "Is There No Help for the Chinese in California" and "The Fourth of July and The Chinese Race." Barth writes that the English-language editorials set a precedent that was followed by other Chinese newspapers in California. It was primarily concerned with discrimination and other civil rights violations against the Chinese, while always pointing to evidence of their adaptation to the ways of the United States. The Chinese columns, on the other hand, continued to be filled with commercial notices and other business-related news.[28] By all accounts the *Golden Hills' News* did not publish for a lengthy period. Writing in 1858, Kemble concluded his three-line paragraph on the newspaper by saying, "It did not live long."[29]

Like the other racial minority publications discussed in this chapter, the *Golden Hills' News* established some precedents that have been followed in other Asian American newspapers. One was the use of a bilingual format, which continues in some periodicals today. Another was a column directed toward the English-speaking readers that argued for fairer treatment of the Chinese and pointed to the contributions they were making to the overall society. There are, no doubt, other precedents that will be discovered as students and scholars continue to study and analyze the history of the Asian American press in the United States.

ANALYSIS

The first Latino, Black, Native American, and Asian American newspapers in the United States are important for more than chronological reasons. While it is important to establish and record the founding dates of the first media for these groups, it is even more interesting to examine the similarities between these different newspapers begun for different groups at different times and places.

One similarity has already been established: They were all founded in a period when the members of that minority group were facing a crisis of unusual stress or pain that was not being experienced by the majority population. But it is also interesting to note that three of the newspapers, *El Misisipí, Cherokee Phoenix* and the *Golden Hills' News*, were also bilingual, using both their native language and the language of the majority population. Two of the periodicals, *Cherokee Phoenix*, and the *Golden Hills' News*, were founded with the support of religious missionaries, and a third, *Freedom's Journal*, was cofounded by a Black minister. Each of the newspapers was especially attuned to the news and information needs of its target audience and, like minority media today, no doubt delivered both news and analysis that was unavailable in the mainstream press. In fact, *Freedom's Journal* and the *Cherokee Phoenix* were established for the primary purpose of providing a voice that would be an alternative to the established press, and the *Golden Hills' News* appeared at a time when the mainstream media were playing an active role in ridiculing and disparaging members of that group. These three newspapers also all appeared in periods when the members of their audience were victims of legal discrimination, social subjugation, and violent oppression.

The racial minority press did not end with the founding of these four newspapers. In fact, each of these groups continues to have an broad range of newspapers, magazines, and broadcast stations targeted to them. Although many of these media have become increasingly commercial in their content and less fiery in their voices, the minority media have continued to fulfill the tradition of providing news, entertainment, and information that is an alternative to what is available in the media directed at the mainstream White audience.

This minority frustration with the mass-audience press has long been felt and, in fact, was directed at the first mass circulation newspaper in the United States, the *New York Sun*. In the 1840s a Black man, Willis A. Hodges, took exception to editorials in the *Sun* opposing voting rights for Blacks. So he first tried the access approach, writing a reply to the editorial, which the newspaper published for a fee of $15. However, when the newspaper published his message it was modified and carried as advertising. Hodges protested, but was advised, "The *Sun* shines for all White men but not for Colored men." Told that the mass circulation newspaper would be closed to the views of Blacks, he started the *Ram's Horn* in 1847.[30]

As long as there is free access to the establishment of print media in the United States, members of all races will be able to follow the avenue of Hodges and the founding editors of the first Latino, Black, Native American, and Asian American newspapers by starting publications for their own groups and presenting alternatives to the news and viewpoints expressed in the mainstream media.

NOTES

1. Edwin Emery and Michael Emery, *The Press and America*, 5th ed. (Prentice-Hall, 1984), p. 2. For further descriptions of communication in non-European cultures, see Leonard W. Doob, *Communication in Africa* (Yale University Press, 1961); Irene Nicholson, *Mexican and Central American Mythology* (Paul Hamlyn Limited, 1967); Robert T. Oliver, *Communication and Culture in Ancient India and China* (Syracuse University Press, 1971); and Jacques Soustelle, *Daily Life of the Aztecs* (Stanford University Press, 1961).
2. Emery and Emery, *The Press and America*, p. 2.

3. James E. Murphy and Sharon M. Murphy, *Let My People Know* (University of Oklahoma Press, 1981), p. v.

4. Félix Gutiérrez and Ernesto Ballesteros, "The 1541 earthquake: Dawn of Latin American journalism," *Journalism History*, Vol. 6, No. 3, Autumn 1979. Also see Al Hester, "Newspapers and newspaper prototypes in Spanish America, 1541-1750," in the same issue.

5. Julio Jiménez Rueda, *Historia de la Cultura en México, El Virriento* (Editorial Cultura, 1950), p. 222, as quoted by Carlos Alvear Acevedo, *Breve Historia del Periodismo* (Editorial Jus, 1965), p. 79 (translation from Spanish by authors). For a description of *relaciones* in Spain see Henry F. Schulte, *The Spanish Press 1470-1966* (University of Illinois Press, 1968), p. 72.

6. Acevedo, *Breve Historia del Periodismo*, p. 75.

7. Described in Emery and Emery, *The Press and America*, p. 16.

8. All quotes from *El Misisipí*, October 12, 1808, pp. 1-4. For a more complete translation of the issue, see Félix Gutiérrez, "Spanish language media in the U.S.," *Caminos*, January 1984, pp. 10-12. See also Félix Gutiérrez, "Spanish-language media in America: Background resources, history," *Journalism History*, Vol. 4, No. 2, Summer 1977, p. 37; Raymond MacCurdy, *A History and Bibliography of Spanish Language Newspapers and Magazines in Louisiana, 1808-1949* (University of New Mexico Press, 1951), pp. 8-9.

9. Walter C. Daniel, *Black Journals of the United States* (Greenwood Press, 1982), p. 184.

10. Ibid.; see also Kenneth D. Nordin, "In search of Black unity: An interpretation of the content and function of 'Freedom's Journal,'" *Journalism History*, Vol. 4, No. 4, Winter 1977-78, pp. 123-124.

11. Daniel, *Black Journals*, p. 185.

12. Lionel C. Barrow, Jr., " 'Our Own Cause:' 'Freedom's Journal' and the beginnings of the Black press," *Journalism History*, Vol. 4, No. 4, Winter 1977-78, p. 122. Also see Nordin, "In search of Black unity," and Henk La Brie III, "Black newspapers: The roots are 150 years deep," in the same issue.

13. Richard LaCourse, "An Indian perspective—Native American journalism: An overview," *Journalism History*, Vol. 6, No. 2, Summer 1979, pp. 34-35.

14. See Murphy and Murphy, *Let My People Know*, pp. 21-33, for a description of the *Cherokee Phoenix*. See also Barbara F. Luebke, "Elias Boudinott, Indian editor: Editorial columns from *Cherokee Phoenix*," *Journalism History*, Vol. 6, No. 2, Summer 1979, pp. 48-53, and Sam G. Riley, "A note of caution—The Indian's own prejudice, as mirrored in the first Native American newspaper," pp. 44-47 in the same issue. Elias Boudinot apparently shortened the spelling of his last name from Boudinott early in his career, but is referred to with both spellings in writings of the period and subsequent scholarly works.

15. Elias Boudinot, *An Address to the Whites: Delivered in the First Presbyterian Church on the 26th of May, 1826*, pp. 12-13, cited in Murphy and Murphy, *Let My People Know*, p. 24.

16. Murphy and Murphy, *Let My People Know*, p. 25.

17. "Cherokee Laws," *Cherokee Phoenix*, March 13, 1828, p. 1. Reprinted in *Journalism History*, Vol. 6, No. 2, Summer 1979, p. 46.

18. Luebke, "Elias Boudinott, Indian editor," p. 48.

19. Ibid., p. 51.

20. Riley, "A note of caution," p. 45.

21. Gladys C. Hansen and William F. Heintz, *The Chinese in California: A Brief Bibliographic History* (Richard Abel & Company, 1970), pp. 7-8.
22. Jack Chen, *The Chinese of America* (Harper & Row, 1980), p. 3.
23. Gunther Barth, *Bitter Strength* (Harvard University Press, 1971), p. 174.
24. Emerson Daggett, ed., *History of Foreign Journalism in San Francisco* (Works Project Administration, 1939), as cited in Hansen and Heintz, *The Chinese in California*, p. 45.
25. Edward C. Kemble, *A History of California Newspapers 1846-1858* (Talisman Press, 1962), pp. 117, 118-119.
26. Barth, *Bitter Strength*, pp. 174-175.
27. "The Chinese Exodus,"*Golden Hills News*, May 27, 1854, p. 1. Translation of copy on columns in Chinese by Stanley Rosen and Stanley Chung.
28. Barth, *Bitter Strength*, pp. 175-176.
29. Kemble, *History of California Newspapers*, p. 117.
30. I. Garland Penn, *The Afro-American Press and Its Editors* (Willey & Co., 1891), pp. 61-65, as cited in Don Dodson and William A. Hachten, "Communication and development: African and Afro-American parallels," *Journalism Monographs*, No. 28, May 1973, p. 25.

9

ADVOCACY: PRESSURING THE MEDIA TO CHANGE

THE YEAR WAS 1827 and the words appear in the first issue of *Freedom's Journal*, the first newspaper published by Black Americans:

> The peculiarities of this Journal, renders it important that we should advertise to the world our motives by which we are actuated, and the objects which we contemplate.
>
> We wish to plead our own cause. . . . Too long has the publick been deceived by misrepresentations, in things which concern us dearly. . . .
>
> From the press and the pulpit we have suffered much by being incorrectly represented.[1]

Thus from the beginning it was obvious that one of the primary objectives of the Black press was to protest and counter the negative and false reportage of the White press. We shall see that Blacks were not alone in exercising the option of "advocacy" of their own cause as a response to White media and, furthermore, that minority media advocacy has long-standing historical roots. But first, let us put the issue in perspective. We have established in previous chapters the nature of White-owned media and their treatment of ethnic minorities. The social and cultural imperative that minorities communicate *en masse* is an issue of survival. Faced with majority group mass media tainted by racism and insensitive to their needs, minorities in the United States have three options: (1) They may seek access into the majority media through employment; (2) they may develop and maintain their own communications media; and (3) they may apply pressure techniques of various forms to effect changes in majority media content as it relates to them. These three options are related and have been used, both independently and in concert with others. For example, minorities who have obtained professional employment in White media often form organizations that work to change the portrayal or news coverage of ethnics. Or a minority-owned medium may protest inequities it finds in White media, as was the case with *Freedom's Journal*. We have discussed the first two options in Chapters 7 and 8. In this chapter we shall look at the advocacy option and complete the circle of minority media activism.

Nearly a century after the appearance of *Freedom's Journal*, the Black press was still publicly defending its constituency against denigrating reporting in the White press. In 1919, the Black weekly *Wichita Protest* complained about the racial coverage of the Associated Press:

> Every newspaper editor of our group in the country knows that the Associated Press, the leading news distributing service of the country, has carried on a policy of discrimination in favor of the whites and against the blacks, and is doing it daily now. The Associated Negro Press is in receipt of correspondence from editors in various sections of the country decrying the way in which the Associated Press writes its stories of happenings where Colored people are affected.[2]

Even renowned Black spokesman Booker T. Washington spoke frequently of the poor coverage his speeches received from the White press. A Black journalist reported in 1916 Washington's lament that his successful speeches before large crowds, normally expected to receive front-page attention in the White press, would be relegated to the last page and given an inch or so of space. Instead, the front page would invariably be given to considerable reporting of a Black person involved in a minor criminal offense.[3]

There was minority advocacy for change from the earliest days of the motion picture industry. In 1911 the Spanish-language weekly *La Crónica* of Laredo, Texas, launched a campaign against the numerous movies shown throughout the state that denigrated both Mexicans and Native Americans. The period marked the beginning of the heyday of western movies. Movie screens were filled with images of "greasers" and "savage" Indians who were brought to justice by the White cowboy hero. Several prominent members of the Native American community wrote letters to the Bureau of Indian Affairs in Washington, D.C., protesting the images such movies projected of their people. *La Crónica* wrote:

> We are not surprised about the complaint of the North American Indians . . . because the Mexicans can make the same complaint . . . and other Latin races, who are generally the only and most defamed in these sensational American movies [such as are seen on the Texas border] . . . that serve only to show the level of culture of the learned makers of films, who have no more ingenuity except to think of scenes with many bullets, horses, "cowboys" and then it's over.[4]

La Crónica proceeded to call for support from other Texas Mexican newspapers in urging an end to the offensive movies. Earlier the paper had addressed the negative effects such movies had upon its community:

> We judge these with much indignation and condemn them with all our energy . . . all exhibitions that make ridicule of the Mexican . . . because the showing of these facts are indelibly recorded in the minds of the children and this contributes very much to the development of the dislike with which other races see the Mexican race, who the film company has chosen to make fun of.[5]

In addition, the paper sought to persuade Texas theater owners not to acquire and show the films and to follow the lead of two Latinos who wrote letters to filmmakers to cancel further shipments to their theaters. *La Crónica* wrote that Latino families often reacted to negative stereotypes by leaving the theaters when they saw such portrayals and roles that "in reality [don't] fit us."[6] The paper noted that it would publish "with pleasure" the names of film companies that rejected movies denigrating Mexicans.

The first generation of Chinese immigrants who settled primarily in California were, for the most part, unsophisticated laborers whose immediate concern was survival in a new and hostile

Anglo-Saxon world. Because they were not made to feel a part of American culture and because most were from the uneducated working class in China, they did not express displeasure of their treatment by Whites in written form. As small Chinatown enclaves developed in settlements in California and the Far West, the Chinese immigrants sought internal refuge and protection from the ravages of racism. They dared not, given their small numbers and immigrant status, publicly protest against their hosts, whose image of them as inferior precluded tolerance of criticism. However, the second generation of Chinese immigrants included a number of representatives from China's upper classes. These people were educated and were not affected by the anti-Chinese immigration laws passed prior to 1900. They were diplomats, scholars, and prosperous merchants, and despite their interest in promoting closer economic and political ties with the United States, some expressed disapproval of White racism against them in writing. One such writer was Wu Tingfang, a Chinese diplomat who lived in America for nearly a decade. Wu wrote his book *America Through the Spectacles of an Oriental Diplomat* in 1914. By that time Sax Rohmer's fictional and diabolical Chinese character, Dr. Fu Manchu, was four years old and the negative stereotype had found White Americans eager to adopt his imagery to existing racial prejudices against the Chinese. Ever the diplomat, Wu asked forgiveness if his "impartial and candid observations" should offend American readers:

> American readers will forgive me if they find some opinions they cannot endure. I assure them they were not formed hastily or unkindly. Indeed, I should not be a sincere friend were I to picture their country as a perfect paradise, or were I to gloss over what seem to me to be their defects.[7]

Despite this early warning in his book, Wu's criticisms were generally innocuous. He made it clear, however, that he opposed the racism against Blacks and Chinese he had observed in America. He tried to appeal to rationality among his White readers by arguing that they could not be racially superior to the Chinese, whose rich culture and intellectual history merited respect throughout the rest of the world.

There are numerous other incidents throughout American history in which minorities expressed their disfavor with White media as a means of advocating change in White attitudes. Such activity has included every ethnic minority group and every form of mass communication media. The methods of advocacy have ranged from boycotts to letter-writing campaigns and from monitoring White media content to seeking legal redress of grievances, as well as other techniques.

Minority advocacy activists received a major boost when the Civil Rights Act was enacted in 1964. For the first time the weight of law added clout to the cause of media activists who sought change via minority employment in the media. Interestingly, it was often difficult to convince minority activists that necessary changes could be made in media by pursuing legal channels. The period from the late 1960s through the mid-1970s was marked by sit-in demonstrations, street rallies, marches, and picketing, and many of those techniques had proven effective. On the other hand, the legal establishment, which included law enforcement agencies, prosecutors, lawyers, and judges, were seen by most minority activists as major factors in the problems they were addressing. That working through the legal system would result in the changes they sought was a difficult proposition to sell. Ultimately, however, the legal system paved the way for successful minority advocacy on mass media issues.

As we have noted elsewhere in this book, minorities were able to effect changes much more rapidly in broadcasting because FCC employment guidelines for broadcast licensees are much more stringent than those of the Equal Employment Opportunities Commission, the federal body to which newspapers are answerable. In addition, other social, economic, and political forces began to bear upon mass media institutions. Although he was referring to the political process, futurist John Naisbitt captured the essence of why minorities are able to exert considerable leverage in the effort to improve their lot in media. The issue is related to racial diversity and the trend toward decentralization in the United States. According to Naisbitt in his book, *Megatrends*:

> The key to decentralization of political power in the United States today is local action. Localized political power is not delegated from the federal level to the state, municipal, or neighborhood levels. Rather, it stems from the initiatives taken by the state or neighborhood in the absence of an effective top-down solution . . . . Successful initiatives hammered out at the local level have staying

> power. Local solutions are resistant to top-down intervention and become models for others still grappling with the problems.[8]

How decentralization through technology and economics is generally affecting mass media in America is more thoroughly discussed in the next chapter. Here, we shall examine how minority advocates, working at the local level and using the force of law, began making an impact on mass media in the late 1960s. In some respects their successes are reminiscent of how the populist movement of the 1830s drastically altered mass media and entertainment in the United States, with the exception that meaningful change often had to be won in hard-fought courtroom battles.

BROADCASTING

The advocacy story for minorities in broadcasting begins with the United Church of Christ's Office of Communication. The United Church of Christ (UCC) has had a long standing interest in both civil rights and freedom of religious and other forms of expression. It has committed its resources to such efforts in the United States and in various other nations. Generally, the organization, a coalition of Protestant denominations, has dedicated itself to the proposition that media should operate under Judeo-Christian principles. It considers mass media to be a missionary sphere of interest. UCC's Office of Communications is the organizational arm assigned to the task of media advocacy. It is responsible for landmark legal decisions that have changed the American broadcasting industry and its regulatory agency, the Federal Communications Commission (FCC), in ways even beyond the scope of minority concerns.

The first major case involved station WLBT in Jackson, Mississippi. WLBT had incurred the wrath of Jackson's Black community for a number of years because of its discriminatory racial practices, which included on-air references to Black people as "niggers" and refusal to carry a network show on race relations by airing a sign that read, "Sorry, Cable Trouble" during the scheduled time slot. Black people made up some 45 percent of the station's service-area audience. The station openly advocated racial segregation. UCC became involved, among other reasons, because it had a congregation in nearby Tougaloo, Mississippi, a significant proportion of which was Black. When WLBT began to attack local civil rights activity involving UCC church members, UCC took up the legal challenge of the station's right to hold an FCC license by filing a petition to deny its renewal in 1964. UCC's involvement was important because under the social, political, and economic conditions of the time, local Blacks faced reprisal and likely violence had they attempted to challenge WLBT strictly as a local effort.

The crux of the legal case was the FCC requirement (established by the Communications Act of 1934) that all licensees broadcast "in the public interest, convenience and necessity." On the surface, it appeared that Black residents of Jackson and the UCC would have little trouble preventing WLBT from retaining its license, assuming their well-documented case was adequately presented. Unfortunately, although FCC rules allowed for license challenges, only a miniscule fraction of challenges had ever been upheld since the agency's inception. As the subsequent legal developments showed, the FCC had evolved into a protector of broadcasters instead of a protector of the public's rights. When the UCC and representatives of Jackson's Black community appeared before the FCC, the agency denied them "standing" even to present their petition on grounds they had no "interest" (financial) in the license renewal procedure. The FCC renewed WLBT's license, but the UCC filed suit in the U.S. Court of Appeals, which granted standing to the complainants and ordered the FCC to hold a full hearing on their case. The court maintained that members of WLBT's audience most certainly had standing because as consumers they had an interest in local broadcasting content over public airwaves. In fact, the court's position was that the FCC could not do its job without the assistance of the public in determining public interest. Despite participation in the hearing process, the UCC was distressed when the FCC granted a license renewal to WLBT on a one-year probationary status.

Believing the FCC decision to be improper and unfair, the UCC once again took the issue to the Court of Appeals and found relief. In harsh language that took the FCC to task for its shoddy treatment of the petitioners, the court took matters into its own hands and denied WLBT the license. Significant also was the court's ruling that public petitioners should not bear the burden of proof in such cases, but rather that the licensee must be able to show it handled its license privilege in a responsible manner. Moreover, the court ordered the denial on the grounds that the Fairness Doctrine had been violated, and that WLBT practiced racial discrimination in programming and hiring—all extremely important issues for minority groups. Another important right, the right of standing in FCC license hearings, was, of course, won in the initial phase of the case.

The UCC was also instrumental in a case involving Native Americans in Rosebud, South Dakota.[9] Rosebud is a Sioux reservation, the inhabitants of which undertook a legal action against two South Dakota television stations, KELO and KPLO, that reached a combined 90 percent of the broadcast audience in the state during the 1950s and 1960s. KPLO became a virtual satellite to KELO and by the mid-1960s was originating little or no local programming to serve the interests and needs of the Rosebud Sioux. The UCC assisted in filing a petition to deny license against KELO, which resulted in the negotiation of agreements with both stations. The agreements called for program changes and the employment of five Native Americans in full-time positions in broadcasting.

The concept of advocacy groups and broadcast licensees they have challenged reaching agreement via negotiated settlement set the stage for the last major UCC-inspired milestone we shall consider. In a 1968 case involving local citizens' groups in Texarkana, Texas, with support from UCC, the license of KTAL television was challenged by a petition to deny its renewal. The station's owners negotiated a settlement that resulted in withdrawal of the petition. Part of the agreement called for reimbursement of legal expenses to UCC incurred during the process. The FCC, however, refused payment of the reimbursement, citing the possibility of encouraging frivolous lawsuits in the future and the potential for overpayment of such expenses. The FCC also feared that the public-interest merits of petition-to-deny cases could be overshadowed by the financial ramifications. Again, UCC took the issue before the appeals court and was granted a ruling that held negotiated reimbursements to be valid in instances where the petition-to-deny case is bona fide and the public interest has been served. The ruling gave advocacy groups added bargaining power (broadcasters have more at stake if they choose to draw out a proceeding in hope the citizens would exhaust their funds) and encouraged challenged licensees to negotiate settlements more quickly to avoid the more lengthy and expensive process of a fully litigated case.

A capsule review of the typical minority advocacy group (or other local citizens' group) procedure for prompting change in broadcasting is basically as follows. If it can be shown that racial discrimination exists in programming, employment, or other areas detrimental to the public interest, a "petition to deny" the station's license renewal may be filed with the FCC. If the petition reaches a hearing at the FCC, the licensee bears the burden of showing how its practices are, indeed, in the best interests of the community it serves. That is because local citizens' groups have "standing" as interested parties to the license renewal process. If the citizens' advocacy group challenge is upheld, the broadcaster may lose its license or an arrangement may be made to ensure that the wrongs are rectified. If, however, the challenging group and the licensee negotiate a settlement prior to a hearing before the FCC, the challengers may withdraw the petition-to-deny action and may be entitled to reimbursement of legal expenses incurred. More than 100 such actions had been undertaken by citizens' groups by the mid-1980s, some by nonminority groups benefiting from precedents established by racial minorities.

NEWSPAPERS

Although newspapers come under the less demanding guidelines of the Equal Employment Opportunities Commission and their response to ethnic minority grievances has been slow, the advocacy movement has made inroads. Some of the credit also must go to the advocacy efforts directed toward broadcasting stations, because many of them are owned by large media organizations with properties in both print and broadcast media. In 1980, for example, the Times-Mirror Company (owner of the *Los Angeles Times*, *Dallas Times-Herald*, and *Newsday*, among other newspapers) reached a negotiated settlement with the National Black Media Coalition (NBMC) over a purchase transaction of several broadcasting stations. The settlement not only addressed rectification of minority employment and programming shortcomings existing in the broadcast operations Times-Mirror was purchasing, but included the appointment of a Black and a Latino to the company's board of directors. The company also agreed to provide scholarships for journalism and broadcasting students attending predominantly Black colleges located near the newly acquired broadcast stations. In addition, several other employment and training programs were funded as a result of the agreement. (The agreement was made possible because citizens' advocacy groups may also intervene when broadcast licenses are transferred, as in a change of ownership, as well as when licenses are considered for renewal.)

In the early 1980s two major events may have signaled the beginning of a more committed effort to increase ethnic diversity in American newsrooms. Legal actions brought against the *New York Times* and Associated Press forced the two news organizations to improve their minority employment numbers, and the result should be more diversified coverage nationally in the newspaper press. That hope is founded on the premise that successful legal action, particularly when large, respected institutions are involved, may spur others because of the fear that they, too, may be vulnerable to similar legal actions.

A significant advocacy movement of the 1980s involves the resource of minority professionals who have succeeded in White-owned newspapers but who are keenly aware of the problems ethnics encounter on the job. At the same time, they maintain a commitment to see other people of color join them in the profession. The result has been the formation of national professional associations for minority journalists. Among them are the National Association of Black Journalists, the National Hispanic Journalists Association, and the Asian American Journalists Association. Each works separately but cooperatively to improve working conditions, increase job opportunities, and sponsor scholarships for promising minority students. In 1984 a Native American Press Association was formed, thus constituting the first step toward a national advocacy presence for American Indians. Most of the organizations hold national and regional conventions, where seminars and workshops are presented on issues relevant to minority news professionals. In addition, numerous local and regional professional journalists' organizations have been formed since 1980, most of them affiliated with national associations.

Individual activists also have aimed their efforts directly at newspapers and achieved some success in keeping the issue before the industry. Among the leaders who emerged in the mid-1970s to mid-1980s were Robert Maynard and Nancy Hicks (instrumental in founding the Institute for Journalism Education, among other efforts), Jay T. Harris (who conducted studies of minority employment in newspapers for the American Society of Newspaper Editors from 1978 to 1983), Gerald Garcia (an executive with Gannett Newspapers), and Albert Fitzpatrick (an executive with Knight-Ridder Newspapers).

Perhaps most influential of all is a White, Gerald M. Sass, vice president for education of the Frank E. Gannett Newspaper Foundation, who spearheaded the expenditure of more than $4 million for minority programs in the newspaper industry between 1975 and 1985. Sass, who joined the foundation in 1978, gave financial support to the Institute for Journalism Education, The Consortium (a program facilitating graduate study for students from predominantly minority colleges), the California Chicano News Media Association, and the Asian American Journalists Association, among others.

The efforts of these and other spokespersons for ethnic diversity in American daily newspapers are responsible for most of the progress that has been made in the last decade. They prompted the American Society of Newspaper Editors (ASNE) to adopt in 1978 the goal to have the nation's minority newsroom population equal in percentage to that in the general U.S. population by the year 2000. By 1985 it was estimated that at current employment rates the goal would be achieved approximately three generations late. ASNE has maintained a Minorities Committee since 1977. The American Newspaper Publishers Association (ANPA) Foundation supports minority fellowships and the Associated Press Managing Editors (APME) has a Minority News Committee. The Dow Jones Newspaper Fund has several programs for aspiring minority newspaper journalists, including efforts aimed at high school students. Minority advocates who focus their attention on the newspaper industry, however, are primarily educators or professionals who serve as advisers and catalysts for the generation of programs to meet specific needs as they are identified. As we noted in

Clockwise from top left: *Robert Maynard*, editor and president of the Oakland, California, *Tribune*, is a founder of the Institute for Journalism Education, which has trained and placed numerous minorities into news media professions; *Gerald Sass*, vice president, education, Frank E. Gannett Newspaper Foundation, had oversight of more than $4 million expended for integration of journalism education between 1975 and 1985; *Jay Harris*, an advocate of integration of journalism education and the newspaper industry when he was assistant dean of the Medill School of Journalism at Northwestern University. He joined the Gannett News Service staff in 1983; *Gerald Garcia*, now a vice president with Gannett Newspapers in Tucson, Arizona, has been an advocate of media integration for more than a decade; he is one of the highest-ranking Latinos in American newspaper management.

the discussion of newspaper employment, editor attitudes concerning integration of their news staffs are not encouraging.

FILM AND ENTERTAINMENT TELEVISION

Anyone who looks at film and television roles for minorities in the mid-1980s would find ample cause for change. The employment of ethnics in the various trades and crafts responsible for movies and entertainment television is low. The number of strong, meaningful character roles and script plots is virtually nonexistent. However, that state of affairs is not for lack of activism and effort on the parts of minorities who are part of the industry. Minority caucuses have been organized in the Directors Guild, the Writers Guild, and the Screen Actors Guild. Professional actors and other artisans speak out frequently on the plight of minority artists, but it is difficult to ascertain their effectiveness. The question is whether conditions would be worse were it not for the efforts of those who speak out for diversity. Among the many groups addressing these issues on the West Coast, where they could apply direct pressure to Hollywood, are the Media Forum, Nosotros, and Asian Americans for Fair Media.

ADVOCACY IN EDUCATION

The Association for Education in Journalism and Mass Communication (AEJMC) is the primary organization representing college and university journalism and mass communication education in the United States. Nationally, some 98 percent of all full-time academic instructors in the discipline are White. Obviously, within that enclave are few minority advocates, but there are some. In 1968, under the prodding of Lionel C. Barrow, Jr. (who had written an "open letter" to the organization's convention urging the journalism education establishment to end its de facto segregation against minorities), an ad hoc committee was formed by resolution to bring "minority group members into [the AEJ] pipeline."[10] A comprehensive set of minority-related goals was established by AEJ ("Mass Communication" was not added to the organization's name until 1982). Goals included raising money for 500 minority student scholarships for 1969-1970 and developing curriculum changes to reflect the role of minority groups in America and media reporting of that role. In 1971 the association's Minorities and Communication (MAC) division was created. Barrow, who became dean of the school of communications at Howard University, was the division's first head. MAC's membership came to reflect diversity and, of course, had a number of active White members. Increasingly over the years the division became the conscience of the larger body and the ideals and goals under which MAC was founded became distant memories. The ambitious goals were never achieved, but the attitude of the association paralleled that of American society when the initial rush of the civil rights movement had passed. Basically, the association members responded as if it was MAC's job alone to handle minority affairs. In 1978, 10 years after the creation of the ad hoc committee that lead to MAC's birth, AEJ enacted another "Resolution on Minorities," but by 1985 much of its promise was unfulfilled. The Minorities and Communication division of AEJMC continues to press for the integration of journalism and mass communication education through improved teaching, expanded research, and the maintenance and development of service programs. However, the number of minority doctoral graduates in journalism and mass communication is less than a trickle for the "pipeline" mentioned in the 1968 minorities resolution.

ANALYSIS

Throughout their experiences as minorities in American society, the subject ethnic groups have expressed their discontent with the treatment they received from majority media. Minorities believed it was necessary to protect themselves from the harmful effects of the distorted portrayals and negative news reporting of American mass media. Their responses took many forms, but the object was the same—they were offended and disturbed. Each group developed advocates who fought for changes and reform of White media. With the passage of the Civil Rights Act in 1964, legal avenues were opened along which the advocacy activists could drive their point. Through the leverage provided by federal regulation of the broadcasting industry, major legal victories were won and some of the worst offenders were driven off the air. Meanwhile, the American business philosophy, which encouraged multiple business ownership and the development of conglomerates, ushered in the concept of cross-media ownership. Where broadcast licensees and newspaper groups shared common ownership, minority advocates had an opportunity to affect the slow-to-integrate newspaper industry.

Individual professional activists stimulated major White media organizations and trade associations to fund newspaper integration efforts. They served to "keep the industry's feet to the fire" on the issues of minority hiring, training, and coverage. Meanwhile, ethnic professional journalists, who had benefited from the activists' efforts to open doors to employment, began forming organizations on the local, regional, and national levels and, in turn, became advocates themselves.

Although the film and entertainment television industries have many minority advocacy groups as well as articulate spokespersons among Hollywood actors, little visible progress is apparent when the end products are considered. Technology and the trend toward specialized audience media may force changes in the industry as minorities become a desirable target audience.

College and university educators responsible for the training and ethical development of young mass media professionals have been slow to meet the challenge of integration for an increasingly diverse American society. In fifteen years the record shows little more than two resolutions and the creation of a minorities division, which has small rank-and-file support across the spectrum of journalism educators. The academic professionals in journalism and mass communication remain virtually all White, and course offerings, for the most part, remain void of contextual recognition of the minority experience.

Much work, therefore, looms ahead for those who would actively pursue the challenge of integrating mass media in the United States.

NOTES

1. "To our patrons," *Freedom's Journal* (New York), March 16, 1827, p. 1.

2. Frederick G. Detweiler, *The Negro Press in the United States* (University of Chicago Press, 1922), p. 149.

3. Ibid., p. 150.

4. Translation from Spanish cited in José E. Limon, "Stereotyping and Chicano resistance: An historical dimension," *Aztlán*, Vol. 4, No. 2, Fall 1973, p. 263.

5. Ibid.

6. Ibid.

7. Cited in Elaine H. Kim, *Asian American Literature* (Temple University Press, 1982), p. 31.

8. John Naisbitt, *Megatrends* (Warner, 1982), p. 112.

9. Emil Ward, "Advocating the minority interest: Actors and cases," in Bernard Rubin, Ed., *Small Voices and Great Triumphs* (Praeger, 1980), p. 250.

10. Lionel C. Barrow, Jr., "The Minorities and Communication Division: The beginning," presented to the Minorities and Communication Division, Association for Education in Journalism, at the 63rd Annual AEJ Conference, Boston, August 1980.

SUGGESTED READING

"American Indians and the Media: Neglect and Stereotype" [Special Issue], *Journalism History*, 6 (Summer 1979), pp. 34-53.

"The Black Press: Roots 150 Years Deep" [Special Issue], *Journalism History*, 4 (Winter 1977-1978), pp. 109-153.

Bullock, Penelope L. *The Afro-American Periodical Press 1838-1909*. Baton Rouge: Louisiana State University Press, 1981.

Chamberlin, Vernon A. and Ivan A. Schulman. *La Revista Ilustrada de Nueva York*. Columbia: University of Missouri Press, 1976.

Detweiler, Frederick G. *The Negro Press in the United States*. Chicago: University of Chicago Press, 1922.

Gutiérrez, Félix (Ed.). "Spanish Language Media Issue" [Special Issue], *Journalism History*, 4 (Summer 1977), pp. 34-68.

Hester, Al. "Newspapers and Newspaper Prototypes in Spanish America, 1541-1750," *Journalism History*, 6 (Autumn 1979), pp. 73-77, 88.

LaBrie, Henry G. "The Black Press: 150 Years Old," *Negro History Bulletin*, 11 (May-June, 1977), pp. 705-707.

Lewels, Francisco J. *How the Chicano Movement Uses the Media*. New York: Praeger, 1974.

Oak, Vishnu V. *The Negro Newspaper*. Westport, CT: Negro Universities Press, 1948.

Suggs, Henry Lewis. *The Black Press in the South, 1865-1979*. Westport, CT: Greenwood, 1983.

V

Conclusion

"The social role of the media has undergone a fundamental change. The communication media system that once built a mass audience by looking for commonalities in a heterogeneous society. . . . But now, the media seek, find, and reinforce the distinctions between groups in society. The media are no longer mass media, but segmented media . . . reinforcing differences between the segments to enhance the delivery of the advertising message."

10

RACIAL DIVERSITY AND THE END OF MASS MEDIA

THE 1980s HAVE BEEN a decade of evolution and change for racial minority groups and their relationship with communication media. Though obstacles remain, the growth of racial minority groups, the hiring progress spurred by pressures on the communication industry, the increased importance of minority audiences to advertisers, and the new opportunities afforded by new communication technologies all have combined to construct a media mosaic that is more racially diverse than the past. The mid-1980s witnessed a Pulitzer Prize Gold Medal awarded to Latino reporters for the *Los Angeles Times* for their series on Latinos in Southern California; the satellite distribution of cable television programming to Blacks by the Black Entertainment Television network; the founding of the *Navajo Times*, the first daily Native American newspaper; and the continued growth of print and broadcast media directed toward Asian Americans, much of it fed by entertainment and news content imported by new technology from the Asian continent.

As the United States moves into the twenty-first century, the development of communications media and their relationship to racially diverse groups in the nation will continue to evolve and will be increasingly influenced by three major forces. The importance of these forces can be determined through past developments and projected future changes. They are not the only forces exerting influences in this arena, nor is their impact entirely predictable, but it is clear that they will exert a great deal of influence on the ways in which media develop and interact with racially diverse populations of the United States. These three major forces are

(1) continued growth of racial diversity in the United States;
(2) technological changes in communication media; and
(3) continued segmentation of audiences through the media by advertisers.

In this chapter we examine these three forces and analyze both their current and their potential impact on racial minorities and the media. Information on some of these factors has already been covered in previous chapters. Here we examine that information and discuss the way it is likely to affect the future of communication media and racial minorities in the United States.

GROWTH OF RACIAL DIVERSITY

As the data in the chapter on demographics clearly show, since 1970 the United States has experienced its greatest population growth rate in the non-White populations. Lower median age, slightly larger anticipated family sizes, and continued immigration from Asia and Latin America all point to the development of a society in the United States in which racial minorities constitute a much larger percentage of the population than in the past. In some of the nation's largest cities it is already statistically incorrect to apply the term "minorities" to the non-White population, given that non-Whites make up a majority of the people of those cities.

While it is impossible to predict when the population lines will cross, it appears the United States will become a nation in which non-Whites constitute the majority of the population sometime before the year 2100. As the racial makeup of the nation continues to change, the media and other institutions in the United States will have to respond to racial diversity more than they have in the past.

Projections of the available data also clearly indicate that Whites will continue to be in the majority during the lifetime of most people born in the twentieth century. Even when they are outnumbered by the collective strength of individual non-White groups, Whites will continue to be the largest single racial group in the United States for the near future. In many cities in which racial "minorities" make up the majority, Whites are often still the largest single racial group and, in most cases, wield the largest share of economic and political power. The numbers a racial group represents in the population of a city, state, or nation does not directly translate into the amount of power that group exercises, particularly in media ownership and policymaking. For all the growth of minorities in the past two decades, in 1984 there was only one metropolitan general circulation daily newspaper owned by a minority person, the *Oakland Tribune*, owned by Robert Maynard. There was only one general news organization headed by a racial minority, United Press International (UPI), which named Luís Nogales its president in 1983.

Finally, the growth in racial diversity will have an enduring impact on the nation only if racial minorities remain "beyond the melting pot." Other groups have come to the United States and, after a generation or two, blended into the majority society both culturally and racially. Because of social and legal barriers in the United States, non-Whites have not melted into the mainstream society. In fact, for many years their integration was severely restricted by laws limiting immigration, legislation and court rulings curtailing their legal rights, and institutional and personal acts of social and economic discrimination. Those members of racial minority groups who have succeeded in penetrating predominantly White educational institutions, professions, and residential districts are still identifiable by physical characteristics that distinguish them from the White majority.

Some members of minority races have gained access through race-conscious admissions or hiring policies that have placed a special priority on affording minorities access to educational and employment opportunities. While these members of the non-White population have achieved access to educational and professional arenas that were once closed to racial minorities, it is too early to predict if such advantaged minority persons will have the ability, or the desire, to shed the identity, culture, and, sometimes, language, they share with others of their race. However, it is clear that the growing racial diversity of the United States will have a long-lasting impact on the media and other institutions only if members of racial minority groups continue to retain a higher degree of cultural identity than the European immigrants who came to the United States in earlier decades.

TECHNOLOGICAL CHANGES IN COMMUNICATION MEDIA

Perhaps even more important than the racial changes taking place in the society of the United States are the worldwide changes in communication media that have been triggered by technological advances. The past generation has witnessed fundamental changes in the technologies used in producing newspapers, television, radio, and video. Technical advances such as offset printing of daily newspapers in color, satellite transmission of cable television channels, stereo programming on AM and FM radio, and the widespread use of videotape in entertainment and news programming have become commonplace in only the past decade. Before 1970 the technologies needed to make them a reality were known to only relatively few persons with enough foresight to envision how they could be applied in the future. By the mid-1980s the changes wrought by these technological advances were taken for granted by most people living in the United States.

But as wide ranging as these changes have been, they are merely the first wave of technological advances that have the potential to transform communication media in the near future. The United States is in the process of becoming what has been called an "information society," a society in which the collecting, processing, storing, transmitting, and receiving of visual and printed information outstrips manufacturing or agriculture as the central economic activity. The movement of North American society into the information age has been greatly accelerated by technological advances at all steps of the information process. These new applications of technology have greatly broadened the range of communication media available and the ways in which they are used.[1] In the mid-1980s a bewildering array of communication technologies are under development by large corporations and smaller entrepreneurs, each device being promoted as the communication technology that could dominate the others in the future.[2]

Some of the technologies are completely new consumer applications, such as *cellular radio*, which offers enhanced communication for mobile telephones; *silent radio*, which transmits messages scrolling across video receiving screens; and *videotex*, which permits two-way communication between a central computer and a home receiver built into a television set. Others are technological extensions of existing communication technologies already in place, such as *cable television*, which was extended into the suburbs and cities; *direct broadcast satellites*, which use satellite transmission to beam television signals directly to homes, rather than transmitting through stations or cable systems; and *bilingual television*, which allows the audience to choose between two audio signals for the same program. Still other new media are merely technological or regulatory changes that appeared to create new communication opportunities, such as *AM and VHF drop-in stations*, which uses enhancements in telecommunications technology to allow licensing of additional radio and television stations in communities already given their quota of stations under earlier rules designed to prevent interference between stations; *videocassette recorders*, which allow the audience to record television programming and replay it in the future; and *low-power UHF stations*, which make use of an unused portion of the broadcast spectrum to allow licensing of television stations to a restricted geographic area.

The new technologies afford new opportunities to racial minorities and other groups that have not enjoyed equal participation or service from existing communication media. But racial minorities will probably take part in the new technologies more as employees or users than as owners or developers of the new media. This is because the major communication conglomerates have invested heavily in developing commercial applications of the new technologies. Unsure about which technologies will eventually become big money makers, major telecommunications corporations have spread their investments across several technologies that look promising. If an investment in one technology fails to pay off, such as CBS's investment in a cable arts channel or RCA's experiment with videodiscs, the conglomerates still have money invested in technologies that may eventually produce profits.

But most minority investors have neither the seemingly infinite financial resources of large corporations nor steady incomes generated by newspapers, magazines, or broadcast stations capitalizing on the new technologies of the past. With less breadth of experience and expertise, it is difficult for them to capitalize on the new technologies at a level competitive with the major conglomerates. Members of racial minority groups also have fewer financial resources to invest in developing commercial applications of the new technologies. For them, the new technologies represent a one-shot, all-or-nothing, proposition. They can invest in a specific area, such as the low-power UHF television stations now airing Spanish-language programs provided by the Spanish International Network or cable television programming such as that distributed by Black Entertainment Television. Unlike the major corporations, they are unable to spread their limited capital and expertise across several new technologies.

While the new technologies afford racial minorities new entry points into communication ownership, employment, and programming, minorities who enter the arena find themselves competing with major corporations. As with everything else in the free enterprise system, there are no guarantees of success. Members of minority groups will most likely continue to be the takers of the greatest risks in the new technologies field. If their enterprises fail, they will have to fold without being able to pick up profits through another investment or proceeds from a previous venture. If their use of new technology succeeds, they risk being taken over or copied by one of the major communication conglomerates.

Members of racial minority groups do have an advantage in their understanding of racial minority communities that have not been well served by the communication media in the past. These gaps in telecommunication service provide the best entry point for minorities into the communications opportunities afforded by the new technologies. With a knowledge of racially and linguistically different communities, they can develop innovative uses of new technologies to serve segments of the audience that have been overlooked by the mass audience media.

In the past, minority entrepreneurs have succeeded by adapting "new" technologies such as printing and broadcasting to the unique social and economic structure of their communities. There is no reason for the future to be any different, particularly since the technologies vastly expand the opportunities for "narrowcasting" media content to specific audiences. As the range of outlets in radio, video, print, and other media continue to expand, it will become increasingly important for the media to compete for audiences by narrowing both their content and their appeal to attract specific segments of the mass audience, including member of racial minority groups.

CONTINUED SEGMENTATION OF THE AUDIENCE

Market segmentation, the strategy of dividing the potential consumers of a product into identifiable segments and then directing advertising through media that reach those audiences, has been an important advertising strategy since the new technology of television emerged as the most effective medium for reaching the mass audience in the early 1950s. Radio and magazines, which once delivered the mass audience to advertisers, were forced to survive by abandoning general audience content and, instead, targeting their media to specific segments within the mass audience. As a result, listeners turning the AM and FM radio dials in most cities will find that each station has a different programming format designed to attract a specific group of listeners. By the same token, a visit to the magazine section of a supermarket or convenience store reveals a plethora of magazines, all vying for the attention of potential readers with predefined interests. The only two mass audience magazines still surviving were begun as offshoots of other media: *Reader's Digest* and *TV Guide*.

Market segmentation is a consumer-driven sales approach in which corporations subdivide the total heterogeneous potential market for a product into smaller segments, each of which has its own homogeneous characteristics.[3] Audience segments are broken out in a number of ways, such as place of residence, socioeconomic status, sex, age, education, and race. Segmentation has become increasingly important for advertisers as they have found they can increase both their penetration of the audience and the sales of their products if they design advertisements geared to market segments and place them in print and broadcast media reaching those segments.

More than population growth and technological advances, it is the economic mechanisms of support that control the development of media in the United States. Print and broadcast media are largely supported by advertising. When advertising is increased for a particular segment of the population, the media that reach and influence that segment gain increased advertising dollars. These dollars also make it more profitable for managers of existing media to consider changing formats and content to try to attract that segment and the advertising dollars that will follow.

Minority-oriented media have gained increased advertisement placements and profits because of this change in marketing strategy by major corporations and their advertising agencies. Since they often reach audience segments that are growing faster than the White majority, they will be even more important to advertisers in the future. Media directed to racial minorities will continue to grow as long as major corporations and advertising agencies divide the mass audience into segments and place advertising in media that penetrate and persuade the racial minority segments of the overall population. This makes ownership of media directed toward racial minority groups more profitable and stimulates growth in minority media, by both Whites and minority owners. For instance, in 1981 the nation's largest newspaper chain, Gannett, purchased New York's Spanish-language daily, *El Diario/La Prensa*. Similarly, *Players*, a magazine for Blacks generally formatted along the lines of *Playboy*, was started by a group of White investors in the 1970s.

The outlook for growth in media for racial minorities is further enhanced by the first two factors mentioned in this chapter: the growth of the United States as a racially diverse nation and the advances in communication technology. Together, these three factors point to a racially heterogeneous nation that can be divided and reached by a much wider array of communication technologies. While such an outlook is favorable for the economic success of the minority-formatted media, it also represents a fundamental change in the role of the communication media as they relate to both the racial majority and the racial minorities in the United States.

COMMUNICATION MEDIA AND THE SEGMENTED SOCIETY

The development of communication media in the United States for many decades was based on mass communication, the breaking down of differences in sex, age, education, geography, race, and other differences in the audience and delivering to that mass audience entertainment, news, and advertising that would attract many and alienate only a few. But now the sales approach of advertisers is the opposite. Rather than wanting to address an undefined mass audience, advertisers prefer to target their messages to specific audiences whose demographic profiles are known to them. They want to be able to tailor their advertising to men, women, specific age groups, the affluent, and other definable groups within the mass audience. As a result, the audience strategies of the media that depend on advertising for their revenues have changed. Media must attract the audience that advertisers want to reach if they hope to continue to sell space and time on their stations and publications. The commodity they sell to advertisers is not the amount of space or time for the advertising message, but the size and composition of the audience that will be exposed to the advertising message.

Following the lead of the advertisers, the emphasis in media is now on market segmentation; the ability to define certain segments of the audience, describe their demographic characteristics, and zero in on them through media content that will attract members of those segments. Rather than trying to blend all members of society into a mass-audience melting pot, the advertisers have found they can have more impact with the advertising dollar if they can target their advertising messages to specific audience segments and place advertising in media which reach those consumers.

Even mass audience media, such as newspapers and network television, are divided to reach specific audience segments. The television week and day are divided by programming designed to attract different audiences at different times of the day and different days of the week. Network prime-time television is often cited as the last mass audience medium in the United States. But prime-time television programs are increasingly dependent on the percentage of men, or women, or city dwellers, or young urban professionals in their audience. This is because figures from the A. C. Nielsen Co. which measures television audiences, showed that the top prime-time network television series suffered a 17 percent drop in audience ratings from 1974 to 1984. As a result of this audience loss and competition from new technologies, analysts now talk of modeling television programming after *narrow*casting to audience segments, rather than *broad*casting to the mass audience.[4] Faced with a steadily declining audience, network television executives and programmers now promote their audiences in terms of the demographic profiles of the people who do watch their programs. Television programs now have a better chance of staying on their air with moderate ratings *if* they pull demographic groups advertisers want to reach into their audience. In 1985 the executive producer of the NBC program *Miami Vice*, whose audience ratings were in the bottom half of the Nielsens, boasted, "Our demos [demographics] are incredible."[5] This meant that the detective program, which incorporated a slick musical and video format, was successful in attracting a strong percentage of urban dwellers under 35 years old, a group of affluent consumers who usually don't watch television during *Miami Vice's* Friday-night air time.

The emphasis on market segments and audience demographics has forced network executives to search for more refined ways of measuring and describing their audience. Raw numbers describing the size of the audience and percentage of viewers who are watching a particular program were sufficient when television was purely a mass-audience medium. But the declining primetime numbers and the increased priority of advertisers on audience demographics led television executives and audience measurement firms to experiment with more sophisticated devices and methodologies that could provide advertisers with what a *Daily Variety* reporter described as "more detailed demographic data that can tell them not just *which* households are watching a program in which they have purchased commercial time, but *who* is watching in that household."[6] One European company, AGB, promoted its "people meters," which, a representative of the firm claimed, could tell which women 18-34 who watched the first *Dallas* episode also watched the last episode. The people meter, which was also being tested by other rating firms, assigns a number to each member of the household and asks each one to "key-in" his or her number when beginning to watch television and "key-out" when he or she leaves the room. In true Big Brother fashion, the people meter also requires the household members to verify their presence at regular intervals. But, unlike the characters in George Orwell's novel, *1984*, the viewers are asked to verify their presence for the sake of audience demographics, not for government control.

Daily newspapers, while serving a defined geographic area, were also thought to be somewhat immune to audience segmentation as long as their circulation figures could demonstrate that they attracted a certain percentage of the potential readers in their area. However, overall penetration of newspapers (the percentage of potential readers who actually read the newspaper) has declined steadily. Newspaper advertisers also demand more demographic information on who is being exposed to their advertising messages. Newspaper executives have become increasingly concerned not only with the size, but the composition, of their readership. A key 1979 study financed by the American Newspaper Publishers Association led researchers to describe the newspaper audience not as a mass audience, but as an audience of numerous subsegments of the population.[7] Newspaper publishers are particularly concerned about younger, affluent readers between the ages of 18 and 34. Members of that age group are a prime target for advertisers looking for new customers, but they also read a newspaper less regularly than older and less demographically desirable members of the potential audience. In a 1984 article for the advertising trade magazine *Madison Avenue*, Janet Bamford commented on the importance of 18-34 readers to newspapers and advertisers:

> But younger readers remain a desirable and lucrative audience for newspaper publishers. Advertisers want to reach them because they often have more disposable income than older adults, who may earn more, but who are also supporting a mortgage and children. Young adults are willing to try new products, say marketers, and since they're often setting up housekeeping for the first time, they need just about everything.[8]

As a result, newspapers have sharply increased their use of color and added special sections with emphasis on such topics as entertainment, health, sports, science, and business to draw younger readers and other desirable audience segments. The *New York Times* introduced five once-a-week sections in the late 1970s: "Weekend," "Living," "Home," "Sports Monday," and "Science Times." The use of special sections has been particularly effective in attracting younger readers and, at the same time, helping advertisers place their commercial messages next to editorial content that is targeted by topic to a specific audience segment.

The most commercially successful newspapers are clearly divided each day of the week into separate sections so that the newspaper can be easily taken apart and distributed to members of the household that section should reach. The current strategies of general-circulation daily newspapers do not call for attracting the mass audience to every section of the newspaper. Just because a newspaper reaches a home does not mean each member of the household should read all of it. In fact, newspaper marketing departments and advertisers would prefer that different sections of the newspaper go to different members of the family with different demographic profiles. The old mass-audience magazines, such as *Life*, *Look*, and *Saturday Evening Post*, operated under the editorial philosophy that when the magazine came into the home "Nobody reads all of it, everybody reads some of it." Large newspapers today operate on a latter-day variant, with the advertising parceled out to specific sections that are supposed to subdivide the various demographic groups in the household. To reinforce this point, the *Los Angeles Times* in the early 1980s ran a television advertisement featuring a housewife parcelling out the different sections of the newspaper to the seats of different household members at the breakfast table, describing what each person liked best about his or her section.

Audience segmentation, since it is a marketing tool, implies that the segments that will be addressed are the ones that have the potential for returning advertising dollars back to the advertisers and, in the long run, a record of doing just that. It is not enough for an audience segment to be identified, measured, and addressed. Those who are in that group must also respond to the advertising by purchasing the products that are advertised.

As advertising agencies continue to favor media that deliver the specific audience segments they want to reach, the social role of the media has undergone a fundamental change. The communication media system once built a mass audience by looking for commonalities in a heterogeneous society. It was the ladle that stirred the melting pot and refined or set aside those ingredients that did not mix, such as members of racial minority groups. But now, the media seek, find, and reinforce the distinctions between groups in the society. The media are no longer mass media but segmented media, playing to different segments of the audience and reinforcing differences between the segments to enhance the delivery of the advertising message.

Segmentation can be based on several criteria, such as geography, age group, gender, and position in the family life cycle.[9] In order for a portion of the audience to be segmented, it must be

(1) identifiable;

(2) measurable;
(3) accessible; and
(4) substantial enough to be potentially profitable.

For many years minority audiences met the first three criteria, but were thought to be either too poor or too small to warrant attention by major advertisers. A 1981 marketing textbook by William Cunningham and Isabella Cunningham cites segmentation based on race, religion, or national origin as possible segmentation bases in addition to the more commonly cited criteria:

> Ethnic and racial factors have been effectively used as a basis for segmenting markets. Although the U.S. is known as a great melting pot, certain groups have not been assimilated into society as quickly as others. In these situations, it has proven beneficial for firms to modify their product and promotion mix to fit the specific ethnic market.[10]

As print and broadcast media directed to minority audiences have poured out surveys arguing that both the aggregate size and the collective wealth of their audiences can be translated into profits for corporations, advertising agencies have directed more and more dollars to those media and their audiences. Racial minorities meet the apparent criteria for segmentation, the minority media and their advertising agencies contend. They are identified, counted, and described by no less an authority than the U.S. Bureau of the Census. They are addressable through minority-formated media and, to the extent that large numbers of Latinos and Asians use languages other than English, they are unreachable through mainstream media. Finally, because they are racially different from the White majority in the United States, they will carry a racial, if not cultural, identity with them for the rest of their lives.

MINORITIES, MEDIA, AND THE SEGMENTED SOCIETY

Immigrants coming to the United States in the nineteenth and early twentieth centuries were greeted by a plethora of newspapers aimed at integrating them into the society. Later, radio and television served the same purpose. The aim of the communication media was to build a mass audience based on commonalities. Differences between members or groups in the audience were overshadowed by the new interests and loyalties depicted and reinforced by the mass media of communication. Where the foreign-language media existed, they mainly served first-generation arrivals and steadily declined in number and importance as the new arrivals and their children learned English and assimilated into the mainstream of mass society. The same was predicted for racial minority publications. In a 1954 book, one author predicted that the Spanish-language press would be extinct within fifteen years. Instead, in 1970 *Editor & Publisher* reported on the continued health and expansion of Spanish-language newspapers.[11] Over the years the number of Black newspapers has declined, but the number of radio stations and magazines targeted to the Black population has increased. Media directed toward Asian Americans are experiencing a percentage growth in the 1980s similar to the expansion years of Spanish-language media in the 1970s.

Recent editions of the *Editor & Publisher* and *Broadcasting/Cablecasting* yearbooks[12] document the continued importance of minority media. *Editor & Publisher* lists 2 daily and 159 weekly newspapers geared toward Blacks, 5 dailies and 24 weeklies in Spanish, 10 dailies and 2 weeklies in Chinese, 6 dailies and 4 weeklies in Japanese, and 1 Filipino weekly. The list, which is incomplete, does not include the *Navajo Times* or several Korean dailies published in the United States. In radio broadcasting there are 4 stations listed as having a Native American format, 275 programming to Blacks, 2 in Japanese, and 130 on the United States mainland broadcasting in Spanish. In addition, *Broadcasting/Cablecasting Yearbook* lists several pages of radio stations airing programs to these groups for fewer than 20 hours a week.

It could be said that these print and broadcast media directed toward racial minorities will go the way of the immigrant and foreign language media of the past, that they are a mere offshoot of the immigration from Asia and Latin America and the recent upward mobility of some Blacks. It could be argued that, as in the past, these media will serve only a transitional role in reaching racial minority audiences that are too small for the mainstream media. But such analogies would be shortsighted.

This is because references to the past are inadequate models for explaining the media of these racial minorities and the current communication system in the United States. Since 1965 about 80 percent of the immigration to the United States has come from Asia and Latin America. These immigrants and their children are not just entering the United States at a different time and place. They are also encountering the communication media at a different stage in their evolution. When the waves of European immigrants entered New York's Ellis Island the communication media of the United States were truly the mass media. Their role was to address the new arrivals and the rest of society at the lowest common denominator; providing news and entertainment that would cut laterally all groups—men and women, old and young, rich and poor, East and West, farmer and city dweller—by providing content that would attract many in the potential audience and alienate only a few. The audience of the masses was essential to the media because advertisers demanded that they attract a large and somewhat undifferentiated audience that could buy a wide range of products and services. But now, with audience segmentation, the approach of the media to their audience is the opposite. The media now look for differences and ways to reinforce them.

The impact of continued market segmentation on society is also affected by the advent of new technologies in the field of telecommunications. When television became widely available in the early 1950s, it supplanted radio and magazines as the dominant mass audience medium when about 30 percent of the people in the United States had purchased receivers. But the new technologies now being developed are not being promoted as the new key to the mass audience, although all of them would like to maximize their penetration of the segment to which they are directed. Instead, they are billed as increasing the media's ability to address narrow audience segments that are not profitable for mass-audience media. Therefore, it is possible that the new technology, when coupled with a market segmentation philosophy, will be able to serve racial and language minorities and still be profitable.

As a result, cable television (which is already available to more than 30 percent of the television viewers in the United States) has developed as a series of specialized channels offering a somewhat predictable fare of sports, movies, religion, and local programming. Like format radio, which delivers a consistent sound to its audience, cable television stations are designed to provide a predictable blend of programming to those who tune in. The new technologies, which already are widening the array of media available, will be more quickly exploited if they are able to survive on a smaller audience.

The most immediate implication of audience segmentation in a racially diverse society is that minority groups will be more fully addressed than they are in a mass-audience media system. A wider range of minority-formated media will carry both advertising messages and content to groups that were previously thought to be too small or too economically disadvantaged to merit serious attention. Racial minorities will no longer have to depend on mass-audience media that consider them only a secondary audience, if they consider them at all. To the extent that the minority-oriented media provide entertainment and information content that serves the needs of their audiences, racial minorities will benefit from this growth in media diversity.

Segmentation also means labels, labels that may mask the complexities of the people to whom they are applied. Just because a person is a member of a certain race, age, or sex does not mean that he or she thinks, lives, speaks, or consumes in the same ways as other members of that group. Labels based on race, while they may describe shared physical characteristics, do not adequately describe the complexity of Blacks, who are becoming increasingly polarized at the tops and bottoms of the economic ladder; Native Americans, who live in very different environments on the reservation or in the city; Latinos, who share a range of language ability and a variety of national backgrounds: and Asians, who, in addition to other differences, do not share the same language. Each group is also divided by the geographic, educational, age, sex, and economic differences that divide members of all racial groups in the United States. Minority-oriented media dependent on market-segmentation advertising act to identify characteristics that separate the minority groups from the majority and from each other, then reinforce those factors in their content and advertising. They also must prove that the audience they draw constitutes attractive potential consumers. Advertisers may want to target their advertising to media that reach only the affluent members of the racial group, or those in the age categories that buy their products. This means that the future of minority media could be dictated by their ability to attract the most lucrative segments of their racial group, not those in the greatest number or need.

Segmentation, because it is a marketing tool, will benefit those strata of the racial minorities whose size make them easily measured and reached, such as Blacks or Spanish-speaking Latinos. Racial minority groups that are smaller or harder to reach will probably receive less attention, such as English-speaking Latinos and Native Americans in urban areas. Market segmentation does not mean that all minority groups will be addressed by the media or addressed equally well. It merely means that those strata of the minority audience that the advertisers want to reach have a better chance of being courted by news and entertainment content.

But there are deeper implications to the segmentation of racial minorities in social fabric of the United States. Audience segmentation can also mean that minorities become further separated and, possibly, distanced from the rest of society. Segmentation points to a society in which people may be integrated in terms of the products they consume, but do not share a common culture based on the content of the entertainment or news media they use. Segmentation means that society will no longer be as strongly bonded together by the media. This is a trend that affects all people in the United States who use the media, not only minorities. The "global village" envisioned by Marshall McLuhan is developing as one in which people are not so much drawn together by the media content they read, hear, or watch, but by the products they consume.

Market segmentation through the media has even greater implications for society, and particularly the role of communication media in the society. For more than a century the communication media have been the "glue" that helped keep most of the society together. They built and developed a common culture, albeit commercial, that fed a similar diet of news and entertainment to people in different walks of life in different parts of the country. To be sure, this catering to the majority meant that certain segments of the population, such as racial minorities, were often either left out of the mainstream content or portrayed in ways which interpreted them through Anglo eyes. But the same media also served to transmit the culture and language of the dominant group to the new immigrants. Some immigrants, because of physical characteristics such as color or geographical proximity to their mother country, were outside of the melting pot.

True, the media sometimes built common interests where they did not already exist, developing a surface culture or generating interest in events or personalities that were not of real importance to the readers, viewers, and listeners. And the emphasis on the lowest common denominator often meant that the mass media acted to lower public tastes rather than elevate them.

But the bottom line was that the media sought and built an audience based on common interests rather than differences. And out of this was forged the society that most Americans live in today. Now, with the emphasis on marketing and audience segmentation, the media play a very different role. The media, rather than trying to find commonalities among diverse groups in the mass audiences, look for differences and ways to capitalize on those differences through content and advertising. The force in society that once acted to bring people together now works to reinforce the differences that keep them apart.

Based on growth of numbers alone it would appear that both the mass-audience media, which will need to attract an increasing share of a racially diverse population to claim it is truly mass media, and the media targeted to racial minority groups, which will have a growing target, would undergo cosmetic, if not basic, changes by the end of the twentieth century. Mass audience media will have to include more minorities in a wider range of visible roles in entertainment and news content if it hopes to attract shares of the growing minority groups. Minority personalities with "crossover" appeal to all races, such as Bill Cosby, will have the greatest opportunities for success. The media directed toward minority audiences will most likely become more targeted to specific strata within the market segment, such as Black teenagers or bilingual Latinos. As advances in technology make the media more plentiful, they will become more targeted, which will benefit minorities and other segments of the population that are identifiable and potentially addressable.

Not only is the United States becoming more racially diverse, but the divisions that have accompanied racial diversity are being reinforced by the communication media of the country. This division means that racial minorities will be more fully served by an expanding communication media system than were racial minorities in the past. But it also means that the socialization function of media in developing and transmitting the common culture of the society will be less important.

NOTES

1. For a description and analysis of new technology and the information society, see Loy A. Singleton, *Telecommunications in the Information Age* (Ballinger, 1983).

2. For a brief description of the range of new technologies with implications for communications, see John R. Bittner, *Mass Communication: An Introduction* (Prentice-Hall, 1983), pp. 312-360.

3. For general descriptions of market segmentation and its application to racial minorities, see William J. Stanton, *Fundamentals of Marketing* (McGraw-Hill, 1981), pp. 65-86; and William H. Cunningham and Isabella Cunningham, *Marketing: A Managerial Approach* (South-Western, 1981), pp. 184-203.

4. David Crook, "Age of 'narrowcasting' dawns," *Los Angeles Times*, September 10, 1984, p. VI-1.

5. "Miami Vice: Pop and cop," *Newsweek*, January 21, 1985, p. 67.

6. Mike Silverman, "Ratings services look for more detailed data via people meters," *Daily Variety*, January 9, 1985, p. 4.

7. Ernest F. Larkin and Gerald L. Grotta, "A market segmentation approach to daily newspaper audience studies," *Journalism Quarterly*, Vol. 56, No. 1, Spring 1979, pp. 31-37, 133.

8. Janet Bamford, "Wanted: Readers, 18-34, affluent . . . ," *Madison Avenue*, May 1984, pp. 90-98.

9. Stanton, *Fundamentals of Marketing*, p. 78.

10. Cunningham and Cunningham, *Marketing*, p. 193.

11. See John H. Burma, *Spanish-Speaking Groups in the United States* (Duke University Press, 1954), pp. 98-99; Spyridon Granitsas, "Ethnic press alive and well, 440 published in the U.S.," *Editor & Publisher*, November 28, 1970, p. 12.

12. *Editor & Publisher Yearbook*, 1984 ed., pp. 445-448; *Broadcasting/Cablecasting Yearbook*, 1983 ed., pp. F-55, passim.

SUGGESTED READING

"Ad Dollars Increase as More Big Clients Enter Spanish Media," *Television/Radio Age*, December 19, 1983, pp. A-20-A-34.

Kidder, Rushworth M. "The Navajo Times Comes of Age—At Six Minutes Past Deadline," *Christian Science Monitor*, March 23, 1984, p. 1.

Kurtz, David L. and Louis E. Boone. "Marketing Segmentation" and "Market Segmentation Strategies," in David L. Kurtz and Louis E. Boone (Eds.), *Marketing*, 2nd ed. Chicago: Dryden, 1984.

LaBrie, Henry G. "The Disappearing Black Press," *Editor & Publisher*, March 17, 1979, pp. 53-54.

LaBrie III, Henry G. "The Black Press: Recovering from Hard Times," *Editor & Publisher*, March 31, 1984, pp. 12-15.

"Learning the Hispanic Hustle," *Newsweek*, May 17, 1982, pp. 83-86.

Schatzman, Dennis. "The Black Press and Its Role in Modern Society," *Editor & Publisher*, April 21, 1979, pp. 16-18.

Sing, Bill. "Four Goals for Asian Americans Indicate Needs for Services," *Press Woman*, November 1983, p. 9. Also has articles on Blacks, Latinos, Navajos, women.

Wilkie, William L. and Joel B. Cohen. *An Overview of Market Segmentation: Behavioral and Research Approaches*, Working Paper, Report No. 77-105, Marketing Science Institute, June 1977.

Zotti, Ed. "An Idea Whose Time Has Not Quite Arrived: Spanish Sections in Newspapers Still Struggling," *Advertising Age*, February 15, 1982, pp. M-29-M-33.

INDEX

ABOUT THE AUTHORS

Clint C. Wilson II is Associate Professor of Journalism, University of Southern California. From 1980 to 1983 he was Director of the Media Institute for Minorities at USC. He is a professional journalist and editor in addition to being an educator. His professional experience includes the *Los Angeles Times, Los Angeles Herald-Examiner, Pasadena* (California) *Star-News* and the *Los Angeles Sentinel*. He was formerly the Executive Editor of *Sepia* magazine. His scholarly work on ethnic minorities and mass media has been published in such periodicals as *Journalism Educator, Columbia Journalism Review*, and *Change* magazine. He is on the board of directors of the Los Angeles Black Media Coalition and is former head of the Minorities and Communication Division of the Association for Education in Journalism and Mass Communication. He is a founder of the Black Journalists Association of Southern California. He holds the doctorate in higher education administration and a master's degree in journalism from the University of Southern California, in addition to a bachelor's degree in news-editorial journalism and public relations from California State University, Los Angeles.

Félix F. Gutiérrez is Associate Professor of Journalism at the University of Southern California School of Journalism. A member and the former Executive Director of the California Chicano News Media Association, he is a founding member of the National Association of Hispanic Journalists. His recent professional media experience includes reporting for the *Star-News* in Pasadena, California, and the Associated Press bureau in Los Angeles. He is coauthor of *Spanish-Language Radio in the Southwestern United*

States and coeditor of the *Telecommunications Policy Handbook*. He has written more than thirty articles and book chapters on Latinos and media published in such periodicals as *Communication Research, Journal of Communication, Journalism History, Columbia Journalism Review, Nuestro,* and *Agenda*. His degrees include a doctorate and a master's in communication from Stanford University, a master's in journalism from Northwestern University, and a bachelor's in social studies from California State University, Los Angeles.